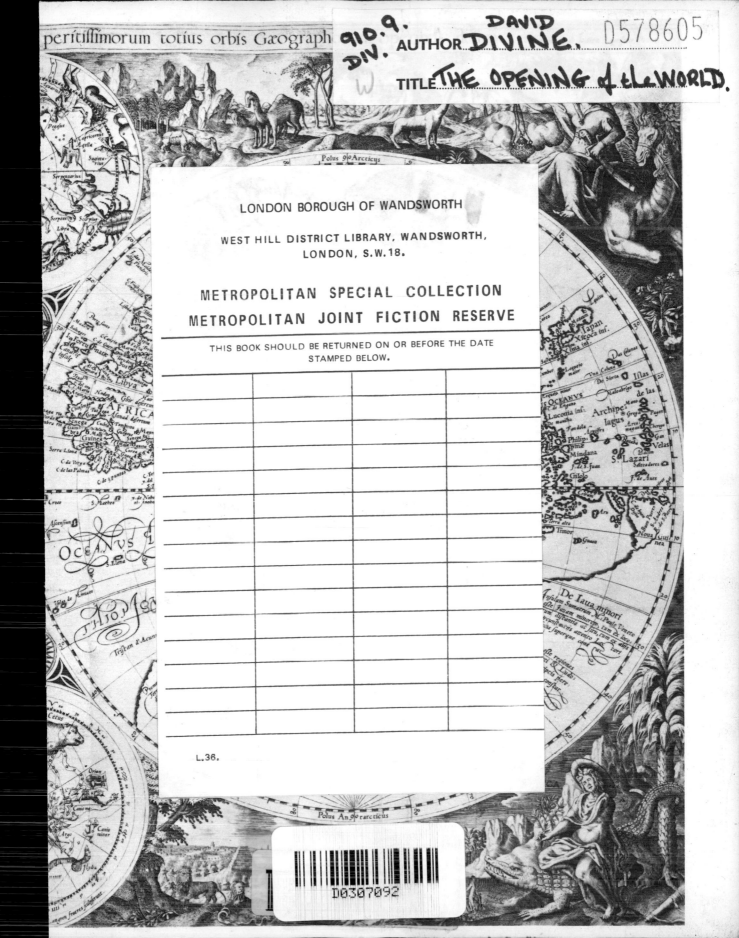

The Opening of the World

David Divine

The Opening of the World

Collins, St James's Place, London

This book was designed and produced by
George Rainbird Limited,
Marble Arch House,
44 Edgware Road,
London W2

House Editor: Caroline Benwell
Designer: Trevor Vincent
Cartographer: Tom Stalker-Miller
Indexer: Vicki Robinson

© David Divine 1973
First published in the United Kingdom
in 1973 by
William Collins, Sons & Company Limited,
14 St James's Place, London SW1
and 144 Cathedral Street, Glasgow C4

ISBN 0 00 211169 1

Text set by
Cranmer Brown (Filmsetters) Limited,
London

Printed and bound by
Cox & Wyman Limited,
Fakenham

Colour plates printed by
Impact Litho Limited,
Tolworth

Printed in Great Britain

To Elizabeth Ann

With acknowledgments to Strabo of Amasya,
father of the literature of exploration,
and those who have followed him.

Contents

List of Colour Plates

List of Maps

I **The Renaissance of Exploration** 12

II **The Fundamental Ship** 30

III **Crete and the Classic Voyages** 38

IV **Oar Thresh** 54

V **The Portuguese Initiative** 74

VI **Primary Rewards** 90

VII **The Triumph of Guinea** 106

VIII **The Cape of Good Hope** 130

IX *Otro Mondo* 148

X **India Achieved** 166

XI **The Globe Encircled** 178

XII **Elizabethans** 194

XIII **Genocide** 214

XIV **The Rise of the English** 230

XV **The World Refashioned** 240

Illustrations and Acknowledgments 265

Index 268

Colour Plates

25 Portuguese ship of the fifteenth century

26-7 Medieval version of Ptolemy's world

28 Thirteenth-century map of the world

37 *(above)* Ship model from the tomb of Tutankhamun

(below) Twelfth-dynasty Egyptian ships

38 Mosaic landscape of the Upper Nile

55 An Anglo-Saxon view of a Dragon ship

56 The prow of the Oseberg ship

81-3 The Catalan Atlas

84 João I entertaining John of Gaunt

93 João I

94 Saint Vincent panel

111 Lisbon quayside

112 Detail from *Landscape with the Fall of Icarus*

129 Prester John fighting Ghengis Khan

130 The Cape of Good Hope

147 Portuguese sailor in a crow's nest

148 Columbus

165 Map of the New World in 1500

166 Da Gama

183 Magellan

184 Map of South America in 1558

201 John Hawkins

202 Francis Drake

219 Cortés' march to Tenochtitlan

220 Ecuadorian wearing gold ornaments

245 European traders in Golconda

246-7 Saint Francis Xavier arriving in Japan

248 An Englishman at leisure in Bengal

Maps

31   The First Discoveries

48   Classical Voyages

64-5   Viking Raids

126   The Portuguese under Henry the Navigator

261   The Triangular Trade

262-3   The World in the Sixteenth Century

The Renaissance of Exploration

Opposite
The Infante Dom Henrique
of Portugal, 'Henry the
Navigator'

The headland of Sagres thrusts strongly southward into the Atlantic, a gale-swept plane of level rock, its cliffs cut sheer to the broken water 180 feet below. Seas stream past it on either hand, giving the illusion of movement. It has, in a wind, the contained excitement of the flight-deck of an aircraft carrier at the instant of take-off. Navigators, Greek and Roman both, said Strabo, called it the Sacred Cape, 'the most westerly point of the inhabited world'.

Strabo is not infallible, there are other headlands, farther west, but what he meant was to establish that as late as his day men believed the *promontorium sacrum* to be both the end-place of geographical knowledge and the outer limit of mythology.

There is a singular appropriateness then in the decision of the Infante Dom Henrique of Portugal, styled in English 'Henry the Navigator', to adopt it as his base for the indefatigable succession of adventure that opened the world to Western man.

If, in 1418, when Henry began to examine the possibilities of a southern voyage public opinion polls had existed, a survey of Western belief would have produced an overwhelming majority for the proposition that the earth was flat. In coastal areas where the ordinary man had contact with seamen, there would probably have been a reasonable level of 'don't knows'. Only an educated minority drawn from the universities, the advanced thinkers in the upper levels of the church, a reading population – which may have been larger than is ordinarily accepted – and the professional seamen, would have opted confidently for a sphere.

Early Greece had visualized its earth as flat, with its *omphalos* – its navel – at Delphi. Pythagoras had destroyed that concept with mathematics. Aristotle had corroborated his theoretical assumptions with observations of the earth shadow on the moon in eclipse. Eratosthenes used the justly famous well at Aswan to measure its circumference with surprising accuracy. Poseidonius absorbed it into geographical precept. Herodotus and Strabo, writing for the ordinary man, popularized it.

Rome, in accordance with practice, built on the Greek foundations.

Christianity, in its early formative centuries, utterly rejected it. Lactantius Firmianus, tutor to Constantine's son, thundering against it with all the authority of the Ante-Nicaean fathers, said:

> The idea of the roundness of the earth is the cause of inventing this fable of the antipodes ... for these philosophers having once erred, go on in their absurdities, defending one another. Is there anyone so foolish as to believe that there are antipodes with their feet opposite ours; people who walk with their heels upward and their heads hanging down? That there is a part of the world where the trees grow with their branches downwards; and where it rains, hails and snows upward?

Incredulity is contagious. Lactantius was followed by a lucent succession of saints: St Basil, St Jerome, St Chrysostom, St Gregory; even St Augustine, who argued that the idea was incompatible with the historical foundation of the Christian faith, whose origin was with Adam, since nations in the antipodes 'could not be descended from Adam it being impossible for them to have passed the intervening ocean'.

Christian man followed his saints. Mapmakers followed belief. Wind-blowing cherubs in the Greek mode surrounded the outside world. 'Beastes' disported themselves in the outer sea. At some point it became widely accepted that by simple logic the ocean, following immutable laws, poured roaring over the undiscovered edge of the earth.

John Holywood of Halifax in Yorkshire, and a lecturer in mathematics at the University of Paris, brought back the Globe over the haloes of the saints. In 1230 – he had translated his name to Sacrobosco – he completed an abstract of Gerard of Cremona's version of the Almagest, *De Sphaera Mundi*, which became the standard work on the earth for three centuries. It endured to be bound with the Portuguese navigating manuals in the sixteenth century and it did more than any other work to break down the entrenched position of the flat-earth theorists.

Its first section defined the terrestrial globe, its second dealt with 'circles great and small', its third systematized the rising and setting of stars, and its fourth the movement of the planets.

It is the fountainhead of Renaissance navigation.

Enchantingly it was reinforced by one of the most splendid hoaxes of the Middle Ages. *Mandeville's Travels* was the world's first best-seller in the field of travel fiction. Sir John Mandeville was not a knight, not an Englishman, and not an explorer. His detailed and death-defying journeys were lifted from other people's travelogues, with elements of simple invention, but the result was eminently readable; the book had an immediate and widespread circulation in manuscript editions, and came to its triumph in the sixteenth century in print. Translated into innumerable languages, Spanish among them, it must, like Sacrobosco's work, have been available to Henry. In its twentieth chapter Sir John says:

> And men may wel preuen be experience and sotyle compassement of wytt that yif a man fond passages by schippes that wolde go to serchen the world, men myghte go be schippe alle aboute the world and abouen and benethen, the whiche thing I proue thus after that I haue seyn.

Sir John may have been spurious, his dictum has an evidential truth: in 1357, when it was written – probably at Liège – it was authentic prophecy.

The climate of opinion in the fifteenth century has its origins in these attitudes, but any attempt to assess the Portuguese achievement must be judged against a still massive opposition of Christian tradition.

Henry the Navigator was the third son of João I of Portugal (1385-1433), the

Ractado da Spera do múdo tirada delatim em lingoagẽ portugues Com hũa carta que huũ grãde doutor Allemam mandou a elRey de Portugall dom Joam ho segundo.

Frontispiece from Sacrobosco's *Treatise of the Sphere*

bastard of Pedro I by Teresa Lourenço, who, as the people's champion in a frantic era, broke the regime of 'the infamous and adulterous' Queen Regent Leonor, founded the House of Avis, defeated Castile at Aljubarrota, and secured the independence of Portugal for 200 years. It was an uninhibited age.

Henry's mother was English, Philippa, daughter of John of Gaunt, time-honoured, throne-hungry Lancaster, who had played her as a pawn in the vast chess game that had, for its ultimate intended prize, the crown of Castile.

That her father in due time lost the game made small difference to Philippa. She was a forthright queen and she bore her husband five remarkable sons and a daughter of beauty. Dying of plague at Lisbon at the crucial moment of the preparations for the Crusade to Ceuta, she heard from her death-bed the wind

In this family tree, defaced by the removal of the coats of arms, Philippa stands in the centre. Above her is her husband, João I of Portugal, and below her father, John of Gaunt.

for Africa – the north wind – blowing, and ordered her husband and her sons to sail, giving them first their swords.

They buried her and sailed.

The status of Portugal at the beginning of the fifteenth century is of an immense significance in the history of European civilization. A strip of indifferently fertile land scarcely ever more than 100 miles wide along the unconsidered Atlantic coast of the Iberian Peninsula, she was a minor nation, her population just over 1,000,000. On land, as a consequence, she was subject to stringent limitations: the first, a perpetual lack of manpower; the second, the vulnerability inherent in a narrow country unable ever to exercise a realistic strategy of defence in depth; the third, a perpetual imbalance, economic and financial, against a combination of Leon and Castile.

At sea she had wider options. Already, during the reign of Afonso I in the twelfth century, when Portugal became a separate kingdom, actions at sea are reported as distant as the Straits of Gibraltar. Lisbon itself was captured by an amphibious expedition; so later was the Algarve, when forty ships, mostly galleys, carried and covered the force that took Silves.

Diniz 'The Farmer' (1279-1325), greatest of the early kings, regularized the navy under Nuno Fernandes Cogominho and planted pine forests for shipbuilding. When Cogominho died, Diniz brought in the Genoese, Manoel Pessanha (or Pezagno) with twenty *sabedores do mar* – experts of the sea – to sharpen it as a weapon of strategy.

Maritime trade balanced the naval effort. There was a traditional commerce with the Mediterranean, conditioned, inevitably, by the changes in Mediterranean power and in this period dependent either on Genoese or Venetian goodwill or surreptitious arrangement with the Moor. Simultaneously, however, a trade with Northern Europe developed: first by way of the Biscay ports and France; then with the Low Countries – there was a Portuguese House at Bruges, very early; finally with the Hansa towns and England. At the beginning of the thirteenth century Portugal was applying for as many as a hundred safe conducts for English ports in a single year.

Once the disruption of civil war was over, Portugal had a strong sea potential. Relations with Castile had been stabilized. João was able to contemplate the tempting alternative of war by sea.

A high romance legend, basically created by the chroniclers, claims that João's three eldest sons – Duarte, Pedro and Henry – on reaching the appropriate age for knighthood, were offered a year of international tournament in the opulent late-medieval manner, with their accolades at the end of it.

Stimulated by Henry, according to the legend, they rejected the offer with a demand to be permitted to win their spurs in war against the infidel.

It has a fine boyish zest about it, but an attempt to secure a point of power at the entrance to the Mediterranean had been proposed as early as 1409 by the King's Treasurer, João Afonso, who possibly estimated that a seaborne assault would scarcely cost more than a year of tournament and might secure an inestimable prize. Three objectives offered: Tangier at the Atlantic mouth of the Straits, Gibraltar at the Mediterranean mouth, and Ceuta, to the south.

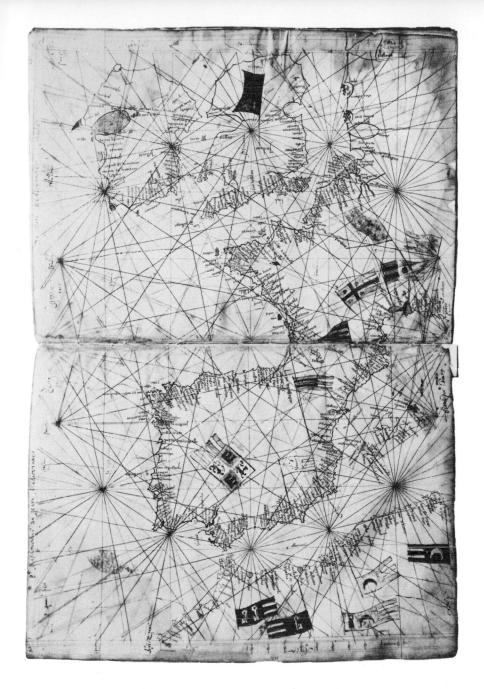

Portolan chart of the
Atlantic coasts of Europe
and Africa in about 1327,
attributed to Petrus
Vesconte

Capture of any one of these would immensely enhance Portugal's reputation, greatly please the Church as a defeat for Islam – and offer gratifying possibilities for trade. Knighthood for princes fell sharply below that level of aspiration,

Henry was just sixteen when in 1410 João considered his preparations sufficiently advanced to send his personal confessor to Rome to inform the Pope. Tangier had faded early from the target list. Its landing places were inadequate to an amphibious operation. Gibraltar lay in Castile's sphere of influence. Ceuta remained. One of the twin Pillars of Hercules, it had a manifest importance in any attempt to gain control of the Straits. Phoenicians or Carthaginians – the

17

point is arguable – had settled it. Greeks followed. The Romans held it and named it, after its seven hills, the Septem Fratres; the Moors shortened it to Sebta. It lay on a three-mile peninsula which broadened into the Hills of the Brothers. Abyla, the Southern Pillar, lay in their centre. The town was built on the narrow isthmus which connected it with the mainland.

It was, in addition, the terminus of the ancient and immensely profitable caravan routes through the High Atlas and the Rif which, from the days of the Phoenicians, had brought gold and ivory and slaves from Western Africa. Endless episodes of conquest and reconquest had passed through it. It was Islam's gate to Africa. It was still the link port in the short sea passage to Granada, the last Moorish foothold in Europe.

By 1411 preparation was intense. Elaborate operations to secure silver and copper had been inaugurated and new money was being coined to pay for material. Contracts had been placed for ships and warlike stores. The great forests that the foresight of Diniz had planted at Leiria for a future navy were being cut. Food production had been heavily increased, the manufacture of canvas for sails had been doubled, ships' fittings, guns, oars for the galleys, barrel staves for wine and water were being produced in ever-increasing quantities, rope walks were being duplicated and re-duplicated.

Elaborate cover plans had been employed to veil every aspect of the operation but eventually the point was reached where it was necessary to inform the Cortes and the Church. The validity of the operation – as a Crusade – had itself to be decided. In addition the complexity of the preparations overwhelmed the capacity of the normal civil service.

Duarte, the heir apparent, was appointed in overall control of administration. Pedro, the second son, was given responsibility for recruiting in Estremadura.

A late stage in the construction of a fifteenth-century ship

Henry and the King's bastard, the Count of Barcelos, were appointed to the northern provinces – Beira, Entre Douro e Minho and Trás-os-Montes – and as soon as recruitment was satisfactory Henry was sent alone to Porto, his birth-place, to galvanize that great shipbuilding area into productivity.

Inevitably Europe discerned the armaments' build up. Castile and Aragon sent embassies with urgent questions and were reassured. Granada sent an ambassador and was left guessing. Portugal herself sent an ambassador to the Court of Holland to complain of attacks against her shipping off the Low Countries and create thereby an impression that the armada was destined for the North.

The gathering of intelligence on Ceuta was similarly concealed. An embassy was sent to Blanche of Navarre, the widowed Queen of Sicily, who was seeking a husband. Duarte had been suggested but the ambassadors were empowered to offer Pedro, the second son, in the knowledge that he would be rejected. The purpose was to enable the head of the embassy, the Prior of the Order of St John, to call in at Ceuta and make a survey of the harbour under cloak of diplomatic immunity.

Returned to Lisbon, the Prior, with two bags of sand, a bushel of beans, a skein of wool and a silver porringer, built history's first recorded 'sand table' and demonstrated with the model the tactical weaknesses of Ceuta's defence.

By midsummer preparations were complete. The Porto contingent was ready to sail under Henry with fifteen new galleys, fifteen large foists and forty other ships. Lisbon's fleet had assembled. Contingents of chartered ships had come in from Galicia, from Biscay, from Flanders. Ten came from England, five of them with 'Mundy, a rich merchant of London', and fifty archers. By July, according to Matthew of Pisa, there were 242 vessels in the Tagus, sixty-three of them large *naus*, fifty-nine oared *galés*, 120 smaller craft – *barinels* and *barcas* and such – and 45,000 men.

Raymond Beazley, working from contemporary accounts, put the figure higher, at 50,000 soldiers and 30,000 seamen. Ruy Dias de Vegas, envoy of the King of Aragon and a spy of quality, on the other hand calculated it at 19,000 all told. The ships, even the great ships, were not very great, and the little ships were very small indeed.

The conflict of opinion raises, as always, questions as to the reliability of contemporary evidence. The problem is not confined to Portugal nor indeed to the fifteenth century. Medieval figures could serve a variety of ends – often simultaneously. They could impress the home public, they could justify royal expenditures, they could provide a deterrent to future political enemies. Probably de Vegas was near enough to the truth. Later in the period Portugal was served in succession by three chroniclers of most notable quality.

The first of these was Fernão Lopes who, in 1415, was Keeper of the Royal Archives. Commissioned at Duarte's accession in 1434 to write the *Chronicle of Portugal* to the close of João's reign, he earned, justly, the reputation of Portugal's Froissart. In an inaccurate age he was accurate. In a period of artificial conventions he was plain and balanced. He was dramatic when it was essential, and he was easy to read. He was succeeded by Gomes Eanes de

CHRONICA
DELREY D. IOAM. I.
DE BOA MEMORIA
E DOS REYS DE PORTVGAL O DECIMO.
TERCEIRA PARTE.
EM QVE SE CONTEM A TOMADA DE CEITA.
OFFERECIDA A MAGESTADE DELREY
DOM IOAM O IV. N. SENHOR
DE MIRACVLOSA MEMORIA.
COMPOSTA POR GOMEZEANNES D'AZVRARA
Chronista mór destes Reynos, & impressa na linguagem antiga.

Anno de 1644.

EM LISBOA. Com todas as licenças necessarias
A custa de Antonio Aluarez Impressor DelRey N. S.

PROLOGO.

CONCLVSAM he de Aristoteles no segundo liuro da natural Philosophiá, que a natureza, & ó começo de mouimento he de folgança, & pera declaração desto, aprendamos, q̃ cada hũa cousa tem qualidade por a qual se de moue a seu proprio lugar, quando está fora delle, entendendo alli ser cõfirmado melhor, & por aquella mesma propriedade faz assossegamento, depois que está onde a natureza requere. Exemplo disto he a pedra, q̃ por a sua graueza, & pezo, decende ao lugar, q̃ lhe pertence, & depois que o percalça, nom se moue: Assi semelhauelmente cada hum homem tem desejo de conseruar sua vida, á qual saõ necessarias muitas cousas, sobre que elle nom ha possição, & por tanto ha mister que as peça por seu mouimento, a quem entender que as pode outorgar, & depois que as tiuer cobrará folgança, vzando dellas segundo o que deue, & por tanto á grandeza de nosso Senhor Deos, infindamente he liberal, a elle, que em que peçamos esto, se pode mostrar por algũas rezoens. Para conhecimento da primeira, saibamos, que no primeiro liuro da gloria, diz o Philosopho, que se algũa proprie dade conuem a duas cousas, hũa a tem por azo da outra, & he necessario, q̃ atal perfeição comprida mente seja em a primeira, cujo exemplo he aqueste. Certo he, que a quentura nom conué ao frio esquétado, senom por o fogo, porém, nom embargante, q̃ elles

✠3   elles

Azurara (known by the abbreviation Zurara) who had been appointed to the Royal Library in 1434 and shortly became Lopes' assistant. Son of a Canon of Évora and Coimbra – with the obvious implications – his first work was a curious account of the Miracles of the Holy Constable, Nuno Álvares Pereira.

In 1449 he was directed by the young Afonso V to write the *Crónica da Tomada de Ceuta*. Beginning, by his own claim, where Lopes left off, he wrote from official documents and from earlier eye-witness accounts. He discussed the campaign officially with Henry '. . . in whose house I stayed for some days for the purpose by the King's orders for he knew more than anyone in Portugal about the matter.' Beginning to write in the September of 1449, he finished the work with remarkable speed in the following March at Silves in the Algarve.

His style is altogether less balanced than that of Lopes and he has a distressing tendency to panegyric. His accuracy is often at fault and his bias is obvious. Despite these considerable defects, he remains the primary authority in relation to an age of transcendent importance. He retains through all the interruptions and inconsistencies of the explorations a passionate belief in their significance and a reverence for their director.

Title-page and Prologue from Zurara's *Crónica da Tomada de Ceuta*

If he allows that belief sometimes to develop into an uncritical worship, it is to be understood in the *mores* of the day and place. The *Crónica do descobrimento e conquista de Guiné* is one of the essential books of history.

The third of the chroniclers occupies an altogether different pedestal. Diogo Gomes was one of the most brilliant of Henry's captains; a bold man, enormously thorough, infinitely observant, and balanced in all his views.

It is possible that he could not write. Certainly he dictated his part of the record – clear and hard-headed – to Martin Behaim (the cartographer who constructed the earliest surviving globe) in the Azores in about 1484. Behaim wrote in German; it was translated into Latin – and disappeared. 400 years later it was rediscovered in a codex in the Royal Library at Munich. He, or Cadamosto, discovered the Azores. He, and Cadamosto, penetrated the great river systems of Guinea and made the first rational surveys of an unknown world.

Philippa, dying, had predicted that the fleet would sail with a fair wind on the Feast of St James. On 25 July it left the Tagus, the King and his sons not in mourning but in the brilliant colours of medieval war.

With trumpets calling, and the splendid banners of sea pageantry, the van of the fleet surged through the narrows of the Tagus, eased its sheets, and steadied on the long run to Cape St Vincent with the north wind that the Queen had promised.

At the Cape topsails were backed in salute to the saint, and clear of Sagres the fleet hauled its wind and headed in east-north-east for Lagos.

Until this change of course the Expedition of Ceuta may justly be described as a masterpiece of confident maritime organization. For its day and its gigantic size its logistics were perfection, its timing impeccable and its discipline admirable. João's strategic intentions were still triumphantly masked, but to stand in to Lagos was to risk being embayed with any change of wind to the south. To throw away a fair wind is the cardinal sin of seamanship.

João compounded sin with ceremonial delays ashore. Frei João Xeira, his chaplain, preached; masses were said; the Expedition's objective was astonishingly made public. Three days were lost – and the north wind with them. When finally they sailed, light airs forced them east to Faro and for seven days they wallowed in hot and infuriating calms. They were ten days astern of schedule when, on 10 August, the leading ship sighted the Rock of Gibraltar with Ceuta less than fourteen miles beyond. João put in to Algeciras Bay and anchored in sight of the Seven Brothers across the Straits, squandering what was left of the initiative.

He had a great inexperience of the sea (he was always ill, and hated it) and his problems were stupendous. There were no precedents to guide him. A council held in Algeciras Bay advised, unwisely, that the fleet should sail at nightfall, spend the Sunday making preparations at sea and launch the assault in the dawn of Monday.

They sailed in the darkness, with light westerly airs which died in fog off Cape Europa. The surface current that runs irregularly into the Mediterranean caught them and swirled them eastward. In World War II a British destroyer,

H.M.S. *Firedrake*, on anti-submarine patrol, was swept sixty miles in that same combination of fog and current, and grounded in Torremolinos Bay. Some of João's ships fetched up farther still off Malaga. Some of the galleys had clawed their way to Ceuta. The rest were scattered in a vast demilune across the western narrows of the Mediterranean.

As they headed back towards Gibraltar to regroup, the Levanter, the gale from the east, struck savagely.

Tradition says that the disaster brought João victory, that Sala ben Sala, Governor of Ceuta and a soldier of repute, had secured help from Fez and from the mountain tribes and could have held out against any attack, that when he saw the fleet driven back in disorder to the shelter of Algeciras he decided its objective was not Ceuta and that he could safely dismiss his reinforcements.

It is entirely improbable. Fez was 150 miles distant up a winding mountain road, communications were inadequate. Large-scale reinforcement could only have reached him in time by an incredible effort and no garrison commander of long experience would have dismissed it with a hostile fleet – however damaged by storm – at anchor fourteen miles away. Nothing in ben Sala's defence of Ceuta indicates at any point the existence of a coherent plan, everything suggests miscalculation and surprise.

The King's plan, on the other hand, was skilful, imaginative and brilliantly successful. Zurara's account of it is his clearest presentation of an important military issue.

The citadel of Ceuta was built at the narrows of the isthmus, the city on the low-lying flat that stretched towards the hills of the Brothers. The harbour lay to the north but there was a winter harbour to the south after the Phoenician pattern. The citadel was, for its day and place, powerful; the city was walled and the north wall, stretching as far as Abyla, the Pillar, was of particular strength.

At a stormy council meeting, where a new-formed party advocated abandonment, João and his sons carried the day and the assault was fixed for the morning of 21 August. Following the meeting, the King sent for Henry and reminded him of his early plea to be the leading man ashore:

> . . . I will have you land with the first party as their commander. If it is the will of God we will anchor the fleet off the town tonight. You will go round to Almina with your squadron. The Moors, seeing our main strength on the other side, will come to the conclusion that that is the point of disembarkation, and will concentrate there. When I make the signal you will land as swiftly as possible, and when the beach is taken the fleet will move over to your side and follow.

From its precision and for the positive understanding it shows in João's mind, the information must certainly have come from Henry himself in the course of Zurara's stay 'for the purpose . . .' It shows a clear comprehension of the mobility inherent in seaborne forces, a sense of the reality of sea power and a high appreciation of the possibilities of deception. It was not Henry's plan – though Zurara does his best to suggest that it was – but João's, and it worked.

None the less, Henry was baulked of his ambition. Waiting impatiently in his galley for his father's signal, he watched in fury as Ruy Gonsalves, a henchman of the Count of Barcelos, jumped the gun and waded through the shallows. Henry followed impetuously. The landing began in scrambling and unco-ordinate fashion against '. . . Moors who lined the harbour shouting defiance'.

It could indeed have ended in a disastrous reverse, but the Moors appear to have limited themselves to shouting. Zurara makes the utmost of a giant negro '. . . of a most threatening complexion, all naked, who used no weapons other than stones', and who seems in fact to have slowed the progress to the Almina gate. One stone carried away the visor of the helmet of Vasco de Albergaria of the Prince's staff, but the negro was run through with a lance, and the defenders poured back through the gate in panic – and incomprehensibly failed to close it. Henry with his standard-bearer and, according to one account, four men – and, to another, 500 – poured through the opening.

Effectively, Ceuta fell in the first ten minutes. The rest is a story of scrambled street brawls in the complex of blind alleys and narrow lanes that constituted a normal Moorish sea port. Understandably Zurara's account lacks clarity but it does stress, and sometimes overstress, the danger to Henry. It develops always the theme of his achievement, but it also records with a slightly sardonic note that when Garcia Moniz, the Prince's old tutor, reached him at a point of danger, he told him: 'Don't imagine that your men are still interested in fighting Moors, they're all over the town plundering empty houses.'

The Moors attempt to regain Ceuta

Henry did indeed get himself cut off at one point, and may have been slightly wounded, but was rescued by his friend Vasco de Ataide who himself was killed in the skirmish. Early in the afternoon it was over. Henry was summoned to the Great Mosque, where his brothers had installed themselves, to plan an assault on the citadel. Before anything could be decided a countryman saw sparrows (some say swallows) on its parapet and declared that they would not have been so quiet had there been anyone there. When they advanced to batter down the gates, two men inside, one of them a Biscayan and the other from Genoa, called out that the garrison was fled and that they would withdraw the bolts – and did!

Ceuta was firm in the hands of Portugal.

Zurara sums it all up in a splendid essay in panegyric as: 'That most glorious conquest of the great city of Ceuta of which the heavens felt the glory and the earth the benefit.'

Besides Vasco de Ataide, seven men fell in the course of that 'most glorious conquest'.

The butcher's bill is not always the best or even the most appropriate measure of a victory, but this is so inadequate as to be grotesque. An assault against a walled city and a strong citadel, a day's fighting in narrow streets appropriate for ambush and assassins, a force of anything from 19,000 to 80,000 men involved – and no more than eight men dead!

Sala ben Sala was an admired soldier and it is not the least curious facet of this curious affair that he suffered no disgrace in abandoning Ceuta. Twelve years later he was Governor of Tangier when Henry made his lamentable attack. It is impossible to believe that he intended seriously to defend Ceuta. The volume of resistance, the speed at which the small part of the Portuguese forces involved fought its way through the narrow streets makes that altogether plain. There *was* no defence. The five-storied tower on wheels described by de Vegas that was to have made possible the scaling of the ramparts of the citadel, was never brought ashore from the ship that carried it. The new-made bombards were never fired. Very quietly Ceuta collapsed.

The skill, the speed and the silence of ben Sala's withdrawal is the sole evidence of any planning at all in the entire story of the defence.

It is possible that ben Sala gambled on the assumption that a seaborne expedition would not be able to hold the city and that when the ships were gone he could return, quietly, and take over once more. If he did, he misjudged the probabilities. Portugal was determined to hold, 'for of a surety no one', said Zurara with immense emphasis, 'can deny that Ceuta is the key of all the Mediterranean Sea'.

Pedro de Menezes, the young man with the olive stick who volunteered to hold Ceuta for his King, might, as time passed, have dissented. The key failed to turn in the lock. João Afonso's concept of a Portuguese *entrepôt* controlling the rich trade of Moorish Africa was stillborn. The gold, the ivory, the slaves were diverted to Melilla and Gazahouet and Oran. Granada organized new short sea communications. No market for Portuguese goods established itself. Militarily Ceuta became an intermittently beleaguered fortress without a trade to pay for its upkeep.

A Portuguese ship of the early fifteenth century

Overleaf
Ptolemy's concept of the world, formulated in the second century, survived into the fifteenth. This version is from the 1482 edition of the *Geographia*.

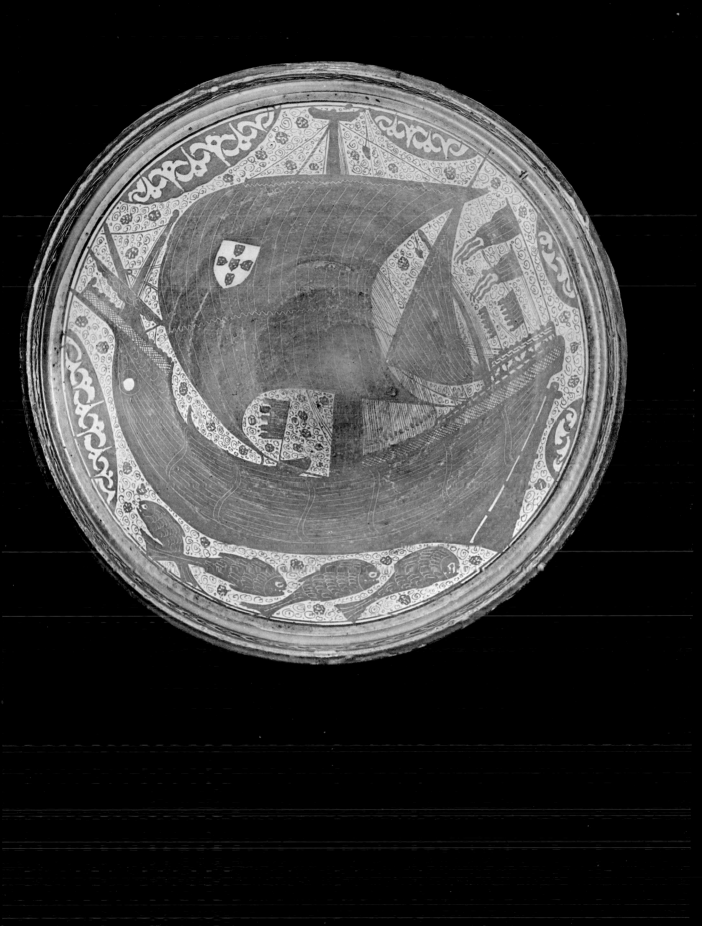

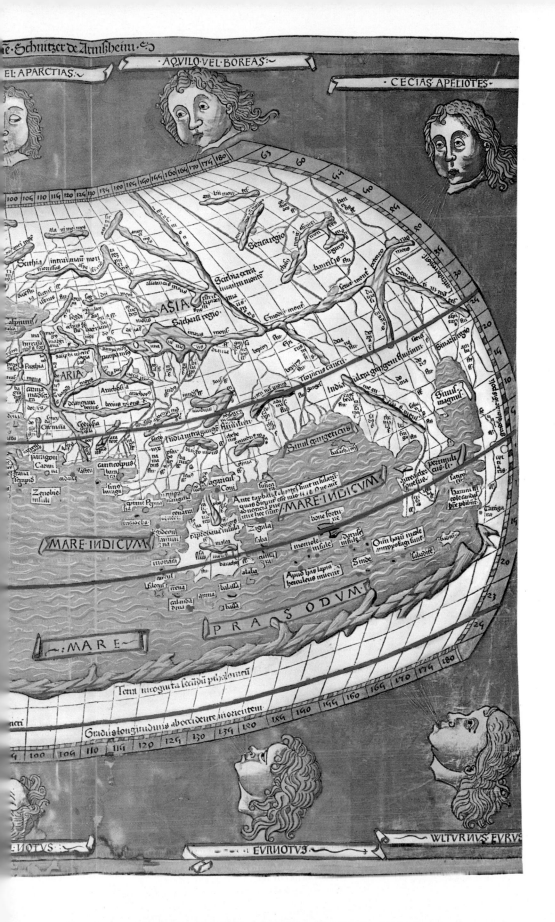

Yet there were consequences that in the end became immeasurable.

A thirteenth-century map centred on Jerusalem

Four of these were immediate. In a new guise as victor in a Western crusade the international status of Portugal was enhanced. In the rich prospect of overseas empire the vision of the Portuguese people expanded outward. In her own eyes – more importantly even than in the eyes of others – the manner and the conduct of the expedition established Portugal as a sea power. Last of all, Henry, flushed with an understandable pride in his own achievement, became in his own mind aware of the possibilities of sea adventure – the idea of exploration would soon follow.

Eventually, however, the quasi-siege of Ceuta drifted slowly into a positive attempt to expel the Portuguese. The Kings of Granada, Tunis, Morocco and Buggu, with a great army (estimated, improbably, by the King's Ransomer of Captives at 100,000 men) and a fleet of 74 ships, invested the city and Pedro de Menezes called urgently for help.

Henry was twenty-four by now, vigorous and experienced. A relief force was assembled at great speed and passage to the Straits was made, reportedly, in four days.

The tendency to anticlimax that marks so much of Henry's proceedings at this time at once came into play. As the relief force reached the Straits, de Menezes, his patience exhausted, mounted a furious pre-emptive strike against the besiegers. It seems quite certain that the King's Ransomer was at fault as to the enemy's numbers. The siege collapsed, the fleet of Granada slipped away, Henry and his rescue force were left with nothing whatever to do.

This in no way inhibited Zurara: 'The Infant was very diligent in succouring it with two of his brothers . . . and the aid of a great flotilla, and after killing many of the Moors and delivering the city, he repaired it and returned very honourable to Portugal.'

He spent three months in fact at Ceuta and it is impossible to overestimate the importance of these months. This is the springing point of all the discoveries. During these months he became aware of Africa. He talked to traders and to camel drivers, to seamen and slaves and shepherds. He gathered, slowly and with great difficulty, the secrets of the gold trade from the south, of the caravan routes, of the great rivers, the ivory, the second-grade spices of Western Africa, and the great black kingdoms of the basin of the Niger. The King of Tunis received for his merchandise gold and slaves. 'Henry resolved to do by sea what the king for many years had done by land.'

When he returned to Portugal fresh reputation had accrued to him. Zurara wrote unblushingly: '. . . seeing how that Sovereign Pontiff, Vicar General of the Church, and the Emperor of Germany as well as the Kings of Castile and England begged him to be Captain of their Armies'.

Precisely what Henry V, busy at that moment besieging Rouen and planning his advance on Paris, actually offered we do not know. It is improbable, however, that he was in the mood for begging.

It is as improbable that Henry the Navigator would have contemplated acceptance. He was already seized of visions of expansion – if not yet of exploration.

Chapter II

The Fundamental Ship

With Homer a split developed between land man and sea man that has been permitted to obscure the significance of the ship in human development.

The stick which became the spear, the club, and the portable personal weapon has been exhaustively appraised. The flaked pebble which was adapted into the hand axe, the chisel, and the knife, has been appropriately recognized. Fire has been awarded its fundamental place. The basic significance of a means of crossing water has, however, largely eluded the assessors.

Its invention is almost inconceivably distant. The origin of man himself has moved back in time endlessly in recent years. Three centuries ago Archbishop Ussher could declare, *ex cathedra*, that man was created 'about eight of the clock on the evening of Saturday, 22 October, 4004 B.C.' and be accepted. To-day, with the astonishing discoveries of the Leakeys, first at Olduvai in Tanganyika, then at Lake Rudolf in Kenya, we accept with almost equal absence of challenge that sentient man existed 2,500,000 years ago. We know that almost as soon as he established himself in relation to his environment he began to move, that in due course he spread across the globe, and that in whichever direction he moved – whether from Lake Rudolf (if indeed he began there) or from whatever fecund nurturing place first gave him being – he had, almost at once, to cross the first of the unfordable rivers which seam the world.

A means of crossing water was palpably among the most urgent of the requirements for man's success as a species. The distribution of primitive artefacts by itself proves that waterways were not, for any length of time, a bar.

Discovery of the means must have been basically simple – a boy in a pool after flood, finding a still buoyant bundle of matted reeds on which he could rest his chest and kick himself across to the other side; a hunting party in pursuit of a wounded beast; an exhausted man pursued by his fellows sighting a driftwood log and propelling it across a stream in desperation. The problem may have been solved in any of a dozen ways, but just such a bundle of long-stemmed papyrus provided the basic flotation gear on the Nile for thousands of years, and just such a log ferried countless tribes across countless other rivers. And the progression thereafter was simple and logical. Three bundles of reeds made a raft, three logs lashed together were stable and could be manoeuvred.

The boat came long after. Its development required conscious thought.

Civilization began with settlement, settlement came with cultivation. The world's first village was possibly Jarmo on the uplands of a tributary of the Tigris north-west of modern Baghdad. Other villages challenge the claim – Hacilar in Anatolia, Tepe Gawra on the edge of the Fertile Crescent, the first of many Jerichos. All owed their origin to the same discovery: that the food grains gathered by nomad women could, if kept clear of weeds and simply cultivated,

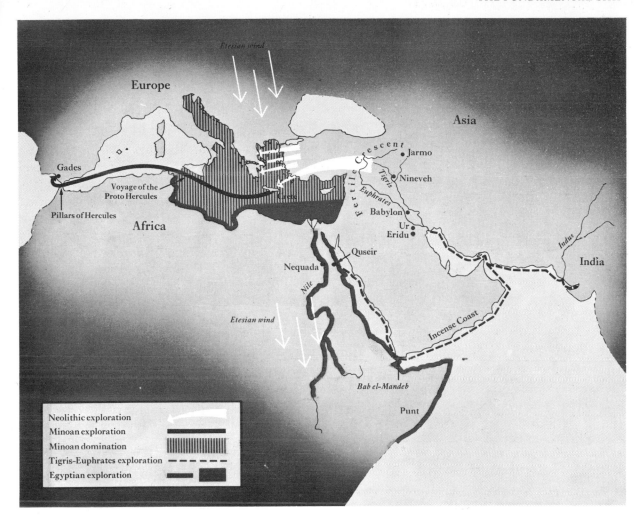

The First Discoveries.
The first voyage of
exploration began with a
migration of grain-
cultivating man from the
Fertile Crescent to the
Aegean coast and Crete. The
map shows the maritime
development of the
civilizations of the
Tigris-Euphrates, the Nile
and the Indus, and the
extent of the sea empire
built up from Crete

produce a climactic rise in food values. Emmer wheat – a type still widely grown in parts of Asia, Africa and southern Europe – and two-row barley readjusted the statistics of survival. They spelt, simultaneously, the beginning of the end of nomadism. Man had to live thereafter season by season with his wheat field. In 7000 B.C. Jarmo had twenty-five permanent houses. They renewed themselves on the same site, generation after generation.

The boat in this phase can have had only a limited importance. Until the villages multiplied and communication problems arose, it would have been useful only in fishing. But Mesolithic man an age before had invented the chisel/ gouges which made it possible to hollow a log into a dugout canoe, and fishermen in the north had perfected a skin boat. At Jarmo or some other village about this time, devising a wicker framework and a skin covering, the village people produced the prototype of the boat that made possible the development of the city.

Tentative expansion downstream towards the great river plains of Mesopotamia began probably as early as 5000 B.C. with the Hassuna culture. Population increases appear to have created demands for cultivation on a larger scale. The great rivers alone in that already semi-arid area offered the possibilities: constant water, level flood plains, seasonal regeneration of the soil, widespread grazing, and the ultimate possibility of controlling water by dams and ditches. Where Jarmo's fields fed a probable average of 150 people, a riverine site might, and in the final outcome did, feed 150,000.

The town, however, could not subsist on husbandry alone.

The development of the late Neolithic trade is complex and fascinating. It had before Jarmo already passed the limited man-portable stage of obsidian from Turkey for weapons or decorative shells from the Persian Gulf for ornament. Surpluses of other kinds were being moved. Land transport barely existed; the ox had just been organized, the onager and the wild ass were still 1,000 years away, and the tamed horse 2,000. The camel had not yet been invented by its committee. The wheel not yet imagined.

The rivers supplied a highway, river craft a vehicle. The first known three-dimensional representation of a boat was found at Eridu, the town that preceded Ur of the Chaldees and the Ubaid culture. It is an eight-inch model – child's toy or votive offering – yellowish-grey in colour, ill-shapen, unlovely. It was made in or about the year 4000 and its importance in the developing history of urban man cannot be measured.

It does not, however, represent the first boat. Its design is already sophisticated. It has a strong mast-step, so it carried a working mast. Holes in its thin sides were clearly for backstays, so it carried a sail. It is thin-sided without ribbing, so it must have been of wicker and skin construction. It can have been anything from 500 to 1,000 years in development – through all the period, that is, that the village required to transform itself into the town – for Eridu is held to be the world's first town.

It could have carried the loads of ten oxen. Fleets of such boats made it possible to enlarge the town into the city – into, inevitably, the chain of riverine cities that in due course fringed the rivers from Nineveh in the north by way of Ashur and Babylon and Kish and Lagash and Larsa to Ur. It was here, in the beginning, that Ziusudra prepared a 'huge boat' and survived the Flood.

Early in this period the river boat went to sea. Eridu was almost in sight of the headwaters of the Persian Gulf. Fishing was an essential part of early economy. How soon and where the first seagoing ship was perfected is not established. Despite the lack of timber in an arid country, it was built of wood (possibly of sycamore and acacia as in Egypt later) and there is plain evidence that the earliest sea trade went south to the Hadhramaut coast – the Incense Coast – to supplement, and in due course to supplant, the dangerous journey involved in bringing that religio-economic substance across the Arabian Desert.

This is the beginning of oceanic navigation. The ships that made the journey to the Incense Coast were the ships, as time progressed, that discovered the Straits of Bab el Mandeb and penetrated into the Red Sea and reached Quseir, the first point of communication with the Nile and Egypt. Quseir was 3,506 miles from the Shatt el Arab at the head of the Persian Gulf. The distance is half as much again as the passage of Columbus from Gomera in the Canaries to San Salvador. It was a voyage of unparalleled magnificence.

Egyptian ship development follows a comparable path. Villages along the banks of the Nile began possibly earlier than along the Tigris/Euphrates when the upland people, grazing the savannahs made by the late Neolithic rains above the valley of the river, moved down to the water as the rains diminished and the pasture vanished. They required boats in order to communicate.

The earliest Egyptian ship model dates from the Badarian period, roughly coeval with Eridu, about 4000 B.C. – a clumsy, ladle-shaped object of rough clay, one end flattened as a platform. Flinders Petrie, who discovered it, considered it to be a papyrus boat, but it is thin-sided and quite certainly a dugout, adapted for coming up against a high bank.

400 years later there is a diagram of a ship with seventeen oars and twin deck-houses drawn with great clarity on the bottom of an oval dish.

300 years later still, pictures burgeon on the pots of the period known as Naquada II, boldly drawn in purple pigment on a buff ground, crescent-shaped vessels with high curved ends, banner poles, innumerable oars, and deck-houses. Probably these were papyrus ships – rafts rather – built of a construction of reeds tapering at either end. Subsidiary sections, shaped like the moon in eclipse, were bonded into the central area.

At the end of the Naquada period there is one last superb pot (now in the British Museum); it carries a plain, careful picture of a ship with a square sail. One theory is that the pot depicts a foreigner – the square sail is sometimes used in heiroglyphics to denote a stranger – and that it records the advent of a visiting ship from the Persian Gulf, the end perhaps of the first foreign-going voyage. It may be so. Naquada was a small town on the bend of the Nile where the ancient track came over the mountains from Quseir by way of the Wadi Hammamet.

Below left
A river boat, of the Naquada II period, many-oared and equipped with two deck-houses

The first known representation of a square sail

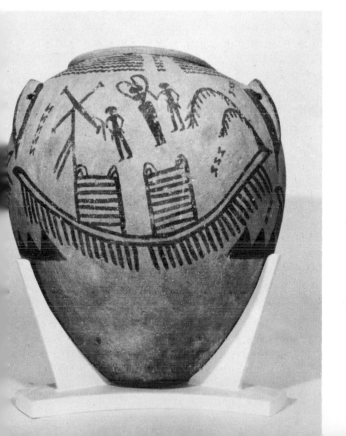

Early Egyptian progress by evidence owes much to Sumer and the Tigris/Euphrates. It moved on, however, without it. It produced wooden ships long before the Pyramids. In 1952 five ship graves were identified at the base of the Pyramid of Khufu – Cheops – two of them intact. One has now been opened. In it, meticulously preserved, was found a funeral ship 140 feet long, 20 feet wide and displacing 40 tons. It had been taken to pieces and stacked with infinite care to be ready for reassembly in the after world. It has been possible to reassemble it in this.

It had had, however, generations of forerunners. Cedar from the Lebanon was extensively imported by Khufu and this ship was built of it, so were the seagoing 'Byblos' boats that carried the trade to and from the Phoenician seaports; but before cedar was imported the Egyptians used the short timbers of acacia and sycamore and they had an immense constructional audacity. The dramatic reliefs on the walls of the temple of Queen Hatshepsut at Dair al Bahri show a gigantic barge, with a length of 200 feet and a beam of 65 feet, carrying a 750-ton obelisk from the quarries at Aswan. It is the high-water mark in ship construction for 3,000 years; nothing greater was attempted until the nineteenth century.

Audacity was limited principally to construction. Despite the enormous enthusiasms of the inscriptions, Egypt seldom displayed a significant interest in the sea – the Great Green. Sahu Re, admittedly, built a substantial fleet for his campaigns against Syria and the Phoenician ports, and it performed adequately. Successful battles at a later date were fought against the northern islanders, the People of the Sea. The north coast of Africa, possibly even as far as Tunis, was visited in trade – and occasionally in war. Queen Hatshepsut in the south, ebullient, dynamic, transvestite (the earliest prototype of Women's Lib), sent down her over-publicized fleet to fetch from Punt '. . . all goodly fragrant goods of God's land. Heaps of Myrrh resin, with fresh Myrrh trees, with ebony and ivory, with green gold of Emu, with cinnamon wood and two kinds of incense.'

A model of a funeral ship found in the ship grave at the foot of the Great Pyramid

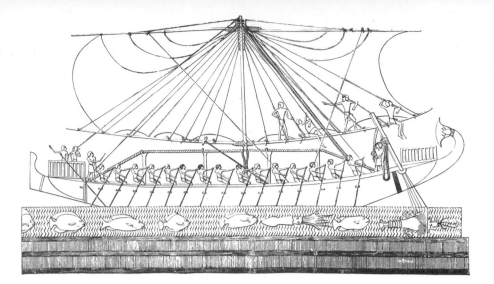

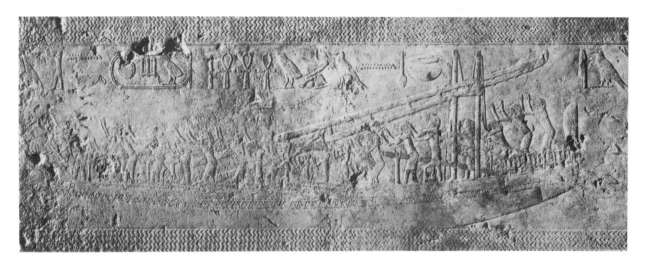

A large sea-going ship of the
fifth dynasty from the tomb
of Sahu Re

Wherever Punt was, the route was already trodden. Ships had passed that way intermittently for 2,000 years since the Sumerians first came to Quseir. Egypt, except for occasional individual ventures, was never an innovator at sea, her ships were adapted from her river craft, her sails remained identical with the sails that moved the great papyrus ship/rafts up the Nile on the infinitely dependable southward drift of the Etesian wind. Surviving models, cautious reconstructions alike suggest that the best of the Egyptian sea boats would have gone to leeward like a child's balloon in anything approaching a blow.

Egypt was, in sober truth, prisoner of the Etesian wind, embayed in the south-east corner of the Mediterranean. From Derna in Libya to El Arish at the northern bend of the Palestine coast she lay on a dead lee shore, and she failed to perfect the sail or the ship which could have freed her from it.

The Nile, on the other hand, was the child of the Etesian wind. The entire, complex and infinitely rich economy which developed between the Nile mouths and Aswan was based with an absolute simplicity on south-north movement with the current and north-south movement on the constant wind.

It is hardly to be wondered at that Egyptian thought, ingenuity, endeavour, even religion, was inward turned; that to Egypt the Nile was visceral; that the Great Green was external and hostile except, effectively, for the narrow triangle between the river mouths, the isthmus, and the ports of the Syrian coast. Despite the inscriptions, there is no positive evidence anywhere of established trade except in that triangle and along a brief stretch of the coast of Africa. Limited finds of Egyptian trade goods on the south coast of Europe could have been carried as easily in foreign bottoms. Minos traded with Egypt, not Egypt with Minos.

Egypt rejected sea power.

There was one other riverine civilization, that of the Indus valley. Much later than with the Tigris or the Nile, Neolithic man on the hills of Baluchistan passed through the same developmental pattern as at Jarmo. Somewhere about 2500 B.C. he appears to have moved down to the river plain, absorbing the indigenous population. Mohenjo Daro – the Mound of the Dead – greatest of his cities, was identified only in 1922. A city of well burnt brick laid out with astonishing modernity in rectangular blocks, it is estimated to have held 50,000 people and it dominated the Indus plain.

Details of its culture indicate contacts with the cities of the Tigris/Euphrates. These may have been maintained by land across Baluchistan, but ruins on the barren pre-oil-age island of Bahrein have yielded Indus seals of great perfection dated, possibly a little early, at 2300 B.C.

If the dating is accurate, they must inevitably have been carried by Sumerian ships. They are in any event proof that there was contact by sea, but almost nothing is known of the Indus ships. That they began, as the others began, as river craft is unquestionable. That the associated skills were part of the contact is reasonably certain. That they ascended rapidly in load-carrying capacity must be inferred from the swift development of cities like Harrapa and the 100 towns and villages known to have been built in the course of Indus history. That the Indus community became a sea-going people is also clear.

At Lothal on the Gulf of Cambay there is a brick basin, 710 feet in length and 120 feet in width, opening on the entrance channel. On the landward side a loading platform flanked it, in the entrance a sill 23 feet wide gave sufficient water to keep ships berthed in the basin afloat. It is the largest 'public work' in the Indus area, but additionally it is the world's first wet dock, one of the major maritime advances outside the tideless Mediterranean. Its technical quality argues an advanced requirement in sea trading. The Indus seaports stretched from Suktagen Dor near to the Persian Gulf in the west to Telod in the south.

In due process of time the riverine civilizations died: the Nile by an endless succession of conquest and recovery from the Hyksos to the Romans, the Tigris/Euphrates by vast swirls of invasion from Asia, the Indus by one immense surge of destruction about 1500 B.C. which wrecked Mohenjo Daro. They left behind them legacies: shipbuilding, port construction, primary navigation, and the urge for exploration.

But even theirs was not the earliest exploration.

Above
Ship model from
Tutankhamun's tomb

Below
Twelfth-dynasty Egyptian
ships

Chapter III

Crete and the Classic Voyages

Knossos on the Island of Crete is the primal city of European civilization. The Minoans built it on a mound made up of layer on layer of Neolithic prehistory. In the lowest layer of all Professor J. D. Evans of London University excavated a camp site with hearths and charred grain, and carbon-14 testing fixed the date of a burned stake from its centre at 6100 B.C. plus or minus (after the custom of such tests) 180 years.

Crete has been an isolated island since the Pleistocene period. The grain at this, the lowest of the ten levels of the mound, was bread wheat, and emmer and *einkorn* and six-row barley. There was no cultivated grain in Europe 8,000 years ago. This came from Asia Minor, through Anatolia, by gradations from the Fertile Crescent. This was the legacy of Jarmo.

The camp site under Knossos is the terminal point of the first known voyage of exploration.

It has to be. This was before Eridu and long before Ur and the earliest tentative thrusts out from the great rivers. Akra Sidheros, the eastern promontory of Crete, is 100 miles from the Turkish mainland. In whatever craft they made the crossing, these people must have taken departure from a point between Samos and Kastelorrizon. Even with island hopping they had to pass in succession Karpathos and Kasos, straits of more than thirty miles in width

We know nothing of their boats. Dugouts are improbable; they must have been of substantial size, for the site yields bones of sheep and goats and cattle. It is likely that they were skin boats on a strong wicker frame of the type that made the riverine development on the Tigris possible.

From whatever point they came, the voyage is one of the earliest triumphs of man.

Fresh waves came from the east as the years passed. By 3000 B.C. there was a nascent civilization. 1,000 years later the people of the Palaces – the Minoans – had a high sophistication, and the sweep and triumph of their story stems from a single geographical circumstance. Crete is positioned centrally at the focal point of the Etesian wind. Theories that it might have been discovered from Egypt or from Libya are discounted by this fact. From the Rosetta mouth of the Nile it is 400 miles upwind. Even from Libya it would have involved a beat against the summer wind of 150 miles. It is inconceivable that Neolithic man could have bucked the prevailing northerlies. The Etesian wind was the genius of Cretan civilization. Constant through the summer, it gave the Cretan people communication with the old lands to the east, and promise of new lands to the west. All Africa was downwind of it, less than four days' sailing. Europe lay across sheltered water with admirable harbours. Because of it the Cretan culture was the mirror-image of the riverine civilizations. Where the river peoples were

Roman mosaic of the first century showing a galley and other craft on the Upper Nile constrained to look inward to their rivers, the Cretans perforce looked out over an open and inviting sea.

It required time to develop. The first Cretans lived in caves – Zeus traditionally was born in one, on Ida. Even before the end of the Neolithic period, however, a primitive trade was functioning just as it had above the Tigris and the Euphrates. Egyptian stone vases, found fragmented in the uppermost Neolithic layers at Knossos, indicate that contact, by whatever route, had already been established with the south. Obsidian from Milos proves contact with the north. The hybrid culture that began to expand about 3000 B.C. with intermittent injections of new blood from Asia Minor, and probably from the slightly earlier Cycladic development, demonstrates a steady accretion of new materials and new techniques that can have reached the island only by sea. In 2000 B.C., when the strong main wave of Bronze Age man flooded in, Crete was conditioned to accept its new potentials.

Maritime expansion moved outwards simultaneously with the Palace culture that burgeoned after 2000 B.C.

When 1,500 years later even the memory of the Palaces was lost, the shadow of its power was so remembered that Thucydides wrote:

> . . . Minos was the first person to organise a navy. He controlled the greater part of what is now called the Hellenic Sea, he ruled over the Cyclades, in most of which he founded the first colonies – putting in his sons as governors after driving out the Carians. It is reasonable to suppose that he did his best to put down the pirates in order to secure his own revenues.

Thucydides' analysis is the first, as it is still the clearest exposition of the origins of sea power. Minos built a navy, secured with it control of the sea, used that control to police the seas between, and created an oversea empire.

Whether Minos was the name of an actual king or a dynastic title is irrelevant. The Palace civilization expanded by administering a novel role in absolute security: it is significant that the Cretan cities were built without defensive walls. Protected by sea power, it flourished; projected by sea power, its dominance was extended in the Late Minoan phase to the mainland of the Peloponnese and to trading posts and colonies spread wide along the littoral of the inland sea. Early and far-reaching exploration consolidated a systematic development of trade and seaports and towns.

Tragically Crete lies in a seismic zone. About 1700 B.C. an earthquake struck. Damage was very wide, but the Palaces were rebuilt in a fantastic surge of energy.

The Second Palace at Knossos is the major achievement of the Bronze Age in Europe. Its courts, its halls, its stores and chambers are past numbering. Possibly it was its complexity that gave rise to the legend of the maze of the Minotaur. Its throne room and its frescoes, its gypsum floors, its ranked gigantic storage jars, its Kemares ware, its gold cups, its jewels, its bull dancers and its bulls are incomparable. It is the fountain-head of European decorative art – and it flowed from the sea and ships.

Exploration expanded in search of trade to finance it, to provide services for it, to secure exchanges. It went to the Hellespont and beyond, to Libya, to Egypt, to the coasts of Africa, the Adriatic, Sicily, into the West; Crete's captains first explored the Mediterranean as a sea, and Hercules was the first of sea captains. His exploits were before Argos and the mainland Greeks who claimed him. He was a Cretan and his achievements derive from the race memories of the earliest voyages of all, overlaid with the boastings, the sex conquests, the brawls and hairbreadth escapes of seamen from the beginnings of time.

Minoan seals frequently showed maritime subjects, like these cuttlefish swimming among fronds of seaweed

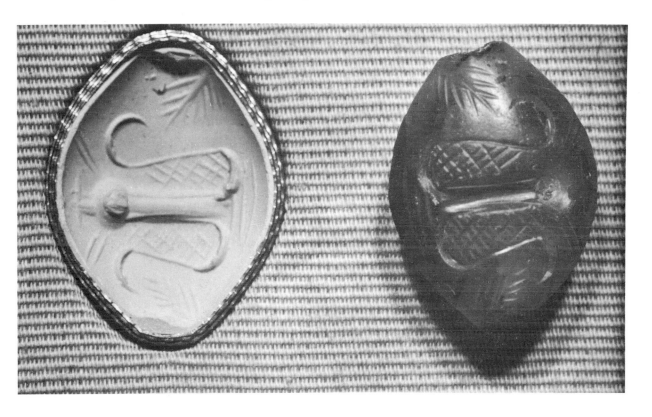

Greek poets, when the barbarism of Greece was purged, filched him. Zeus, his father, was born, it will be remembered, in a Cretan cave.

All Crete was lost in the lacunae of race memory until 1900, when Arthur Evans in one of the masterstrokes of archaeology recovered the magnificence that was the court of Minos.

It had died in a night.

Seventy-five miles to the north of Knossos the caldera of the extinct island volcano of Thera disintegrated in an explosion immensely more violent than that of its nineteenth-century counterpart at Krakatoa. Its tidal wave swept south to wipe out the palaces and coastal towns of Northern Crete. Knossos itself, inland and partly protected by its hills, escaped the tidal wave, but the Second Palace was shattered by the associated earthquakes. What was not shattered, burned.

Two-thirds of Crete was buried under tephra, volcanic ash that choked an ellipse running almost to within sight of Cyprus. No other cataclysm has so instantly destroyed a vigorous civilization. Minoan Crete ended with Thera. In a single night a power vacuum was created in the eastern Mediterranean.

Two nations, Egypt and Mycenae, were positioned by time and achievement to contend for the succession to the Minoan splendour.

Egypt had just extricated herself from the yoke of the Hyksos invaders and Thutmose III, succeeding Hatshepsut, his impetuous sister, had built up a moderate sea potential and a military ambition. When Thera exploded he was campaigning against the northernmost of the Phoenician cities, preliminary to an advance across the desert with boats carried on ox-carts to the Euphrates. He made no bid for sea power.

The campaign was triumphant – and evanescent. Egypt turned back to her river valley.

Mycenae – Golden Mycenae – had begun as a windy village set 'in a nook of Argos' above the track that led from Corinth to the Argolid. Founded by a Bronze Age people who came by way of the islands after the Cretan wave, it was in 2500 B.C. a prosperous town.

Culturally at this period the Minoan influence was dominant on the mainland. Even the beautiful grey Minyan ware that the newcomers had brought took on the patterns that Crete had perfected: the octopus, the argonaut, the dolphin and the fish. 1,000 years later, however, when fresh waves arrived from Asia Minor, Mycenae became powerful as well as prosperous. A working arrangement appears to have been established with Crete. Mycenae coveted, and was strong enough to achieve, a sea trade of her own. It is not ordinarily in the nature of sea power to accept contiguous rivals, but when Thera exploded, Mycenae survived to be the logical successor.

The Peloponnese itself was almost as much an island as Crete. Mycenae lay strategically in the eye of the Etesian wind as Crete had done. Though when first they came to Greece her people had had no word for the sea, she had perfected seamen and sea know-how. How much damage she suffered with Crete from the explosion is uncertain, but Nauplia, her major port, was 100 miles farther from the epicentre than Knossos. Milos and other islands made partial

A leaping dolpin, from a
Late Minoan vase

breakwaters. In addition the coast was west of the great tephra fall. Recent
underwater explorations have revealed submerged buildings along part of it
which may have sunk as the result of earthquake action, but the effects were
marginal. Despite this, it was more than twenty years before Mycenae was able
to reorganize sufficiently for the take-over of Crete, though trade, presumptively, had revived earlier.

The new maritime empire endured for approximately 200 years. Where the
Minoans had established trading posts, Mycenae set up colonies. She set up
power points in the Levant, Cyprus, Northern Greece, Italy and Sicily. Fresh
explorations in search of trade opened up the western basin of the Mediterranean as far, probably, as Ceuta and Gibraltar, and as her vision expanded she
acquired an increasing sea power. Mycenaean raids are recorded against the
coasts of Libya and Egypt, on Asia Minor and the islands.

There is a surviving record of her potential. Linear B, the script on the clay
tablets first discovered by Evans at Knossos and in quantity at Pylos, was
deciphered by the amateur Michael Ventris in an intellectual exercise that is a
major adventure in archaeology.

Initially the results were disappointing. The tablets were civil service records;

administrative documents of the Palaces; lists of arms and armour, flocks and herds, jars of wine and oil. Then, with the Pylos finds, they revealed by inference something of the final predicament of Mycenaean power. In an acrimony of scholarship that matches the internecine wars of the Aegean, they built up a picture of the movement of women and children in the face of threat, gave details of preparation for invasion: ration allowances, the dispatch of bronzesmiths to naval bases, the positions of coast watchers, the stations of the fleet. And in doing so, they revealed the organization and methods that earlier must have readied the ships for the Trojan War. Pylos itself had been one of the concentration points. Homer made that clear: 'Next came the men from Pylos and lovely Arene; from Thyron where is the ford across the Alpheus; from Aepy . . . . Nestor was in command of these men. His squadron numbered ninety hollow ships.'

More than 700 vessels sailed for Troy, and the Trojan War as a whole is one of the splendid oddities of history. With the most profound respect towards Homer and for Helen – who must have had a singular loveliness – and for the dramatic traditions of heroism and sacrifice and treacheries that it established, it was a trade war, fought to ensure the freedom of the trade routes that crossed at the Hellespont: the north-south land route from Europe to Asia Minor, the even more vital sea route – for the Aegean cities – through the narrows of the Hellespont to the Euxine Sea.

That particular destruction of Troy marked the apogee of Mycenaean power. Within 100 years the Bronze Age had ended. In the sequential collisions of the vast migrations that followed it the Dorians forced a way on to the Peloponnese, and Mycenae, on its mountain, burned. The sea throne of the Mediterranean was once more empty.

Tyre, said Strabo, describing its recovery from Alexander's depredations '. . . restored itself both by means of the seamanship of its people, in which the Phoenicians in general have been superior to all people at all times, and by means of their dye houses of purple.'

There was no other contender for the vacated throne and the Phoenicians created a wide market for their specialized skills. They had invented the carrying trade. Originally they came perhaps from the Persian Gulf, a vaguely Semitic people who set up on the seaward slope of Palestine, were ousted by more powerful newcomers, and, battling in succession with Assyrians, Hittites and Egyptians, secured themselves in fortress cities on islets or promontories along the coast. They selected defensible points, preferably with a winter and a summer harbour. Having no hinterland, they carried other people's goods for hire, and built warships to protect that trade. At Nineveh there was a relief, now lost, of the flight of Luli, King of Tyre and Sidon. Six round ships – traders – and six beaked biremes are withdrawing from Tyre's harbour. A child is being lowered from a temple to the last ship. It is the world's first Dunkirk.

The cities retained their identities, there was no unitary commonwealth, but there were *ad hoc* alliances. They endured defeats. The intrinsic nature of the carrying trade made them a difficult prize to exploit. As Strabo said, 'they

The legendary beginnings
of the Trojan War: the
bottom picture on this
Athenian vase shows Paris
presenting Helen to his
father at his court in Troy.

A beaked Phoenician bireme
of the seventh century BC

The evacuation of Luli,
King of Tyre, from a relief –
now lost – showing beaked
fighting ships and 'round'
hulled traders

restored themselves' and they expanded – first in known areas like Cyprus and Libya with secure markets, then gradually west to Leptis Magna and Sabratha. They founded Carthage and Melilla and Ceuta. They were everybody's carriers: Malta, Sicily, Sardinia, Italy, Massalia. Herodotus claims that they settled Gades, which is Cadiz. As explorers in search of trade, they opened the way to Ocean.

Strabo is specific. The Cassiterides – the Tin Islands – are, he says, ten in number. They lie 'north of the port of the Atabrians', which is Corunna, or 'in the open sea approximately on the latitude of Britain'. Their people

> . . . wear black cloaks, go clad in tunics that reach their feet, wear belts around their breasts, walk around with canes and resemble the goddesses of Vengeance in tragedies . . . as they have mines of tin and lead, they give these metals and the hides from their cattle to the sea-traders in exchange for pottery, salt and copper utensils . . . it was the Phoenicians alone who carried on this commerce.

There was never exploitable tin on the Scillies, but the evidence is that the Phoenicians traded as far north as 'the latitude of Britain'. It is at least as probable that they traded as far south as the 'Western Aethiopians', who had woolly hair and were black, and must have been a negroid people south of the sand desert – which means as far south at least as the Senegal.

It is at all times difficult to separate the Phoenician achievement from the Carthaginian in the west. Dido brought the Phoenician skills with her when she fled from Pygmalion: the alphabet, arithmetic, a navigational knowledge of the stars, the use of Cynosura as a fixed point in the night sky, and an immense inheritance of ship techniques. But the first of the great circumnavigations is beyond question Phoenician. About 600 B.C. Necho, King of Egypt, began a canal to connect the Red Sea and the Nile. When he had spent the lives of 120,000 slaves digging, he was warned that he was building it for the barbarians and abandoned it,

> . . . and when he ceased digging he sent certain Phoenicians in ships, commanding them to sail back into the Northern Sea through the Pillars of Hercules and so return to Egypt . . . and whenever it was autumn they put in to land in whatsoever part of Libya they were at that time. Then they waited for the harvest and when they had gathered in the corn they sailed on, so that when two years were spent, in the third year they turned the Pillars of Hercules and came to Egypt . . . .

Herodotus' account of the voyage is the first clear record in the great succession of the explorations. It has provoked wide scepticism, yet nothing in it is inherently improbable. The distances involved, obviously, were immense, 16,000 miles out and home; but a normal commercial voyage from Tyre through the Pillars to north-western Spain or down to the country of the Western Aethiopians would have involved 6,000 miles for a single trading venture – a third of the African distance. Moreover much of the route was already known. The Mediterranean was the Phoenicians' wash-pot. Traditional voyages had gone to Mogadishu on the Somali coast for ivory. To the west they knew it as far as the Senegal. 7,000 miles of the 16,000 was already known and it would

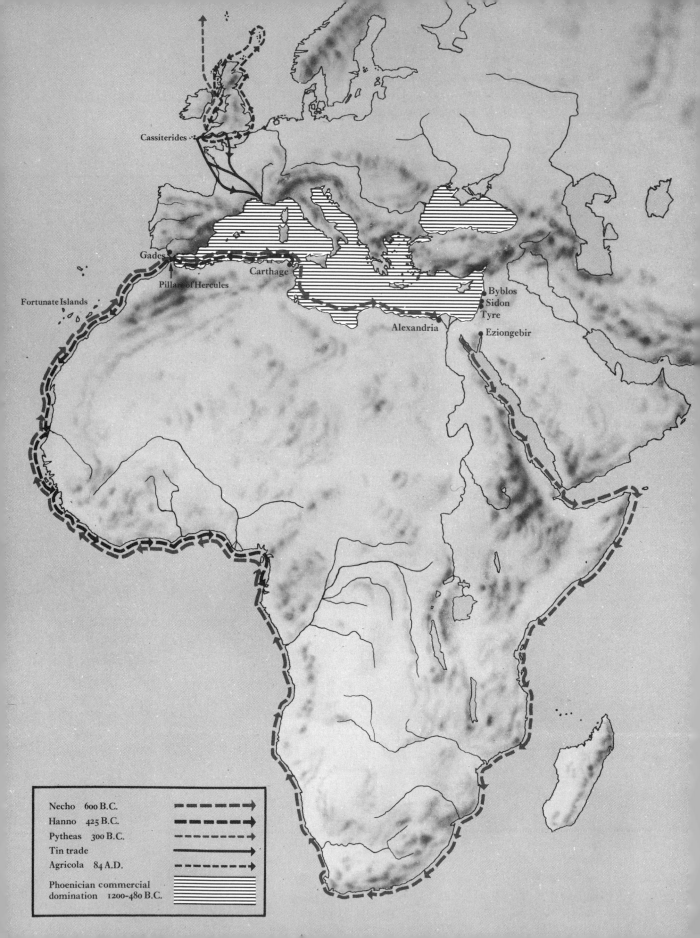

Cassiterides

Gades

Pillars of Hercules

Carthage

Fortunate Islands

Byblos
Sidon
Tyre

Alexandria

Eziongebir

Necho   600 B.C.

Hanno   425 B.C.

Pytheas   300 B.C.

Tin trade

Agricola   84 A.D.

Phoenician commercial
domination 1200-480 B.C.

be wrong to overestimate the effect of ignorance of the remainder. These were the toughest seamen of their world, their ships had been tested in innumerable trades, their sails and rigging were altogether adequate to the task, their pilotage and navigational skills were at least sufficient. They were experts in the northern stars and the Mogadishu voyage had given knowledge of the southern hemisphere, of the stars used by the seamen of India – Canopus which shone over Ceylon, and the great constellation of the Southern Cross.

Herodotus says that they took three seasons. It is entirely possible. Two autumn crops were enough for grain. Fish was in permanent supply. Some meat might have come from hunting. Allowing two periods of five months each for grain crops, they would have had approximately 800 days of rowing and sailing – an average of twenty miles a day with the Moçambique and the Benguella currents to help them round the heel of Africa.

Necho made no use of the knowledge they brought. Possibly it was not encouraging. Africa was basically still a Stone Age country and there were nearer sources of ivory. They would have brought no reports of gold.

Necho was an Egyptian, he turned back to the Nile.

The darkness that followed the burning of Mycenae lasted for approximately 400 years. The Dorians who destroyed it were the collision consequences of one of the broad front migrations that convulsed Europe in the early Iron Age. They were not themselves barbarians. They had the military and technical competence to plan a seaborne invasion across the narrows of the Gulf of Corinth which destroyed the Peloponnese, and to build the flotillas which made it possible. They lacked, however, inspiration to develop their conquest. Thucydides says, '. . . when they had pillaged the Mycenaean Cities and burned the Palaces, the migrating hordes broke up into groups which wandered far and wide.'

There was no spirit of resistance left, however. Even the city states that had lain off the main invasion route like Attica and Arcadia collapsed slowly as external markets disappeared, and the Dorians, after one thrust across the Aegean which established a toe-hold on Asia Minor, neglected the sea and diminished.

Nothing of significance is recorded of Greece until, in the ninth century B.C., the Phoenicians re-established contact. Almost certainly it must have been because they scented a reviving trade – they were a profoundly commercial people – but the contact linked a new Greece with an outside world. Homer was its voice, and Strabo declares positively, 'The Phoenicians, I say, were the informants of Homer.'

Whether Strabo was correct or not, the new Greeks emerged accoutred in a mythology that was Minoan, armoured with a proto-history that was Mycenaean, and invested miraculously with an infinite capacity for intellect and for the arts.

Led by the Ionians, they perfected as early as the first half of the ninth century the *apoika* system, the independent colony, sited on a sea coast, serviced by a functionally balanced merchant fleet with, ultimately, powerful sea-going ships of fifty oars protected by fast naval vessels. It stretched from Pithekoussai on the Bay of Naples to the Black Sea coast.

Opposite
Classical Voyages. The sea heroes of the classical period, the Phoenicians, determined the shape of Africa 'on contract' to Necho, colonized its West Coast, and dominated the Mediterranean until the collapse of Carthage. In the north there was remarkably little exploration; the Phoenicians operated tin routes to Cornwall; Pytheas voyaged to the edge of the pack-ice; and Agricola's fleet circumnavigated Britain.

The Vulci vase with its lively pictures of Athenian ships, one of them a beaked bireme of about 540 BC, the other a merchantman with her sails in brails

When Persia challenged the destiny of Europe in 480 B.C. with a fleet, according to the propagandists, of 1,400 ships, Greece was strong enough to shatter the power of Xerxes at Salamis.

Victory at Salamis was climactic. The Persian army remained for a season, but Xerxes returned to Persia and the threat to Europe lifted. Sea power operated throughout the tumultuous history of Greece but it operated always within absolute limits. It was tautly controlled. It exercised no independence. There is no record of any major enterprise beyond the Mediterranean. Only two Greeks, Scylax the Carian and Pytheas of Massalia, take their places in the roll of the explorers.

Scylax was commissioned by Darius to survey the Indus and the sea route to the head of the Red Sea. He spent two years examining the intricacies of the Indus and made a detailed study afterwards of the coast to the Persian Gulf, and by way of the Hadhramaut and Bab el Mandeb to Heroonopolis at the head of the Gulf of Suez. He recovered the lost knowledge of the Sumerians. The *Periplus of Scylax of Caryanda* is a late work incorporating some of his writing, but the fragments of his first record constitute the earliest Pilot Book in history.

Pytheas operated independently. He appears to have been a Greek merchant of Massalia – which is Marseilles. He certainly examined the Atlantic coast, he unquestionably went to Britain and probably to Ireland; and he claimed to have gone to Thule and beyond it to the frozen sea which he said was '. . . a thing in which the earth, the sea and all the elements are . . . in a sort of bond to hold all together which you can neither walk nor sail upon.'

He said it resembled a sea-lungs and the phrase worried generations of scholars, but the Greek sailor's name for a jellyfish was sea-lungs, because of its rhythmic breathing motion. It is transparent, it shines at certain angles of the sun, young ice forming at the edge of the pack is oddly like it, and Pytheas' description is in fact masterly.

50

Strabo, never notable for generosity towards his geographical predecessors, maintains a constant venom against him. Strabo refused to believe in Thule at all. Ireland, which lay to the north of England, was, he was certain, the northern limit of the inhabited world: '. . . its inhabitants are more savage than the Britons . . . they count it an honourable thing, when their fathers die, to devour them and openly have intercourse, not only with the other women, but also their mothers and sisters.'

Pytheas' book *On Ocean* is unhappily lost. He is known basically from Strabo's acidular quotations but he has his place in history. He was the first explorer of the Arctic.

There were lesser men, Eheumerus the Messanian, for example, and Eudoxus of Cyzicus, and Panchea – though Strabo says he never existed – but the principal contribution of Greece to maritime perfection was neither with its few explorers nor in its wider tactical accomplishment. The contribution of Greece was science.

Thales of Miletus brought and elaborated geometry from Egypt. Anaximander drew the first effective map. Pythagoras evolved the concept of the Global World. Parmenides divided it into zones and latitudes. Eratosthenes, using the fortunate well at Aswan, measured it. Mathematics, astronomy, theoretic geography, everything that is encompassed by philosophy, came first through her to the Western World. She named the winds: Boreas from the North, Notus from the South, Zephyr from the West, Apeliotes from the East. The Tower of the Winds at Athens recognizes eight. Seamen used them or their local equivalents in their sailing directions for giving courses: '. . . from Carpathus is fifty miles with Africus to Rhodes'. With astronomy they learnt to use fully the Great Bear and the Pole Star. With the new geometry they learnt to calculate angles and distances. They were able to accept maps as soon as maps became intelligible.

Greece rationalized seamanship.

The original contributions of Rome to maritime evolution are minimal. There was a port at the mouth of the Tiber as early as 600 B.C., but the vast and highly efficient merchant fleet that grew with Rome's power borrowed its fundamental blue print from the trading system of the Greek *apoika*, its seamanship from the Phoenicians, and its ship design from both. Even the distant trade with India was derived from the discovery by the Greek Hippalus of the periodicity of the monsoon, and the trade itself had been developed by Arabs.

Rome's navy was plagiaristic.

At the outset of the hundred-year dementia of the Punic Wars Appius Claudius, faced with the urgent need to move an army to Messana, was compelled, for the lack of a navy, to shuffle it across the four-mile strait to Sicily on improvised rafts and local boats. Faced with the flexibility of an army transported efficiently by sea, Rome reversed strategic concepts and determined on Instant Sea Power. A navy was built with extraordinary speed on an unashamed copy of the Carthaginian bireme, backed up by quinqueremes duplicated plank by plank from a Carthaginian ship wrecked off Bruttium. Rome added boarding

ladders and assault gangways and spar-operated grappling irons, and sent it valorously to sea under Cnaeus Cornelius Scipio. Contrary to hallowed tradition, it failed to achieve immediate victory – in fact it was captured off the Lipari Islands.

A small Roman boat, from a mosaic at the Piazza Armerina

A second fleet was built. Victory came off Mylae and Rome defeated Carthage in what became essentially a complex maritime war.

Carthage promptly reversed strategic concepts.

Four years after her culminating naval defeat off Drepana, Hamilcar determined on the conquest of Rome by land. In 237 B.C. an immense army marched – west! A year later Hamilcar was at Ceuta, his army in turn was being shuffled across the Strait of Gibraltar on improvised rafts and local boats. It is unnecessary here to catalogue this staggering campaign. Hamilcar died, Hasdrubal was assassinated. Hannibal succeeded to the command and translated what had been hardly more than a vision with Hamilcar into a reality. He launched the invasion of Italy.

Rome was briskly active at sea. In one of the ironic episodes of all war, a vast amphibious force disembarked brilliantly at the mouth of the Rhone to bar it against Hannibal four days after the last of his idiot elephants had disappeared up the defile that led to the Col de la Traversette and the crossing of the Alps.

Hannibal's campaign down Italy is masterly or mad, according to individual loyalties. In 215 B.C., just twenty-two years after Hamilcar marched from Carthage, Hannibal won control of the seaport of Crotone at the toe of Italy 3,000 miles by mapped distance from the start point; 10,000 by the marching and the countermarching of twenty-two campaigning years. Crotone was just 500 miles from Carthage harbour – six days' sailing on a moderate westerly wind.

Rome had wholly failed to seize the opportunities of sea power, Hannibal had missed the opportunities of the land. Half a century later Carthage was destroyed and her ruins dedicated to the infernal gods. It is almost unimportant.

Rome fought other sea wars but they followed established precedents. She executed only one sea exploration of significance, when Agricola, after the Battle of Mons Graupius in Northern Scotland, ordered the fleet that had been his flank guard through the campaign, to circumnavigate the Isles of Britain.

It went north and discovered the Orkneys and, as it turned south, the Hebrides. Neolithic man had been there before them, and beyond question Pytheas too!

There remains one great Mediterranean power.

Byzantium, 2,000 miles from the Straits of Gibraltar, had little contact with Ocean, and perhaps less interest. Byzantium's contribution to the sea and ships is limited to one single astonishing invention.

As she stood almost single-handed against the advance of Islam, Callinicus, an architect, fleeing from the seige of Heliopolis, reached Byzantium and perfected Greek Fire. Three years later a Saracen fleet approaching Constantinople was attacked with it and destroyed.

Its constitution even today is unknown, but it helped for long to keep the Infidel at bay. It was the first modern weapon. All else derives ultimately from it – even the multiple independently targeted nuclear re-entry vehicles of a Trident submarine.

The use of Greek fire: an attack with a Byzantine 'flame thrower'

Chapter IV

Oar Thresh

Early in 793 dragons were sighted flying high over England. Horrific lightning succeeded them. Famine spread. Blood dripped from the timbers of the church at York.

At first light on 8 June following these portents Dragon ships swept in to the quiet beaches of Lindisfarne – the description in the *Anglo Saxon Chronicle* is commendably clear – their crews, roaring, broke like a wave against the abbey of St Cuthbert, fired the church, murdered the monks who opposed them, looted the sacred treasure and withdrew.

There may have been raids (the Norwegian word was *Strandhugg*) before Lindisfarne, unquestionably there were reconnaissances, but the burning of the Mother Church of Northern England is, by definition, the start point of the explosion of the Northmen.

Fifty years after Lindisfarne Turgeis slashed deeply into Ireland and established himself at Dublin, the Rus reached Byzantium, Charlemagne's empire was battered and bruised as far as the Loire, Paris had been captured and the Dragon ships looted as far south as Cadiz and Seville in the heart of the caliphate of Cordoba.

By the end of another century Leif Ericsson was constructing his huts in Vinland on the coast of North America, England was facing the inevitability of the Norman invasion, and in the south the Normans, controlling Apulia and Calabria, were hoping with 'the Grace of God and St Peter' to take Sicily.

The pattern of the time is as intricate, as involuted, as astonishing as the illumination of an Irish manuscript or a Jutland brooch. Three small nations, none of them historically belligerent, all of them isolated from the great collisions of the *Völkerwanderung* and unaffected by the final collapse of the Roman Empire, had suddenly and simultaneously in a surge of raid and trade and exploration uncovered the mysteries of the Northern World.

Diverse theories flourish to explain it: an ungovernable population explosion – a dramatic recognition of the military potential of the amphibious raid – the abrupt appearance of an effective sea-going ship.

Despite Johannes Steenstrup's careful exposition, it is difficult to accept the population theory. Sweden was a wide country. Even with contemporary agricultural systems it must have been able to support a larger population than the archaeological evidence indicates. Norway was a narrow country, but its economy was effectively balanced between the riches of an interminable sea coast and the potentials of mountain pasturage and mountain iron. Denmark may have needed living space, for much of its mainland was sandy waste and scrub pine impoverished perhaps by improvident farming; but nothing in the early advances to the south by any one of the three suggests the compulsive action of a desperate nation.

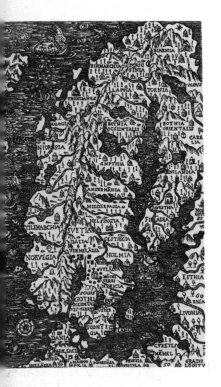

Opposite
Anglo-Saxon view of a Dragon ship, from a tenth-century manuscript

Olaus Magnus' map of Scandinavia

54

ost canis igitur magni cauda sed
constituta e. qua fabule poetaru in astra
mi   nerua que primu ea excogitasse
              mutum fuerat hominib: priu
              habet autem stellas   in pupe
              mo mali .iii. sub cari   na

stellaru ordinem nauis
collocata dicunt . ppt
dicit et mare qd antea
nduali ingenio fecisse
. iiii . in latere . v . in sum
. v . sunt . xvii .

tednis ad la   uda serpens plabitur argo .
onuerans pse portans cumlumine puppim .
on alie naues ut in alto pondere proras
nte solent rostro neptunio prata secantes
edconuersa retro caeli se ploca portat

Certainly the military potential of the amphibious raid played an important part in the subsequent acceleration of the explosion, but the temptation to match this fact with the tactical superiorities achieved by the climactic introduction of the iron sword and the battle-axe (which had brought about the collapse of the Bronze Age civilizations) must be resisted. Raiding was only in part a matter of tactics.

One factor alone is fundamental to all aspects of the explosion and common to each of the three countries involved: the achievement of the sea-going ship.

It was not attained abruptly, the northern ship has a long and respectable ancestry. Extensive finds of dugout canoes in the waterside hamlets of the Maglemosian culture place its origins firmly in the Mesolithic period. The earliest surviving boat – as differentiated from the canoe – was found near Als on the Flensborg fjord in Southern Denmark and is dated at approximately 300 B.C. – just half a century before Rome first began to build a navy against the Carthaginians. Vestiges of dugout construction survive in it, but it was sizeable, forty-five feet in length, built up of five planks and stiffened with primitive ribs lashed to cleats left on the planks when they were shaped by the adze. The assurance of its constructors indicates that – like the clay boat of Eridu – it must have been long in development to reach its level of competence.

The Nydam ship is the oldest surviving ship – as differentiated from the boat – in Northern Europe. Found also near Flensborg, the date is six centuries later, 300 A.D. The distinction 'ship' is justified by her length, seventy-five feet, by the substantial advances in design – she has admirably proportioned stem and stern posts – by the fact that her planks were nailed and that, though she still lacked an effective keel, she was fitted with a well balanced single rudder on the steer board side. She was equipped for thirty oars and had no mast.

The Kvalsund ship was built 300 years later still, about 600 A.D. Her draught is shallower than that of the Nydam vessel, her beam greater, she still lacks a true keel but she has provision for a rudimentary mast. Sail had moved, slowly and tentatively, to the extreme north.

The Oseberg ship was built about 790 A.D. – contemporaneously with the raid on Lindisfarne. Preserved as in amber in the clay and peat of the burial mound of Queen Asa in the Oslo fjord, she is one of the great masterpieces of art in the early Middle Ages. Her curves have the intricate mathematical perfection of Hellenic architecture. She is the epitome of the genius of Scandinavian shipbuilding, the ultimate flowering of a thousand years of progress.

She was not a Dragon ship but a ceremonial vessel, designed primarily for work within the fjords. Her significance rests unarguably in the fact that she represents the supreme refinement of the slow-growing mastery of construction, and that the men who built her must have built before her the plain, tough workaday war vessel that was called generically the Dragon ship. From the Gokstad ship, lower down the Oslo fjord, we know precisely what the Dragon ship was like. She carried no ornamentation, she was about 80 feet in length, she had a keel made from a single oak timber, she was fitted for thirty-two oars, and her mast-step shows that she could carry a square sail of workmanlike size. She was a good sea boat. Magnus Andersen sailed an exact replica of her across

The prow of the Oseberg ship

The Vikings attack
Lindisfarne, from a picture
stone of the eighth or ninth
century

A ceremonial axe-
head inlaid with
gold and silver

the Atlantic in 1893 and proved the type capable of ten to eleven knots in a
following wind. Throughout the period the Viking ship remained effectively
unaltered except in size. The *Ormen Lange* – the Long Snake – was 164 feet in
length, reputedly the largest ship ever built in the north. By whatever name she
was called – Dragon ship – Long ship – Black ship – she was the common factor
in the Scandinavian explosion.

The Swedish historian Askeberg suggested that the vast canvas of the explosion could best be divided into four periods: the raids, the political expeditions,
colonization, and commerce. They overlap inextricably. The brutal raiding of
the *Strandhugg* terrified the coastal villages of Europe until the end of the tenth
century. Canute landed with what was in effect a vast colonizing expedition in
1013. The Vikings of Vinland had withdrawn by then to Greenland. Commerce
was being pursued over the whole area at all times.

It is simpler to consider the explosion geographically, dividing it between
three cardinal points: the east which was wholly Swedish; the west, wholly
Norwegian; the south, a monumental confusion of Norwegian, Dane and
Swede, sometimes allied, often hostile, always operating in a ferocious rivalry.

In the east the early Swedish movements were in reality a continuation of
trading systems which had begun in Neolithic times. The Jutland amber which
the Minoan ships had collected at the interchange points of the transcontinental
trade, had started south along this route. Despite the fall of Rome, there was

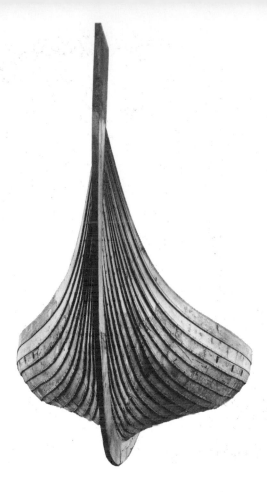

The Gokstad ship, a true
Dragon ship

The Nydam ship of 300 AD

still a well-defined transit pattern from Birka in Sweden to the island of Gotland
and thence to Truso where it divided, one fork going to Danzig, the other to
Drobin on the Latvian shore. Individual traders had established themselves pre-
cariously along this coast and as the century closed, trade expanded and the
settlements grew steadily towards the east. Five thousand of the 7,000 Roman
coins found in Scandinavia have been recovered on Gotland, 40,000 of 57,000
Arab coins, and the greater part of the Byzantine and German money.

The hull of the Oseberg
ship in the course of
excavation and, *below*, the
reconstructed whole

By the early ninth century the Swedes had reached Lake Ladoga to the east of modern Leningrad. The Slavs called them Rus – the word means rower; Sweden was known to the Slavs as Ruotsi, the country of the rowers, which suggests that the trade began long before the introduction of sail. On the layers of an ancient Finnish occupation at the southern end of Lake Ladoga they built the city of Aldeigjuborg. The Russian *Primary Chronicle* says that they were called in by the Slavs '. . . because dissension broke out among them . . . so they went across the sea to the Varangians, to the Rus, and said . . . our land is large and fruitful but it lacks order, come and rule over us.'

As the years of occupation passed, the country, though Russian scholars still argue the derivation, took its name from them – Russia.

The 'Academician' head-post from the Oseberg find

There is a grim remorselessness about the Swedish advance. It went first south by the Volkhov to Lake Ilmen, then to Polotsk, the source area of the great rivers from which the Dvina runs north-east to the Gulf of Riga, the Dnieper south to the riches of Byzantium, and the Volga east and south to the Caspian and the wealth of Asia. It is possible that they used portages in early days between river and river, dugouts are mentioned in connection with the Dnieper, but the dimensions of the trade soon demanded substantial craft. At the end of the 2,300 slow-flowing miles of the Volga was a 600-mile sea passage to Rasht across the Caspian, and at the end of the Dnieper, with its seven rapids, was a sea passage of 350 miles to Byzantium. The problems of cargo-carrying and defence required all the resources of the Scandinavian shipbuilder for solution.

These river ventures must unquestionably be numbered among the great feats of exploration. The area through which they passed was already inhabited, primitively civilized, and therefore known, but the rivers presented stupendous difficulties. Yet within half a century there was an elaborate trade in Arctic furs (sable, ermine, seal and beaver), in amber and walrus tusks, hawks, honey and hazel nuts – and slaves! From Baghdad and Byzantium the Rus went north again with eastern silver and Byzantine manufactures, with gold, silk, cotton and captives. They had initiated the economic miracle of a two-way traffic, not in trade goods simply but in human flesh.

It began, modestly enough, with prisoners taken in the fighting advance along the river routes. It became organized with lamentable speed. It put out tentacles on either side of the river line. Its turnover was enormous and immensely profitable. The word slave itself derives from it – the Swedes called the tribes of the east Baltic by the embracing title Slavar.

To the south the explosion has a more complex shape. It opened at Lindisfarne with the Norwegians. A year later Iona, the beacon bright star of St Columba, was burned. Lambay on the coast of Ireland was ravaged simultaneously with the coast of Wales.

The monastic houses offered a target of singular attraction. Rich in a country that was relatively poor – Ireland was the storehouse of the baggage of the collapse of Western Christianity – the loot was exotic, mystic and prestige-making. It triggered instantly a spirit of emulation. Raids multiplied and as

Byzantine cavalrymen overwhelm a group of Rus invaders

An imaginative view of the invaders

swiftly expanded. Single ship ventures or modest group essays became cooperative efforts of the towns of an entire fjord, or of a petty kingdom.

Political aspirations burgeoned as the potentials of the raids increased. Seventeen years after Lindisfarne Godfred of Denmark was able to mount a fleet of 200 ships to attack Friesland in an offensive defensive against Charlemagne.

Godfred was murdered; Charlemagne, with four years of life left to him, spent much of the time allotted in devising a coastal defence against the Vikings. It protected the slow breakdown of the Frankish empire for almost a quarter of a century; but in 834 Dorestad, south of modern Utrecht, the greatest trading centre of Northern Europe, was carried in a violent attack. Five years later the Norwegian Turgeis took a major fleet to Northern Ireland, and the raids became invasions.

Turgeis reached the Shannon and called himself 'King of all the foreigners in Erin', but the ungrateful Irish drowned him in Lough Owel about the time that the Emperor Lothair was compelled to grant the Island of Walcheren to the Danes. The rivers of Europe were their roadways: the Elbe, the Scheldt, the Loire, and the Seine; and it was on the Seine when Ragnar Lodbrok stormed Paris that Charles the Bald initiated the shame-making practice of Danegeld with a gift of 7,000 pounds of silver.

Their energy was matched only by their audacity. They covered the west in this time. In 860 they settled themselves on the Island of Jeufosse and cut off Paris from the sea for seven years. They set up a base at Noirmoutier and raided first the Loire valley, then the coast of Spain, and finally the Tagus. Lisbon fell to their assault, and they went on past Cape St Vincent and stormed Cadiz. From Cadiz they challenged the Moor and captured Seville.

The indignant Moors beat them out of Seville, but fourteen years later the sons of Ragnar Lodbrok went that way again.

The raid of Bjorn Ironside and Hasting is the apotheosis of the *Strandhugg*. They left Cadiz to itself this time, went through the Strait of Gibraltar, pausing only to plunder Algeciras, fcinted to the Moroccan coast, turned north to the

Plunder: the Gundestrup
bowl, probably made by
Celtic craftsmen and
captured in northern
France, and a Roman
drinking service discovered
at Hoby

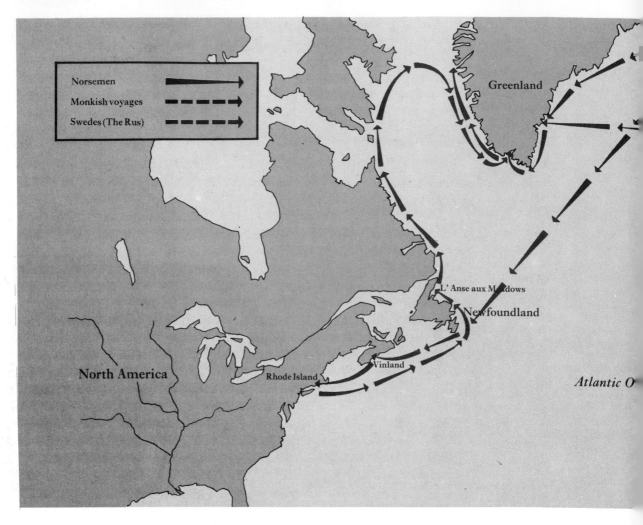

Norsemen

Monkish voyages

Swedes (The Rus)

Greenland

L' Anse aux Meadows

Newfoundland

North America

Rhode Island

Vinland

Atlantic O

Rhone, and set up camp on the stony waste of the Camargue. Arles and Nimes and Valence fell to them. They struck east and looted Pisa. They went south down the Italian coast and sighted a city above the sea and thought that it was Rome. By a ruse – asking for Christian burial for their leader – they entered the city with swords beneath their mourning cloaks. Inside the church Bjorn Ironside rose from his coffin, and they carried the city and sacked it, shouting! Afterwards they discovered that it was not Rome but the now vanished port called Luna.

On the way home they lost forty ships in a gale between the Pillars of Hercules, but they captured and ransomed the Prince of Navarre and recouped their losses.

This was their farthest south.

In the west the story was carried wholly by the Norwegians. There is almost no bloodshed here. Only land hunger and the interplay of natural forces and the first stirring of an intellectual approach to discovery. In the course of it the

Viking Raids.
Not only did the Scandinavians discover the Atlantic coast of America. They also reached the port of Luna in the Mediterranean, Byzantium and Baghdad.

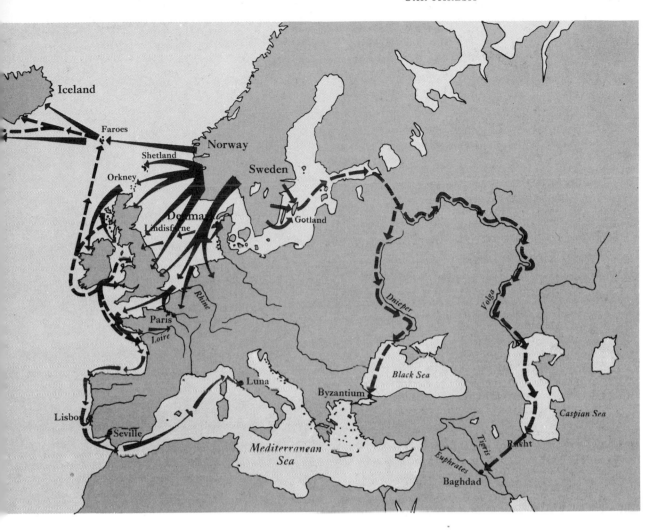

continent of America was discovered by a succession of stupendous accidents.

It begins, formally, with the record of the *Flateyjarbók. The Saga of the Faroe Islanders* preserved in it, says: '. . . there was a man called Grim Kamban. He was the first man to settle in the Faroe Islands – in the days of King Harold Finehair.'

The sagas are not impeccable. There were Vikings settled there before Grim Kamban, and long before they themselves arrived there, there were the Irish.

The Irish navigations have a small and special place in history, a delicate combination of record and legend and plain hard lying. None the less, they happened. Dicuil, the priest, Ireland's first geographer, writing in Paris in 825, describes a group of islands 'lying two days' sail with a favourable wind' from the British Islands. Later, but still long before the Viking explosion, he says that they were inhabited by hermit monks as part of the great northward drift of the sixth and seventh centuries. Certainly monks' cells existed in the Hebrides, the Orkneys and the Shetlands. It seems probable that they reached the Faroes as early as 725. No absolute evidence exists as to the craft they used, although the

A medieval view of Viking invaders

descriptions in Celtic mythology (notably in the *imramha*, 'rowing about stories', but also in the St Brendan legends) suggest that they had wicker and skin boats, hardly more sophisticated if perhaps slightly larger than the boats of that first of all explorations – the voyage to Crete.

The early tin trade to Brittany was carried in such boats. Caesar described the strong, seaworthy, timber ships of the Veneti, but there is no certain evidence that these were used in the Irish trade, and legend leans ribaldly on 'millstones' for the Irish saints.

The Norsemen who preceded Grim Kamban have, despite the *Flateyjarbók*, a great importance. Nadd-Odd, the outlaw, was the discoverer of Iceland in the first of the great accidents of the transatlantic navigations.

Dates, as in most of the sagas, are imprecise but Nadd-Odd clearly was in the Faroes before Kamban, for about the time of Kamban's arrival he made a surreptitious passage back to Norway, despite his outlawry, and returning was caught by a south-east gale and driven past Videro, most northerly of the Faroe Islands. Running for days before the wind in the limitations of square sail and shallow draft, he sighted, in a sudden clearing, snow hanging in the sky – the high and illimitable snow slope of the Vatnajökull.

He returned, calling the new land Snowland.

Gardar a Swede, heading north from Scotland, was blown similarly by a south-east gale and wintered there. He returned, calling it Gardarsholm. Floki, from Rogaland, hearing of the discoveries, fitted out three ships and went in search of it.

Floki is important in that he gives a hint at least of one of the elements in the Norsemen's genius for navigation. The *Landnamabók*, the great record of the settlement of Iceland, says: '. . . he took three ravens with him to sea. When he freed the first it flew aft over the stern. When later he freed the second it circled and flew back to the ship. When he freed the third it flew straightway over the stem in the direction in which they found the land.'

It is a shore-seeking method of an illimitable antiquity. Ziusudra the Sumerian used it, and Utnapishtim who survived the great flood of the Babylonians used it, and passed the tradition down to Noah and the ark. *The Dialogues of Buddha*

The Norsemen were adept at surviving the cold: here they hunt on skis.

66

in a later day say of a bird, 'If on the horizon it caught sight of land, thither would it go.'

Floki wintered on the new land and was very cold and returned, calling it Iceland. Ingar Arnarson took the first settlement party there in 874. He found Papar – the Irish priests – already there, and they left because, as the *Islandinga-bók* says, 'they would not live alongside heathens'.

In or about the year 900 the second of the three great accidents occurred. Gunnbjorn Ulfsson, on passage from Norway to what is now Reykjavik, was swept by another easterly, this time with a good deal of north in it, past Iceland altogether and fetched up in Denmark Strait, one of the world's lamentable stretches of water. A British aircraft carrier, H.M.S. *Tracker*, rolled fifty-two degrees in a gale in Denmark Strait in 1943 and survived. Ulfsson survived also. The seamanship of these men is beyond ordinary comparison.

By this time they were using the *knarr*; or *hafskip*. Nothing was known of the *knarr* apart from mentions in the sagas until 1962, when wrecks of unspecified wooden ships were located on the bottom of the Roskilde Fjord in Zealand. There were six. In a master operation of maritime archaeology the Danes built a coffer dam round them and infinitely patiently separated them from a thousand years of mud. One was a fast cargo vessel fifty-three feet in length, one was heavily timbered for load carrying, one was a passenger carrier. They were not Dragon ships but they were the ships that opened the North Atlantic.

Ulfsson in his *knarr* – she would most closely have resembled the heavily timbered Roskilde ship – sighted a reef, rocks showing in the white spume as the gale abated, wore his ship round in the face of the danger and fought his way back to Iceland, unable to attempt to discover if there was land beyond. What he had seen he christened Gunnbjorn's Skerry.

Eirikr hinn raudi – Eric the Red – named the land beyond it Greenland in one of the earliest of all recorded fraudulent real estate promotions. An Iceland settler, Eric had committed a murder too tough even for the tough Icelanders. In 982 he was exiled for three years.

He could have sailed east to the turmoil of England as it was just before the resumption of the Viking raids, or Ireland with its perennial brawling – either would have suited his explosive personality. He chose instead to go west.

Boat-building

This is the first intellectually determined exploration of modern times. Eric the Red went not to see the 'skerry' that Gunnbjorn had named nearly 100 years before but deliberately to discover if there might be habitable land beyond.

He cleared the skerry and found high land to the west of it and flogged his way down the grim and inhospitable eastern coast of Greenland until he rounded Cape Farewell. There he found the fjord that he named, justly, after himself. The expedition is a model of masterful exploration. From Eric's Fjord he worked his way up the narrow habitable coast below the ice-cap to the latitude of Godthaab. When his three years were spent, he returned to Iceland and invited settlers to go back with him to 'Greenland' because he felt that a name suggestive of warmth and ease would draw more people.

The following year he sailed with twenty-five ships and possibly 600 settlers – men, women, children and domestic animals.

One year after the departure of the expedition Bjarni Herjolfsen arrived from Norway to join his father in Iceland and learnt that he had sailed with the Red Eric. Bjarni consulted his crew: '. . . none of us has ever been in the Greenland sea', he admitted. He might have said as reasonably that none of them had ever heard of it, but they had a splendid rashness. They sailed to follow Bjarni's father.

The third stupendous accident of the easterly gales caught them. This time it must have been a hard north-easter. They drove far to the south of Cape Farewell, missing Greenland altogether. They sailed into an unknown as absolute as the sky itself. They were battered and exhausted and all but overwhelmed when they sighted a 'well-timbered' island.

This was America, before the Vinland voyage.

Inevitably it is difficult to plot courses from the sagas. It has been assumed that Herjolfsen made his landfall on Labrador. The voyage was undertaken in the height of the Climatic Optimum, the warm period that made the first settlement of Greenland possible, but the island was 'well-timbered' and the coast of Labrador even then was unlikely to have been generous of trees. The combination of the gale and the Labrador current makes it at least probable that Bjarni discovered Newfoundland.

He did not land. Well-loaded, he still had ample food; he dared not waste a favourable wind, he headed north and sighted land again and it was still well-timbered – the probability of Labrador recedes even farther. Once more he refused to go ashore. After another 'two days' (time estimates must be taken with extreme reserve) he sighted the coast a third time, high ground with glaciers, and Bjarni said 'this land looks unwinsome and ungainsome', and for the third time he stood away with a fair wind to the north-east.

This is the earliest surviving assessment of the quality of the Americas.

Bjarni reached Eric's Fjord in safety and settled there. Six years later, probably in 992, Leif, Eric's son, bought his ship from him and, after difficulty, persuaded his aged father to lead an exploration to the new land. On the way to the ship the reluctant Eric fell from his horse and broke a leg. Leif sailed as leader.

He found the high land and called it Helluland – the land of slate. He found the forest coast and said '. . . from its good favour this land shall have a name'; and called it Markland. He reached an island '. . . and went ashore in the after-boat and found dew on the grass, and they put their hands in the dew and put them to their mouths and thought they had never tasted any so sweet as it was'.

Leif wintered on the island. The saga says that the German, Turki, his father-in-law, was lost and when they located him, 'rolling eyed, tiny faced and miserable to look at', he had found grapes. Therefore they called the place Vinland: there was 'no frost in the winter and the herbs hardly withered'.

They built huts there, for there was good timber, and they found salmon. They lived well enough and in the spring returned to Eric's settlement at Brattahlid with their news.

In the late summer – or possibly the next year – Thorwald, Leif's brother, borrowed the ship and went west with thirty men. He wintered in Leif's huts on Vinland and the following summer explored the 'western' coast. The designation is important. Except for the inner coasts of Newfoundland, of Nova Scotia, and possibly the St Lawrence bank inside Anticosti, there is no 'western' coast. They wintered a second time at Leif's huts, and the following summer explored the east. Following an accident to the keel of the ship, they sighted a promontory of astonishing beauty and Thorwald said '. . . here I will build my farm'. But when they went in to land there were three skin boats on the beach.

There is a dark inevitability about the fight that followed. Eight of the nine men – the *Skraelingar* – of the skin boats died, and the after pattern of North American conquest was engendered. Thorwald was killed by an Indian arrow, and they buried him on the beautiful promontory and called it Crossness.

Thorfinn Karlsefni followed him with three fresh ships and 160 men – and women. Their first winter was desperately hard, so hard that in the spring Thorhall, called the Hunter, rebelled and took one of the three ships with nine men and left.

The last of the great formative gales caught him and he raced desperately before it to the coast of Ireland, determining, as he battled with the following sea, the extent and the emptiness of the Western Ocean.

Thorfinn went south to the land called Hop, where no snow fell and self-sown wheat grew on the low ground and there were grapes in the hills and the forests were full of game. They were full also of the *Skraelingar*. Thorfinn had taken cattle with him; their bellowing terrified the *Skraelingar* and in the fight that followed there were dead on both sides, and Thorfinn went north again. His son was born that winter at the place they called Straumfjord, and the next spring they won back to Greenland with a single ship.

There is one final venture, macabre and murderous. Freydis, the bastard daughter of Eric the Red, went west with two brothers, Helgi and Finnbogi, as her captains and wintered in Leif's huts. In the winter they quarrelled and she murdered them. Then, with an axe, she cut down, one by one, the other women of the party. There is an elemental horror in the story. Despite it, she got back to Iceland.

Silver-gilt pendant cross of the tenth century

Overleaf
The hotly debated Vinland map. Opposition to its authenticity centres largely on the outline of Greenland which was not determined until long after.

Volent' dei post longu iter ab insula Grocelanda per meridiem ad
reliquas orientales partes occidentani oceani partes tenesse usq;
ad reliquas Indie partes ex leuto[?] profundi oceani venisse aliquad[?]
Videlicet huis[?] insularum quam Vinilanda insidi apellaueruat. Reinen
Grocelanda continuo primum'[?] fide post alios ordinem littonis in hac terra
aperuisse sere de quibus[?] littora te applicauere priora[?] Baldo[?] dereser[?] se venisse de
magnitudo leuto[?] tempore mentes' ebat et binuida poste[?] reliqui merentibus vsa
ad recentiss[?] in insula sterelis[?] vicendum debetur premisit ee[?]
littere reuelle[?]

Vinlanda Insula
a Bnirno repa
et leipo focis

Grønelada

mo filanda
Rornea[?]

Rega
Dorucorum

Manne
Insule
Beati Brandani
Branilie
picte

Desidrate
insule

Randa insula
Rornea[?]

Ingila
terra
insule

Rega
francort

hispaniola ror

Mare Oceanum

Canesio
rex

Bele
Rev
Zilla

Locori

Mare Oceanum

Beat isule
fortune

Pho

The safe return raises important questions of ship handling, and in particular of navigation. How did they find Eric's Fjord?

Ship-handling in the open sea must have been instinct in the Norsemen by this time – they lived by it. Navigation is a different matter. It required elements of absolute knowledge. 'In those days they had not the lodestone . . .' says the saga written 300 years after Floki's voyage. They worked by the sun for daylight courses, making allowances for its extreme obliquity in summer in those high latitudes. The horizon was divided into eight sectors – airts. The Norse helmsman spoke of: Land North, North, and Out North, and on in succession. At night, the relatively brief night of the summer sailing season, they used Arcturus and they recognized the ship star, the Pole Star. Distances between land were seldom excessive (save when Thorhall made his crossing of the Atlantic): 240 miles from the Faroes to Iceland, 350 from Greenland to Labrador, 550 from Eric's Fjord to Markland. Latitude they judged by the noon sun with a rough rule of thumb for the time of year. It must have been highly approximate. Leif reported that the day and the night 'were more equal in length than in Greenland'. Speed and distance run they measured by eye and experience; they had no sand-glass, nor needed one.

No contemporary criticism is made of the fact that Nadd-Odd missed the Faroes and Bjarni Herjolfsen missed Greenland itself – it is accepted reasonably that they were helpless in the power of their gales – but lists of courses and distances were compiled even in these voyages and amended and added to by later experience. 'From Bergen to the Shetlands is two days with a following wind', a kind of embryo *periplus* learned by rote and passed on, for they could not read. Mountain tops were checks along the open sea: '. . . keep north of the Shetlands so that the high ground is just in sight'. They used far-fishing birds, fulmars and eider duck, because their morning and evening flight gave the direction of the firm land of their nesting grounds.

Nothing of any of this is sufficiently accurate to place Vinland with precision.

Late in the 1950s Johannes Brøndsted, completing his masterly book *The Vikings*, wrote: 'It would be interesting if we could trace Wine land by locating Leif's huts . . . like those of other Norse Houses in Greenland . . . by low-flying aerial survey.'

In 1961 Helge Ingstad, who had been Governor of Greenland, and Anne Stinne his wife, an archaeologist, crowned a 4,000-mile search by air and boat of the coasts of America, Canada and Labrador with their discovery at a shallow bay called L'Anse aux Meadows in Newfoundland.

It was the Ingstads' theory that the translation of Vinland was not necessarily Wine land, that 'Vin' may have meant grass, or pasture. In the rough grazing of this bay there were low mounds and hummocks. Four years of delicate archaeological investigation exposed a building of sixty by fifty feet. It had six rooms and a hall with a long fire, and an ember pit. Close to it was a smithy with a stone anvil, small pieces of metal and bog iron. The character of the work and its size matched the excavated houses of the eastern settlement on Greenland where Brattahlid (Eric the Red's house) had been elaborately excavated. A soapstone spindle whorl was found in it. A lump of coal is believed, from analysis, to have come from a surface seam in Rhode Island. Crucial carbon-14 tests produced a date of 1060, plus or minus seventy years; it covers, absolutely, the relevant period. That it was 'Leif's Huts' may never be proved with certainty. That L'Anse aux Meadows was a Norse settlement of the years covered by the sagas is now beyond reasonable doubt.

'The end of the Heroic Age of the Norsemen was an implosion as simultaneous, as world-wide, and only a little slower than the explosion that gave it birth. The battle at Crossness is one of the decisive battles of Norse history. The decision to abandon the expansion was never consciously taken, it was enforced by the non-existence of the resources necessary to make it possible. By the time of Crossness the lines of communication had been overstretched beyond all hope of effective support. At their end was a vast and hostile continent.

Simultaneously the eastern zone of the explosion was in collapse. The breakdown of the Caliphate of Baghdad, with the disruption of the economy of Baghdad itself, sharply reduced the flow of Eastern silver. The rise of Ahmad al Kader and the ultimate intervention of Genghis Khan completed the process. The Baghdad trade broke down, the Volga route was abandoned, the Khaganates of the Rus merged at Kiev and were absorbed ultimately by the Slavs. The trade passed into the hands of Byzantium.

Only in the southern sector was a measure of permanence maintained, and it was maintained only by the paradox of change. The Normanni, who were granted the part of France west of the Seine mouth, became Norman-French. The Danes were absorbed into the English countryside. William the Conqueror's men spoke a dialect of French, and in the final outcome that too was absorbed into the mélange of English. The Irish at Clontarf defeated the Northmen's attempt at hegemony. Even its last historic convulsion – the invasion of Sicily under Roger I – was an affair fundamentally of mercenaries. It ended in the astonishing but oddly practical confusion of a Muslim army, an Arab financial system, a Greek judiciary, and a feudal structure that was largely French. It is epitomized in the exotic beauty of the Capella Palatina at Palermo with its Norman structure, its Byzantine mosaics, and its superb Saracenic stalactite roof.

The hot, hard vigour of the Vikings had altogether passed.

A ninth-century Dragon ship, on figured stone

Chapter v

The Portuguese Initiative

In 1415, the year of Ceuta and of the conception of the Portuguese expansion, Western maritime knowledge was confined sharply to the European coastal fringe.

Access to the southern sectors of the Mediterranean, the Black Sea and the Caspian was limited by hostile Islamic powers; the Baltic was the close preserve of the Hansa towns; the Arctic a precarious summer fishery off a bleak coast inhabited by unfriendly Lapps; the South Atlantic had no known existence and the North Atlantic, with the Viking withdrawal from Vinland and the protracted death of Greenland, had shrunk to an inverted triangle whose base ran from Iceland to the North Cape and whose apex was Bojador on the bulge of Africa. Knowledge ceased at the Canaries.

Maritime exploration has invariably been a discontinuous process. From its beginnings in Neolithic times it has been subject, as earlier chapters have indicated, to gaps and interruptions for causes ranging from the collapse of nations to loss of interest on the part of individuals. The longest and darkest of the gaps of the post-classical period stretched from the fall of Rome to the June morning at Lindisfarne in 793, when the vertiginous flame of the Viking explosion began to light an immense arc from North America to Baghdad. Barely two centuries later darkness fell again and for four centuries little of importance in maritime discovery was attempted, almost nothing achieved.

The Maghrurin – the Lisbon Wanderers – made, according to Idrisi, a prolonged voyage with indeterminate results a little before the Portuguese took back Lisbon from the Moors in the twelfth century. Genoa claims that Malocello, a Genoese ship-master, re-discovered the Canaries a century and a half later. Someone unknown sighted the Azores, for the group appears, inaccurately but unmistakably, in the *mappae mundi*. The Vivaldis unquestionably sailed from Genoa in 1291 and, in the often repeated epitaph of exploration, were not afterwards heard of. And in 1341 an oddly manned fleet of three ships commanded by Nicholas de Recco, its crews drawn from Portugal, Genoa, Florence and Spain, was sent south by King Afonso IV of Portugal.

Following a short and successful passage, it raided the villages of the Guanches, captured four men, brought back a selection of dye-woods, goatskins, tallow and a description of an enchanted mountain, 30,000 feet in height, with a white citadel on its summit.

The Pico de Teide is in fact 12,172 feet high – early exploration tends towards overestimate. The Canaries had been known intermittently since Juba's day, but the rediscovery represents the first stirring of Portuguese imagination at sea. As such it has an important place in history. No settlement was attempted and the principal result of the expedition appears to have been the launching of an endless process of Papal interference in rights and ownerships. Pope Clement

VI gave the temporalities to Louis de la Cerda with the title of King of the Fortunate Islands – a description which infuriated the English ambassador at the Papal court, who held that the description Fortunate Islands referred exclusively to Britain.

In 1346 Jaime Ferrar went boldly south in search of the River of Gold, earned for himself immortality in Abraham Cresques's superb Catalan Atlas (see pages 81-3, 152-3), and disappeared. Almost half a century later Lopez of Seville was wrecked on Grand Canary, and in 1402 Jean de Béthencourt of the very small town of Grainville in Normandy, with Gadifer de la Salle, took down a punitive expedition to avenge the survivors of the Lopez expedition (the Thirteen Christian Brothers), established a colony on Lanzarote and opened the second era of Atlantic expansion.

Substantially before the sailing of the Armada of Ceuta, therefore, there was a history of exploration on the north-west coast of Africa.

In the preceding chapter it was argued that the catalyst of the Scandinavian explosion was the first effective sea-going ship in the north – the Dragon ship that was at Lindisfarne and that survived, in its adaptation as the *knarr*, until the Norman invasion and after.

The catalyst of the Portuguese expansion is more complex. Portuguese legend has enshrined the caravel in the place occupied by the Dragon ship. The name, however, appears in ship lists well before the beginning of the fourteenth century and it is possible that it was used originally for all ships with flush-planking, irrespective of type. It was applied eventually to a small, manoeuvrable and highly useful work ship which evolved in the coastwise trade in company with the *barca*, the *fusta*, the *galé*, the *varinel* and the *nau*. At the beginning of the fifteenth century it was commonly about sixty tons, open except for a forepeak and the spaces under a rudimentary aftercastle. It had a single mast with a simple lateen sail. Cadamosto, the young Venetian who took a distinguished part in a later phase of the explorations, wrote in his journal of the Portuguese attempts to pass Cape Non that Henry '. . . roused himself to accomplish this feat seeing that his caravels did much excel all other sailing ships afloat'. He wrote with the enthusiasm of one who had sailed with them triumphantly. Cape Non, however, was not in any real sense a barrier: its latitude had been passed before the Henrician period began, in the course of de Béthencourt's settlement of the Canaries and its name was not in fact derived from the Latin negative at all but from *nun*, the Moorish word for fish. The couplet about '. . . *ou tornaro ou nam*' seems to have been a late and mistaken attribution. The cape that presented to Portuguese seamen for almost twenty years an insuperable – and incomprehensible – barrier was Bojador, a little to the south of the Canaries.

Gil Eanes defeated Bojador in 1434 in a *barca*, a very small square-sailed ship. Afonso Baldaia, ordered to accompany him on the follow-up voyage, used a *varinel*, a hermaphrodite galley adapted with conspicuous unsuccess for work in the open sea. No mention of a caravel is to be found in the record until 1441 when, according to Zurara, Nuno Tristão was sent south following the discovery

A *nau* (above) and a *caravela redonda*

of the Port of the Galley with '. . . an armed caravel to capture some natives'.

For the first quarter of a century of the operations there is, therefore, no significant reference to the type. Over the next half century it acquired a swiftly increasing importance. It was small, cheap, easy to handle with its lateen rig, capable of a superior performance to windward to that of the square-rigged *barca*. Its shallow draught enabled it to penetrate the mouths of African rivers. It could – and did – venture as much as 200 miles inland. It was suitable for development, and it advanced as the need for it developed to two, three and possibly even four masts. Its size increased proportionately.

Its climactic achievement was the circumnavigation of Cape Agulhas, south and 100 miles to the east of the better known Cape of Good Hope, when Bartolomeu Dias broke through to the Indian Ocean in the most consequential of all Portuguese voyages. After that, astonishingly, it fades from the first place. Dias, appointed to plan and design the expedition destined to take Vasco da Gama across the Indian Ocean to Calicut, abandoned it. Da Gama's voyage was made in *naus*, specially designed and built by Dias to embody the requirements for oceanic exploration established in the light of his personal experience. The caravel, in fact, was essentially a coastwise vessel. The Portuguese seamen of the fifteenth century were, however, a pragmatic race, using the ships that they had, when they had them. It is necessary to look elsewhere for the trigger.

In considering the Viking beginning, the pressure of overpopulation was examined as a possible factor, and rejected. It has been suggested as a comparable factor in relation to the opening of the Portuguese ventures.

In 1415 the population of Portugal was approximately 1,000,000 and the country had just emerged from a siege of the plague. Even in the seventeenth century, when reliable estimates are first available, the total was scarcely 1,200,000. The modern population is 9,000,000 plus, which represents a density of 100 per square kilometre. In 1415 the density was barely ten. Even with the low yield of medieval agriculture, land hunger can safely be ruled out as a primary cause.

A third stimulus was examined in relation to Scandinavia: the abrupt achievement of new and decisive weapons and fresh tactical potentials. The fourteenth

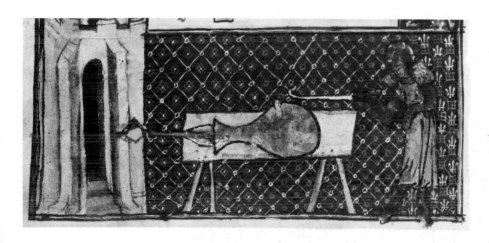

Lighting a *pot de fer*: the javelin is ready in the 'barrel'. From the Millimete manuscript.

century was a period of dynamic advance in arms. A manuscript belonging to the city of Ghent records in 1313: 'Item, in this year the use of *bussen* was first discovered in Germany by a monk.' *Bussen* connotes gunpowder. By 1324 primitive guns were used at the siege of Metz. The Millimete manuscript at Christ Church, Oxford, carries a picture of a *pot de fer* of 1327. In the same year Edward III used *pots de fer* against the Scots. They were called 'crakys of war'. In 1344 they played a small part with the steel-tipped arrows of the long bow at Crecy. By the end of the century the invulnerable medieval castle was already in obsolescence, the end of the *condotierri* was in sight, field tactics were in flux, strategy was readjusting basic concepts, and traditional medieval war was approaching its end.

At sea, on the other hand, the process was retarded by the special difficulties involved with guns on ships. The problem of mounting weapons, the resultant increase in top weight, the practical difficulty of aiming from a moving platform successively inhibited progress. It was not until 1406 that Henry IV of England launched the *Christofer of the Tower*, the first of ocean-going ships to carry 'three small iron gonnes', though Mediterranean galleys had carried bombards earlier.

The problem of gunpowder in the first half of the century still overtopped all else. Early fine-grained powder tended to sift out with motion; charcoal rising, sulphur sinking with disastrous results. Corn-grained powder was not developed until 1440; despite its unquestioned advantages, it must have taken time to reach Portuguese ships. It is doubtful if weapons development at any time by itself significantly affected Portuguese decision-making.

To the short list a fourth and altogether new stimulus must be added and inquired into: the cumulative advances in scientific aids that, by the beginning of the fifteenth century, were actually available at sea. The subject has an immense complexity and is best examined by way of half a dozen of its most notable achievements.

The astrolabe, by which latitude could be determined, was already old on land. Rival schools claim it for the Greeks, for Apolonius of Perge about 240 B.C. and Hipparchus a century later. It was forgotten and revived at intervals down the years; Reginbold of Cologne was inordinately proud of one in 1024, but even then it was not available at sea. The motion of a small ship in a seaway made accurate sights impossible with such a complex astronomer's instrument and the seamen had still to wait for a simplified version. It was not perfected until late in the century.

The magnetic compass, on the contrary, was in wide use as early as the twelfth century. The Englishman Roger Neckham wrote in *De Naturis Rerum* in 1180 that sailors 'also have a needle placed upon to a dart' which enabled them to steer 'when the Cynosura [the star of that name] is hidden in the clouds'. It was not an English invention. Rival schools still argue with furious enthusiasm its attribution to the Chinese (the *P'ing-chou-K'o-t'an* records its existence as early as the end of the eleventh century) and to Amalfi about 1100, though Amalfi's actual contribution may have been no more than to attach the wind rose to the needle. It was familiar early in the Iberian peninsula. In 1294 a ship,

A maritime astrolabe of 1585, showing the solid construction of instruments for use at sea

Opposite
Arab astronomers using a wide variety of the nautical and surveying instruments of the sixteenth-century

the *San Nicolo of Messina*, was seized by pirates and the Prince of Aragon listed a lodestone *'cum apparatibus suis'* as a part of his claim for compensation. Portugal had it at least as early as this, and the inventory of the *São Christovão* on her return from Ceuta included three.

Accurate charts evolved in conjunction with the portable compass. In an age when the *mappae mundi* were picturesque but formless jumbles of misshapen land areas arranged about a central Jerusalem, the maritime chart had an exquisite precision. The unsolved mystery of its existence is its origin. Almost all charts of this brilliant period appear to derive from a single original, so clear, so serviceable, that it required additions as new areas were surveyed but little significant alteration. Working charts produced under this dispensation were plain and clear (elaborate illuminated examples were prestige copies for ship owners and superior officials). A small-boat sailor could navigate today in the Mediterranean with the aid of a normal working copy. It is the graphic presentation of the *portolano*, the pilot book which was the lineal descendant of the classical *periplus*, and the name became interchangeable. The earliest known *portolano* to survive is *Lo Compasso de Navigare* drawn up in 1250, which followed the coast of the Mediterranean clockwise, '. . . first from Cape St Vincent to the river of Seville, 150 miles between east and south-east. From the said mouth as far as the city of Seville is sixty miles by the river . . .'

The pilot books were kept up to date by the constant addition of available information; in due course the Portuguese navigations themselves provided prodigious additions to the coastline of Africa and the charts were expanded to match them. The determination of 'The Rule of the Martoloio' supplied simple mathematical tables by which navigators, working out the bearings of their ports of destination by the use of the rhumb lines always incorporated with the charts, made necessary compensation for the discrepancy between course sailed by the available wind and course made good towards the goal.

80

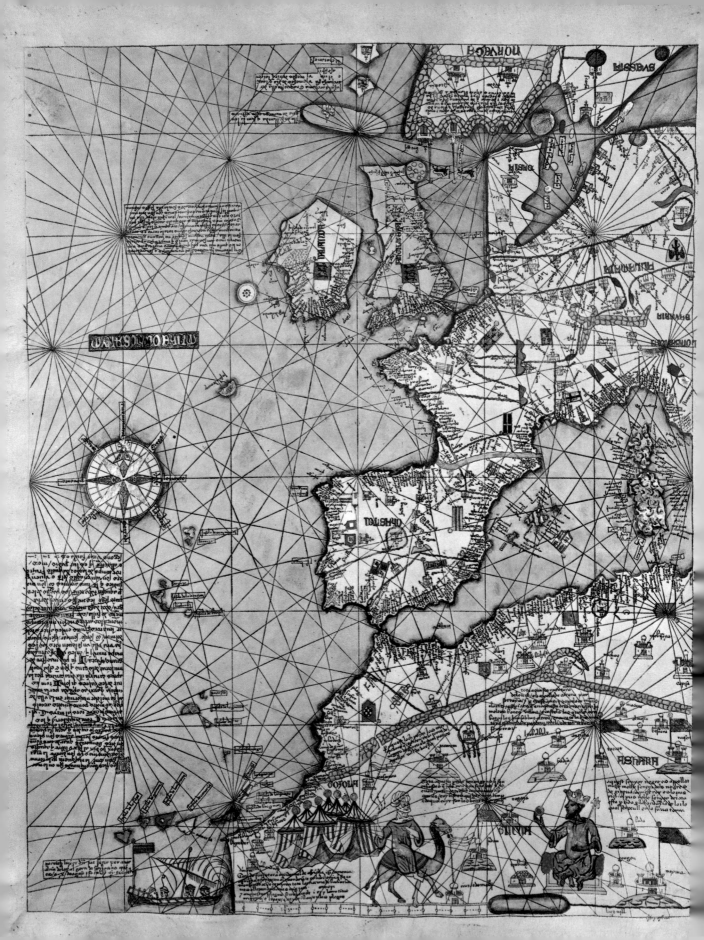

The navigator needed one other instrument to ensure this possibility – the *orologio*, a timekeeper. The sand-glass was developed to fill this need. An English Rutter, the northern and slightly less refined version of the *portolano*, describing a harbour entrance in 1295, said, '... then must ye go south a glass or two because of the rock'. Sand-glasses, exported from Venice in vast quantities, were until the eighteenth century a mainstay of navigation.

All except the seaman's astrolabe were available in 1415. One other was nearing production, the seaman's quadrant. Its origins too go back to the thirteenth century, but the first surviving mention of its use at sea appears as late as 1465, when Diogo Gomes said of the voyage which discovered the Gambia, 'I had a quadrant when I went to those parts'.

No one element in this long catalogue had by itself the quality to trigger this new expansion. It is essential to look elsewhere, and the single parallel that presents itself is that of the genius of Minos, King of Crete, who by the factor of personal control began and dominated an entire period of sea history.

Henry of Portugal, like Minos, was by himself the catalyst of the Portuguese expansion. It is essential for any understanding of his achievement to examine his capabilities, his character and his concepts.

His basic education was that normal to a late medieval prince – the chivalric usage of arms. He seems to have acquired a more absolute understanding of this than did the heir to the throne, his indecisive elder brother Duarte, or than his travelled and literary brother Pedro, but in this the first phase of the stirring of renaissance he absorbed also a reasonable degree of scholarship. João I's court was disposed towards intellectualism. It was provided with 'libraries among the most complete in Europe', as Zurara, who controlled them and who had educated himself in them, makes clear. They were extended by his brother Pedro. We cannot know what Henry read, we do know what was available for him to read, for Zurara, working with them, quotes familiarly from Homer and Hesiod, Herodotus and Aristotle, Cicero, Caesar, Livy, Pliny and Lucan. He was acquainted with the Christian fathers and equally with the emergent contemporary authors.

Despite the traditional lacunae in the classics in late medieval times, it is plain that Henry had access to virtually everything that was necessary to connect him with the past in land history and to most of what was essential in sea history. He was born into the outpouring of material on the subject of the physical world that had begun with John Holywood and that by way of Cardinal d'Ailly and the re-emergence of Ptolemy became the currency of the time.

His brothers profited sufficiently by the same fundamental education to become authors. Duarte wrote on *Justice*, on *Pity* and on *The Loyal Counsellor*. Pedro wrote *The Book of Virtuous Well-Doing*, and is credited with the translation of the *Journal of Marco Polo* which he brought back for Henry from his travels.

Henry himself published nothing. If he wrote at all, his writings perished. No personal statement of his ambitions, his failures, his triumphs remains. Evidence must be dissected from the pages of Zurara – with his unrestrained panegyric –

An early sandglass, from a fourteenth-century fresco by Lorenzetti

João I entertains John of Gaunt prior to marrying Philippa of Lancaster. Prince Henry, their third son, was half English.

from Gomes – with his more balanced enthusiasms – or from the later chroniclers. Apart from these it can only be inferred from his personal reactions at crucial points in his career. What is clear is that he was at least as educated as any medieval prince.

Princely education at the beginning of the fifteenth century did not, however, normally extend to the sea. Herodotus, as has been said, was available to him. Strabo may not have been directly so, but he would have been aware of his main contentions through Ptolemy, when the Greek became accessible again early in the century. A variety of theoretical material was always at hand, but he was never, in any sense, a seaman. The title 'Navigator' was bestowed on him by the English historian R. H. Major in the romantic heyday of Queen Victoria. The

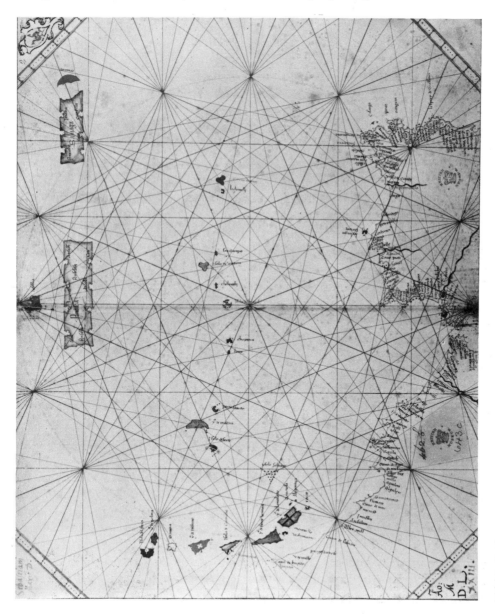

The Atlantic archipelagos and the West Coast of Africa, drawn by Grazioso Benincasa in 1563. Names of headlands cease at Bojador.

86

dictionary definition of navigation is '. . . the art or science of directing the movements of vessels on the sea'. Henry is known to have made four brief round voyages only: the first three to Ceuta for the siege, the relief, and for the attack on Tangier; the fourth and the last to Ksar es Seghir, a few miles to the west of Ceuta. The longest was less than 700 miles – out and home. In the half century of his operations he visited none of the islands that his captains had discovered, not even the long disputed and remarkable Canaries. He never saw his greatest impalpable obstacle, Bojador. He made no personal attempt to investigate either the desert coast or the green splendour that his ships had found beyond it.

It has been confidently asserted that as a Prince of the Royal House he could not reasonably have been expected to reduce himself to the grim indignities of medieval shipboard. The claim is inadmissible. As the third son of a bastard dynasty unencumbered by immemorial tradition, and himself successful in war, he was entitled to make rules for his own life. Master of the Order of Christ, he was in a position to attempt anything at all under the banner of a crusade. He did in fact contemplate at least one personal expedition. A letter of 1441 from the Pope – Eugenius the Bishop, Servant of the Servants of God – in reply to a request for a grant in perpetuity of newly captured land, says: '. . . he purposeth to go in person with his men at arms to the lands that are held by them and to guide his army against them'. He never went. Not, assuredly, from lack of courage – he possessed that beyond question. It is singularly difficult to avoid the simple conclusion that he disliked the sea. As an organizer of issues relating to it, however, he has no parallel. For half a century he controlled an expanding and highly personal empire, providing ships, instruments, gear and expertise, inspiring commanders and men in what at many times must have appeared an endless attempt on the impossible.

How much of his success was owed to his first experience of public service, the mobilization of the Porto element of the fleet for Ceuta, has never been adequately estimated. Under the tough guidance of his much older half-brother, the Count of Barcelos, he learned abruptly the fundamentals of maritime administration and the more immediate urgencies of man-management. In the unquestioned success of the northern mobilization he must necessarily have acquired expertise in shipbuilding, in maritime equipment, in warlike stores, in supply and in appointments to command. Precisely these qualities are inherent in his conduct of subsequent operations at Sagres.

His personal character is less easy to assess.

It is impossible to accept at face value the panegyrics of Zurara. Independent objective material, on the other hand, is obscure. It is appropriate, therefore, to consider him first against the background of his family.

The House of Avis had a complex and ferociously irregular beginning. João, himself the illegitimate brother of King Ferdinand, was Grand-Master of the Order of Avis at the mature age of seven. The dynasty was launched when, a little after Ferdinand's death, João stabbed Andeiro, the ambitious lover of Leonor the Queen Regent, pre-empted the regency, and within two years pressurized the country and the Cortes into accepting him as king. Somewhere

The marriage of Philippa and João I

within this period he found time to father a bastard son and a daughter on Inês Pires of Galicia. By 1387 he was married, as already described, to Philippa of Lancaster and on her fathered five legitimate sons and a second daughter. He was a rugged, rumbustious individualist, but it is an article of English historical faith that his marriage to John of Gaunt's daughter injected an element of stability and good English commonsense into a tempestuous era.

Duarte, her first son, whose primary duty was to ensure the succession in a doubly illegitimate and demonstrably unstabilized dynasty, evaded marriage for almost forty years. Cautious, talented, and in the end melancholic, his first son Afonso was born only a year before King João's death at the age of seventy-seven. In the event of an early death the predictable consequence of a delay such as this – given the tumult and tradition of the time – was civil war. Duarte died early: civil war followed.

Pedro, the second brother, evaded marriage precisely in the manner of his brother. His first child was born in the year of João's death. Practical, travelled, literary, he became in the end an unstable regent caught in a web of intrigue and was in the upshot murdered.

Henry, the third son, evaded marriage altogether. Intelligent, energetic, imaginative, and masochistic, '. . . neither lewdness nor avarice ever found a home in his breast, for as to the former he was so restrained that he passed his life in purest chastity, and as a virgin the earth received him.'

João, the fourth son, also remained unmarried. Alone of the brothers he exhibited a shadowy sense of humour, he even permitted himself a degree of cynicism: '. . . send a thousand gold coins to any of the cardinals and he will give you papal indulgences with far greater blessings'.

Fernando, the fifth son – the Constant Prince – refused a cardinal's hat because he considered that he could not sustain its dignity, and matched, even over-matched, Henry in a young enthusiasm for knightly reputation. He also matched Nuno Álvares Pereira, the Holy Constable, in his revulsion to normal sex: '. . . he had the same cult of virginity, the same horror of impurity, which he considered the worst of sins'.

It would be inadmissible on the basis of the broad tendencies listed here and in the absence of positive evidence to assume a general inclination towards homosexuality in the family of João I. That the tendency, and the practice, existed in other courts and in other royal families – in France, in England, in Italy – both before and after the fourteenth century, should not, however, be ignored.

It would be difficult, on the other hand, to argue on the basis of the shared tendencies against the existence of a significant sexual imbalance. The common factor between the five brothers, the connecting thread, is demonstrably a shared distaste of women.

Henry's 'court' at Sagres was established in the event as a womanless court. It placed in addition a disproportionate emphasis on youth. Henry's selection of captains for his ventures endlessly stresses this: Zarco and Teixeira, who discovered the Madeiras, are described as 'young squires'; Gil Eanes was 'a young squire'; Baldaia, his cupbearer, was 'very young'; Antão Gonçalves was 'his chamberlain and a very young man'; Nuno Tristão 'a very young servitor'; Hector Homen and Lopez d'Almeida 'young noblemen, boys' (they were in fact seventeen). The list can be extended.

Youthful eagerness was no doubt desirable in the adventurous aspects of discovery. Sea experience might conceivably, however, have been even more desirable. The insistence on youth explains much of the early failures.

It is perhaps impossible for the twentieth-century mind to adjust itself to the nuances of fifteenth-century personal moralities. It could certainly be argued from a cold reading of the apparent facts that Henry was a homosexual. It seems equally certain that he exhibited elaborate symptoms of withdrawal. It is undeniable that he had strong masochistic tendencies. It is also, of course, possible that he was a saint.

Some of his contemporaries clearly believed this. The matter is summed up by Diogo Gomes, discoverer of the Cape Verde Islands and hard-bitten leader of heroic ventures. Dictating his personal chronicle to Martin Behaim on the Azores, he told of how he was ordered by Afonso V to examine Henry's corpse months after his death in preparation for re-interment at Batalha: '. . . I found his body dry and intact except in the tip of the nose, and it was encircled by a rough shirt of horsehair; well says the church "Thou shalt not permit the holy one to see corruption".'

Chapter VI

Primary Rewards

An heroic twentieth-century view of Henry and his followers

Accepted legend presents Henry of Portugal as a remote and dedicated figure, self-exiled to Sagres after the conquest of Ceuta and devoted from the outset of his exile to a consecrated search for a sea route to India.

Accepted facts offer alternative possibilities.

Henry did not immure himself at Sagres on his return from the seige of Ceuta. He went instead to north central Portugal, the seat of his new dukedom of Viseu, and apparently spent his time between Viseu and Covilhã, the seat of his secondary title, and the court at Lisbon. Certainly he was at Lisbon when the decision was taken to send him in command of the expeditionary force for the relief of Ceuta in 1418. There is no evidence that he took up residence in the south until his appointment as Governor of the Algarve (his reward for the relief) in 1419, nor did he even then establish himself at Sagres. He appears to have led a peripatetic existence between Lagos, the chief port of the coast, Raposeira, the village that lies like a drift of spume on the hills inland from Sagres, the squat strong chapel of Guadalupe where he prayed, Faro (then a fishing village) and Silves, where eighty years later João II was buried.

The 'court' at Sagres with its palace, its school of navigation, its observatory, its entourage of scientists, cartographers and astronomers is the kernel of a legend. Its survival, even in legend, is singular. In 1453 Zurara, completing the *Crónica de Guiné* thirty-five years after the start of Henry's explorations, declared that he had wished to write:

> . . . an account of that noble town which our Prince caused them to build on Cape St Vincent at the place where both seas meet to wit the great Ocean Sea and the Mediterranean Sea. But of the perfections of that town it is not possible to speak here at large because when this book was written there were only the walls standing, though of great strength, and a few houses.

It is difficult then to accept the 'court' at Sagres as more than a generic name for the widespread establishments which Henry used and the individual experts he brought in as occasion demanded. No satisfactory evidence, moreover, exists by which it is possible to estimate the comparative figures for ships dispatched from the Algarve and the Tagus. Henry, however, '. . . built in the Virgin's honour a very devout house of prayer one league from Lisbon', near the sea at Restello, under the title of St Mary of Belem. It was specifically for the use of his seamen prior to departure, and it postulates a substantial number of sailings from the Lisbon area.

Henry's active career divides quite simply into four major phases. The first, the preparatory period in which he acquired the normal skills and character of a medieval knight and – fortuitously – a capacity for maritime administration. The second in which he carried out a re-exploration of the north-west coast of

The chapel at Sagres where Henry prayed: the oldest remaining fragment of his establishment there

An 'upside-down' *mappa mundi* of 1450 by Borgia, showing the imagined course of the Nile and the vital camel routes across the Sahara: Henry was determined to establish alternative routes by sea.

Africa and the adjacent Atlantic in anticipation of an eventual crusade against the Moorish power. The third in which the crusade was launched and collapsed in disaster and disrepute. The fourth, a triumphant terminal phase in which he engendered an ardour in the people of Portugal for knowledge of the undiscovered world which unlocked the oceans and revealed the continents.

Legend says that he sent his first ship south in 1410. Fact says that in that year he was just sixteen. The third son in a large family, he had limited funds, no known connection with the sea, and no acknowledged interest in exploration. In 1412 (according to Faria e Sousa) he sent a second ship south which cleared Cape Non and reached the vicinity of Bojador. Fact says that in 1412 he had just received his first official appointment – in partnership with his bastard half-brother of Barcelos – to organize the mobilization of the Porto contingent for the Armada of Ceuta. It is altogether improbable that he could have had the time, or again the funds, to spare for an expedition so wholly unrelated to the task in hand. It is just possible that diversionary raids were sent to the north-west coast of Morocco about this time to distract attention from the real objective at Ceuta – Cadamosto asserts that there were minor attacks on both Safi and Messa – but in the nature of the command structure such plans would have originated in Lisbon and the ships would have been dispatched from there. The final claim for the period is that of Diogo Gomes, who states that a major expedition of 2,500 men was sent south under João de Castro in 1415 to invade Grand Canary. The date is palpably a scribe's error. It is inconceivable that Portugal could have mounted two powerful amphibious forces in the year of Ceuta. Other contemporary authors give the year as 1425 and Cadamosto's account of a single-ship expedition in the following year to investigate a current between the islands reported by de Castro must be adjusted to 1426.

No acceptable evidence of exploration or indeed of re-exploration exists in surviving documents within the time scale of the first phase.

The second phase begins with Henry's delayed return from Ceuta in 1418 or 1419 and his appointment as Governor of the Algarve. The vital importance of his three-months' stay in Ceuta and of the information acquired by the interrogation of prisoners, from the questioning of merchants and from spies has already been stressed. The desert tracks were harshly limited by the availability of water, despite this they served an astonishing diversity of country and tapped vast areas of trade. Goods from cities as widely separated as Tangier, Tunis and Cairo are recorded as passing south to be exchanged for cotton, silk cloth, malaguetta pepper, 'elephants teeth' and gold. The life-giving salt route from Araouane canalized the eastern tracks to Timbuktu and the Niger. Widely and eccentrically separated western tracks fed the Senegal and the Gambia.

It is at this point, according to both Gomes and Zurara, that Henry determined '. . . to do by sea what the King of Tunis for many years had done by land'.

It is possible that his determination was accelerated by the fact that King João had banned his plan – hatched simultaneously during the stay in Ceuta – to assault Gibraltar across the strait on his way home. Chagrin seems to have

A panel of an altarpiece showing churchmen, burghers, and soldiers worshipping Saint Vincent, patron saint of Lisbon. On the right, Prince Henry and the future João II.

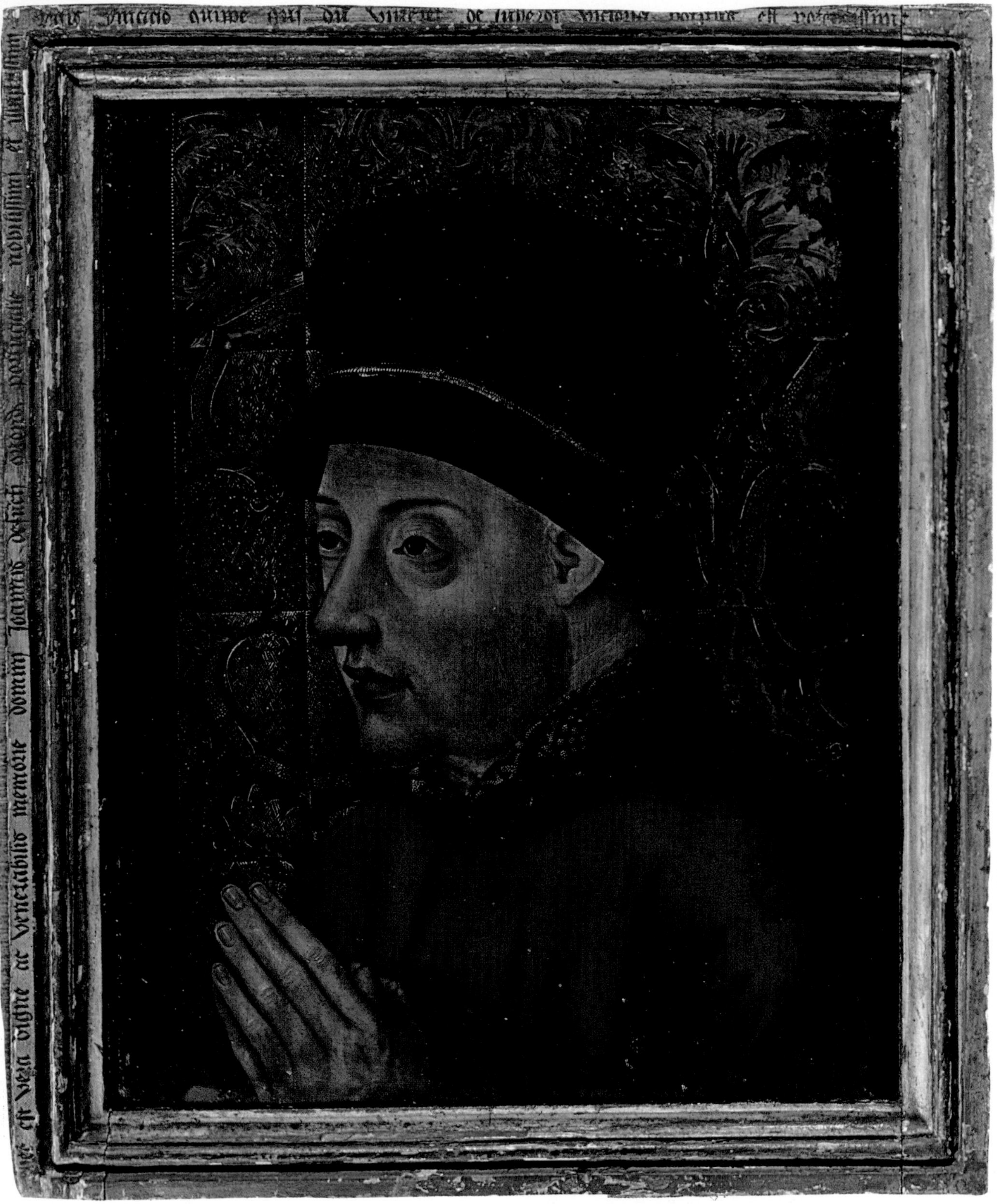

played a discernible part in his decision to separate himself from the court. It may have played an equal part in the first acceptably documented voyage of exploration under his aegis.

Two widely differing accounts exist of its inception. According to one of these, Henry, white-faced 'as one who had seen a vision', appeared to his people at dawn and ordered two ships to be prepared immediately to sail to the south. It may be dismissed as hagiology. Zurara's account is down to earth. Two young squires, João Gonçalves Zarco and Tristão Vaz Teixeira, who had served at the relief of Ceuta, asked for an opportunity to distinguish themselves and were commissioned to fit out a ship to sail '. . . in search of the land of Guiné'.

The parallel between their first voyage and the Atlantic ventures of the Vikings is staggeringly complete. Zarco and Teixeira sailed – in a *barca*, a small coaster with a single square sail – taking advantage of the prevailing northerly. Some days out they were overwhelmed by a violent easterly, a levanter blowing clear out of the Mediterranean, and driven helplessly to leeward. Precisely as Nadd-Odd had been swept past the Faroes to discover Iceland, as Gunnbjorn had been carried to the outliers of Greenland, as Bjarni Herjolfsen had been blown to Labrador, they were swept past the African coast into the empty and unknown Atlantic.

'Guided by God' they made a landfall on a small island and gratefully called it Porto Santo, the Holy Haven. So began the saga of the Madeiras.

Henry reacted with notable speed to the possibilities apparent in Zarco and Teixeira's report. The priority of the Guinea search, hardly established, gave way instantly to a new concept of island colonization. Documentary evidence, as with the greater part of Henry's decision making, is lacking but the factual evidence is that the report was translated at once into a plan for establishing a settlement at the Holy Haven. A third member was brought into the leadership – Bartolomeu Perestrello 'a young nobleman' of the Infant's household who, by the account, commanded one ship. There were possibly two others. Selected colonists embarked in due course with household goods, livestock, seeds and agricultural equipment; Perestrello took with him one doe rabbit, pregnant. The expedition sailed early in 1420.

In the same year Master Jacome, of Majorca, arrived at Dom Henrique's headquarters. An instrument maker and cartographer of reputation, he has been not altogether convincingly identified with Jahuda Cresques, who had been in the service of the King of Aragon forty years before. It is just possible that his arrival stimulated the dispatch of Zarco and Teixeira on the first attempt at the Guinea voyage. It is alternatively possible that he was called in to plot the results of that voyage and to make the consequent additions to the *portolani*.

There appears to have been no Guinea voyage in this year, though the evidence is not entirely reliable. The second Porto Santo voyage, on the other hand, is substantially recorded. The landing was scarcely made before a patch of cloud, perpetually renewing itself in the same quarter, was observed above the horizon. Investigation found another and greater island, cloud engendering, thirty-four miles in length, fifteen miles in breadth, fertile and covered with valuable forest.

It is perhaps carping to call these finds re-discoveries, but the existence of islands in that ocean area was accepted before Zarco and Teixeira were briefed for an attempt down the mainland coast. They may themselves have been unaware of the possibilities, but the Laurentian *portolano* carries islands approximately in that position, other charts and maps indicate them and the curious *Conosciemento de todos los Reynos* lists them. Even if the sad sweet story of the elopement of Ana de Arfet with Machin of Bristol is rejected, there must have been earlier sightings.

The point is perhaps unimportant. What is important is that the settlement was established with remarkable speed at Porto Santo, and expanded almost at once to take in the major discovery of Madeira proper. The new island was divided between Zarco, who took the southern half, and Teixeira, who was granted the northern. Perestrello was given the captaincy of Porto Santo.

Henry has been credited with the establishment of the 'fashion in islands' that continued for the next two centuries. The claim is scarcely justified. De Béthencourt had begun the process of island settlement eighteen years earlier in the Canaries, and the Vikings and the Irish monks had exploited the possibilities as far back as the eighth century. None the less, the setting of Henry's colonies in the Madeiras – unpopulated islands, singularly free of climatic disabilities, disease and pests – was idyllic.

Paradoxically, it produced in miniature three of the major disasters of Western expansion, embryos of the immense tragedies that were to follow in the wake of the great explorations.

On Porto Santo Perestrello's rabbit was responsible for a situation that has invariably been treated in a low comedy key. In reality it was the awful warning of everything that was to follow on the appalling consequences of ecological imbalance. Perestrello's doe littered on the outward passage. She was released ashore with her young. The family interbred and multiplied in the total absence of predators and inherent disease. The young crops of the first sowing were largely destroyed, subsequent plantings were ravaged. Ultimately Perestrello was driven off the island to take refuge for a period on Madeira.

On Madeira itself there were no rabbits, but in the area of Fayal there was little open ground for crops. Primeval forest reached almost to the water's edge, beneath it was an equally primeval deposit of decayed vegetable matter. Zarco determined to burn it out to make clearings for his fields. The subsequent fire is reported to have smouldered for seven years. It did not, as some accounts have claimed, denude the entire island, but it did destroy the traditional ecology of the Fayal area.

The third disaster was in itself innocent. Henry, eager to increase the productivity of the islands, obtained sugar-cane shoots from Sicily and introduced them to both Porto Santo and Madeira. They flourished. The crop produced both a profit and a reduction in the market price of sugar – previously, because of its price, confined to a limited social stratum. Consumption expanded and sugar became a popular taste. The consequential labour demand for its production led remorselessly to the acceleration of the transatlantic slave trade.

The opposite aspect of the picture is beneficently complex. In direct terms of

Henry's establishment a return for expenditure became visible remarkably early. Island crops and introduced products inevitably took time to reach profitability, but island timber and tree products such as dragon's blood (the resin exuded by *draecena draco*, the dragon tree) were exported early and the availability of sound timber of good length made possible the fifteenth-century revolution in Portuguese domestic architecture.

Fallible human judgement acknowledged only the profitable results.

Curiously distinct from the busy-ness of the island traffic, the Guinea Search went on at a lower level of enthusiasm and Prince Henry's next venture of importance had again to do with islands. At an unrecorded date, probably in the summer of 1424, preparations began for an expedition to the Canaries. Henry's finances had undergone a notable change. The income of his estates had been just sufficient to underwrite the first, relatively moderate needs of the Guinea Search and the Madeira settlement. They were wholly inadequate for a large-

João de Castro led the ill-fated expedition to Grand Canary

scale amphibious military operation. In the interim, however, Henry had been appointed Governor of the Order of Christ, the Portuguese Papal order which had replaced the suppressed Templars. The appointment was presumptively in recognition of Henry's services in the two Ceuta expeditions and possibly also by way of solatium for the banning of his planned attack on Gibraltar. The funds of the Order were extensive and a diversion of its activity to maritime exploration reasonable in the view of fifteenth-century opinion.

The expedition to Grand Canary was not an attack on de Béthencourt's successors or even on the Spanish interest, since Grand Canary had not been occupied and could be regarded as technically uninhabited. None the less the expedition had to be planned in substantial strength. Gomes, who claims to have seen the account books and certainly had access to them at the time of Henry's death, says that João de Castro, who led it, was given 2,500 men and 150 horses. The fleet to carry an expedition of that size with stores and fodder can scarcely have numbered fewer than fifty ships. The cost of the transport, according to Gomes, was by itself 34,000 gold *dobras* – doubloons. Exploration within less than six years had moved into the realm of high finance.

The de Castro invasion failed. The tenacity of the Guanche chiefs and the considerable difficulties of the terrain offset de Castro's advantages in horses and armour. The costly expeditionary force re-embarked with heavy loss. In the same year de Béthencourt himself died in France, leaving his rights in the Canaries to his nephew Maciot. Maciot seems to have had the instincts of a Bahamian real-estate promoter. In an inextricable confusion of sale and resale which intermingled rapidly with applications to the Popes for fresh grants of rights, possession in the Canaries is lost in argument. Expeditions to take by force what was not immediately available by favour continued at intervals – in 1427, possibly in 1435, in 1440, in 1445 and after.

Henry's available resources seem to have been diverted almost entirely to these attempts and to a new phase of discovery, or rather of re-discovery, directly to the west.

The Catalan Map of 1429 states that Henry, two years previously, had sent Gonçalo Velho Cabral with two ships in search of distant islands marked on *portolani* of the Atlantic coast. Some doubt exists as to the precise date; possibly they left the following year, after Dom Pedro returned from his travels with Marco Polo's diaries and the new *mappa mundi* given him by the Doge of Venice.

The island of Flores in the Azores, discovered by the Portuguese and stocked with sheep and cattle

Traditionally the expedition sailed from Lagos and extravagant fortune took it directly to the Ants, the close cluster of the Formigas Rocks which are the eastern outpost of the Azores. No high land, however, was visible and Cabral turned back, having covered, fruitlessly, almost a third of the Atlantic.

Henry's stubborn persistence asserted itself. The next year Cabral sailed with a new expedition. On the Feast of the Assumption he sighted the island that he called Santa Maria, and in a slow succession, which continued into the late fifties, island after island was added as far as Flores. Henry stocked them with sheep and cattle. Not perhaps as fertile as Madeira, they were habitable and their climate excellent, and in 1432 sixteen ships were sent 'by the King's orders . . with all kinds of tame animals' and settlement began.

The discovery was profitable, but the profit lay not so much in the productive capacity of the islands themselves as with the fact that they lay at the exact point in the Atlantic essential for a port of call for ships making the return voyage from the south to Portugal on the prevailing winds. They became early the vital staging post of the nascent Portuguese Empire.

The second phase of the explorations divided, with the sighting of Porto Santo, into two wholly dissimilar halves: the Island settlement and the Search for Guinea.

The latter has preoccupied the attention of both historians and romanticists almost to the exclusion of the Oceanic voyages. In cold fact the available evidence suggests that at this period the coastwise voyages were the least regarded element of Henry's effort. The allocation of resources and of cash provides a useful standard of measurement. In one island effort – de Castro's attempt on Grand Canary – more than fifty ships were sent. In the king's venture to the Azores sixteen sailed. Repeated and substantial flotillas were dispatched to the Madeiras. Financially the cost of the assault on Grand Canary must by itself have been immensely greater than the whole cost of the Guinea Search in the fifteen years from 1418 to 1443, for the average over these fifteen years was just under one ship a year. They were indifferently equipped; they were captained by unfledged youths from Henry's entourage; and, despite the panegyrists, their achievement was precisely nothing!

Tradition attributes failure to the terrors of Cape Bojador. Zurara, no seaman, explains it as best he can:

> . . . there was not one who dared pass that Cape of Bojador. Not from cowardice or want of good will but from the novelty of the thing and the widespread and ancient rumour about the Cape . . . . Men said 'there is no profit to the Infante from the perdition of our souls as well as our bodies – for of a truth by daring any further we shall become wilful murderers of ourselves.'

The Portuguese, having passed Cape Non, had in simple fact transferred its terrors to Cape Bojador. Ibn Said's Green Sea of Darkness was moved south of the cape; it was there now that the sun turned men black, the sea boiled, and the mild half-knot Canary current accelerated to a speed at which any ship would be swept helpless to the point where the Ocean roared over the edge of the world.

The Green Sea of Darkness was, in reality, the Arabs' name for the Atlantic as a whole. They had no love of the open ocean and they had bequeathed their fears to Portugal. Even after Cabral had triumphantly found the Azores and de Castro took his fleet in safety to the Canaries, legend survived.

There is for half a generation an astonishing contrast between the confidence of the Atlantic ventures and the successive failures on the coast to the south. Zurara suggests hesitantly that control was not adequately exercised over the youths who were sent on the coastwise attempts and discipline was not always enforced.

The Guinea voyage had in fact been permitted to turn into a racket. The evidence is implicit in the report of Henry's dealings with Gil Eanes after the abortive attempt of 1433.

Eanes, a 'young squire' of the establishment, was sent in that year with the usual injunction to pass Cape Bojador. This was the fourteenth attempt. Zarco and Teixeira, with the first, had finished up at Porto Santo. Twelve others in succession had failed through simple lack of determination or wilful diversion to other and more personally profitable targets.

Eanes cleared Cape Nam without problems, worked down the coast for another thirty miles, then blithely altered course to seaward and headed for the Canaries. Arrived at the islands, he went 'blackbirding', captured a total of eight natives and put back to Lagos to offer them for sale with a bland story that wind and current had made Bojador impassable. Predecessors had altered course much earlier, two are reported as having raided the coast of Granada, one to have reached the Levant. Eanes assumed that he too could get away with it.

Henry interviewed him, listened to a claim that seamen had told him that it was out of the question, and said, '. . . if there were any authority for the stories that they tell I would not blame you, but you have repeated to me only the opinions of four seamen from the Flanders trade or from other well-frequented ports who know nothing of the needle or the sailing chart.'

The interview ended with a *pro forma* 'try again!' The contrast between Henry's laxity towards his fledgling captains compared with the taut handling of the Atlantic voyages has nowhere been adequately examined. That his preliminary enthusiasm for the Guinea search should have been temporarily submerged in the immediate possibilities of the islands can of course be accepted, but that for fifteen years he should have disregarded the flagrant irregularities of the coastwise ventures is difficult to understand except in terms of special relationships.

The failure of Gil Eanes's first voyage ends the second phase of exploration. The third opens with the death of João I – King of Good Memory.

The degree of independence under which Henry operated in the period preceding his father's death is of interest. Until his appointment to the Governorship of the Algarve he seems to have been under normal control as a younger son. His elevation to the Grand Mastership of the Order of Christ gave him, however, financial independence. But the old King kept rein on all his sons, and in relation to the impetuous Henry he seems to have exercised a subtle system of checks and balances. While Henry selected his own objectives and allocated his own resources, he appears to have been warned off Morocco. With the fortuitous discovery of the Madeiras he seems, however, to have conceived the idea of a ring fence round north-west Africa. The Azores development and the attack on the Canaries all had a secondary value as jumping-off points for an attack on Morocco or bases for blockade. In this period Guinea dropped to the bottom of the list of priorities.

The extent of the old King's control is apparent only at his death. He was hardly buried before pressures for an attack on Tangier opened. Apologists after its failure worked ponderously on theories that the pressures came from the youngest brother Fernando. Nothing in the preliminaries justifies it. Fernando was in fact thirty-one years old at his father's death and thirty-five (middle-aged in medieval terms) at the opening of the attack. That he was mystically eager to do battle against the Moor was common form in that day. Henry headed the party of attack – the hero of Ceuta, the master of amphibious warfare, the man of power with the personal account to settle against the Moor. Fernando combined with him, and the royal family was split in two.

Pedro and the Count of Barcelos opposed it. The young João joined them on economic grounds. Duarte, the new crowned King, adopted, characteristically, a neutral stance. The women of the family split at the dynastic level.

Debate raged for a year. At the end of it Duarte, exhausted, joined forces with Henry and Fernando and preparations began, but from the first they lacked the dynamic quality of the Ceuta mobilization. The country, like Prince João, was sceptical for economic reasons, and Barcelos worked underground against it. But the ships were built or chartered, munitions fabricated, levies ordered, and on 17 August 1437 the armada sailed, in divisions – one from Oporto, one from Lisbon. It has been criticized on account of the quality of the ships. In reality they were adequate, though most of them were merchant ships and coasters. What was wrong was not ships but numbers. Accounts vary; a levy of 14,000 was certainly authorized at departure, but estimates of the number of men who reached Ceuta range from 10,500 to 6,000. The mission was indifferently popular.

Duarte had advocated a three-pronged attack on Tangier, Alcácer and Arzila simultaneously, relying on the factor of surprise and the mobility of sea power. Henry rejected it in favour of a time-wasting disembarkation at Ceuta and an advance by land across the northern peninsula of Morocco. The passage to Ceuta was made in the fast time of five days; the transit of the Strait in daylight alerted all Morocco and the landing was delayed, for reasons not explained, until 9 September when it was ascertained that the direct road to Tangier was not passable and Henry was forced to make his move by way of Tetouan – which capitulated instantly – and el Fendek. On 13 September (dates again are uncertain) he reached Tangier. Fernando, suffering from a fever, was there already with ships of the supply train and the reserve, anchored offshore. Tactical as well as strategic surprise had been thrown away. Henry, without waiting for his brother to land, deployed from the line of march and attacked.

He was thrown back with heavy casualties by a prepared and determined enemy. De Menezes, old but wise with twenty years in command of the defence

FERDINANDVS PORTVGALLIÆ PRINCEPS
VIXIT ANN. XLI. OBIIT Aº. M. CCCC. XLIII.

Left
Fernando, Henry's youngest brother, died a prisoner of the Moors

Right
The young João

of Ceuta, had urged him, vainly, to send back to Portugal for reinforcement. Henry now began to pay the price of his impatience.

On 14 September Fernando came ashore and it was decided to send to Ceuta for cannon, scaling ladders and mantlets, and lay siege to Tangier in due form. On 20 September a second and more carefully prepared assault was mounted. The cannon proved ineffective, the attack cost 500 men; and a ship was sent back to Ceuta for two heavier cannon.

The nearer hills were beginning to fill with Moors now as the relief force came down from the hinterland. With stupendous arrogance Henry rejected his brother's advice to maintain one flank on the sea. His camp was entrenched some two miles from the landing place. For this too he paid the price. His last assault appears to have faced two ways: the main weight of it against Sala ben Sala's enduring walls, the rearguard facing the onset of the vast forces of the relief.

Henry and his men, themselves besieged, fought with prodigious courage in a position that they themselves had made untenable. Inevitably they were cut off from the sea. A plan was made for a final withdrawal in the darkness and, incredibly, was betrayed to Sala ben Sala by Mertim Vieyra – Henry's personal chaplain. The ignominious end of the campaign, with Prince Fernando and twelve nobles surrendered as hostages for the promised return of Ceuta, is one of the sombre disasters of the last crusades.

Henry himself withdrew to Ceuta and waited as King Duarte and the Cortes slowly made up their minds on the proposition that Ceuta was worth more than a Prince. He stayed in Ceuta to rationalize his humiliation and not until the following spring did he brace himself to return to the seclusion of the Algarve.

The fourth and final phase of the explorations began, existentially, in the year after João's death. Gil Eanes, ordered peremptorily to make another attempt on Bojador, passed it without difficulty and landed on a peaceful beach. In the turmoil of the time and the growing volume of the Tangier debate it failed to make the impact that it deserved. It is plain that at some moment in the long continuity of failure, different and more rational terrors had been added to the reputation of Bojador. Whether any of these were included in 'the stories that they tell' is not known; it had come to be believed, however, that Bojador was a vast promontory reaching a hundred miles out to sea, so low that it was scarcely visible, that there was a reef stretching out from it for fifteen miles, that the water was so shallow that even a league from land there was no more than a fathom's depth, that a tide race existed for thirty miles from the shore. These were not legends but practical terrors, seamen's dangers. None of them existed!

Bojador is not so much a cape as a bulge in the land. The modern pilot book gives the height of its lighthouse as 229 feet and it is visible for long distances. It has no reef and the current Admiralty chart indicates that the ten-fathom line comes in almost to the low, sandy cliff edge. There are no outlying dangers. It is a remarkably innocent stretch of coast.

Gil Eanes at his second attempt was palpably suspicious of navigational dangers. Somewhere about Cape Juby he stood away from the land to gain sea

The city of Tangier, attacked by Henry in 1437

TINGIS. LVSITANIS. TANGIARA.

room, and stood in again only when dead-reckoning told him that he was clear of the Cape and all possible dangers.

He found no promontory, no reef, no shoals. In gentle weather he landed on a desert coast innocent of any sign of man. At the high-water mark he found a plant 'such as we call in our land St Mary's rose', and gathered it to take back to Henry. The sea, he said in one of the supreme essays in *naïveté* in the history of exploration '. . . was as easy to sail in as the waters at home'.

Henry's reaction was incisive. Eanes was ordered out again 'almost before his report was complete'. Afonso Gonçalves Baldaia, Henry's cupbearer, was sent out in company, in command of a *barinel* for easier handling in coastal waters. The legends had dispersed, the sea dangers were forgotten. In one impetuous thrust the two men moved fifty leagues south of Bojador to a small bay which they called Angra dos Ruivos, and on the desolate sand above the beach they found the footprints of men and camels.

Again they went back to report. Indecision had altogether vanished. Baldaia's ship was re-equipped, and he took on board two horses so that the land beyond the beaches could be investigated. In 1436, a hundred leagues beyond Bojador, he found a deep inlet like the mouth of a great river and assumed, with incandescent hope, that it was the Rio do Ouro – the river of gold.

The horses were swung out and swum ashore. Hector Homen and Diogo Lopes, 'noble youths' of seventeen, rode up the eastern bank of the inlet and clashed with a group of nineteen men, armed with spears. For all that day they skirmished and made contact with the ship again at dawn.

Baldaia went up by boat, sighting vast herds of 'sea wolves', but the spearmen had fled. He filled the ship instead with seal skins – the first cargo loaded in Africa south of Morocco – and continued south. There was no river, and no gold.

Fifty leagues beyond the Rio do Ouro (the distances must not be calculated too precisely) he sighted a high rock like an oared ship and named its doubtful harbour Port of the Galley. In three seasons Eanes and Baldaia between them added to man's knowledge more than the sum of the fourteen voyages that had preceded them! ·

When he reached home enthusiasm had evaporated. Henry was immersed in the politics and preparations of the Tangier campaign. Almost certainly he was in Lisbon, or at Tomar where, as Grand Master of the Order of Christ which was deeply implicated in the new crusade, he had a palace.

For five years exploration was suspended.

The Tangier campaign was a military disaster; its aftermath was human tragedy. Fernando, the last calculations as to his value made, the final attempts at ransom aborted, began his slow approach to death in the atrocious confines of a Moorish prison. Henry, entrapped in remorse – or injured pride, according to his enemies – disengaged from the world in his territory of the Algarve. Duarte, on an unhappy throne, diminished in an agony of indecision and died within the year – of plague according to the doctors, of a broken heart according to his friends. The regency made inevitable by his early death opened its lamentable course, and Portugal moved by jolting and uncertain stages towards civil war.

Two ships only went south in this period, both private ventures. One returned through stress of weather, the other loaded seal skins at the Rio do Ouro and came home. Two others, described (probably incorrectly) as caravels, started out but '. . . because they had hap that was contrary', gave up.

In 1441 Portugal was quiescent. The troubles of the Regency had been for the time adjusted; Queen Leonor was safely in exile in Spain; Pedro was firm in the saddle; the Cortes had asserted itself; and Henry, drawn out of his seclusion, returned to something approaching normality.

Exploration was resumed. There was no urgency about it, no explosion of enthusiasm, but he sent south '. . . a little ship, which he gave to Antão Gonçalves, his chamberlain, only charging him to load a cargo of skins and oil. For because his age was so unformed and his authority of needs so slight, he laid all the lighter his commands upon him . . .' Gonçalves reached the Rio do Ouro without problems, located the 'sea wolves', clubbed enough of them to make up his cargo of skins and oil, and called his ship's company together. He was, he said, '. . . ill content with such petty merchandise' but he felt that if they would support him (there were twenty-one of them all told) they might have the fortune to capture prisoners for the Infant, in which case their reward would be commensurate with the result. Support was unanimous.

They landed at night, Gonçalves and nine others. In the darkness they felt their way inland. At dawn, well away from the sea, they found a path and the tracks of a group of perhaps forty men, leading in the wrong direction. Returning in the heat, and short of water, they came upon one naked man, driving a camel. He defended himself, was wounded by a javelin, and surrendered . . . the first African captive! Returning with their prisoner to the ship, they sighted men on the crest of a hill, and a woman below and captured her also.

When they reached the beach there was a new ship in the inlet. For the first time Zurara uses the description 'caravel'. She marks not only the introduction of a new type, immeasurably better equipped for the requirements of coastal exploration, but of a revived enthusiasm!

Her commander, Nuno Tristão, '. . . who had been brought up from boyhood in the Infant's privy chamber', had explicit orders to take prisoners '. . . by every means in his power'. That Gonçalves had forestalled him independently appears to have been approved; 'They met with great joy.' The prisoners were questioned but the interpreter provided by Henry could get nothing from them for they were Berbers and spoke 'Azeneguey of the Sahara', and Tristão at once proposed a second raid, each ship supplying ten men led by their captains. After debate – Gonçalves feared that the previous night's clash might have aroused the entire area – the proposal was agreed. In the darkness they located two encampments and fell on them crying 'Portugal and St Iago!'. Five men were killed, ten taken prisoner despite a resolute defence.

One of them, Adahu, a Berber, 'was nobler than the rest' and communication was established, but attempts to make further contacts failed. The Azenegues withdrew inland; Nuno Tristão continued south in obedience to prior orders while Gonçalves headed for Lagos with his cargo of skins, his oil – and the first captives brought out of Africa.

The Renaissance slave trade had effectively begun.

Chapter VII

The Triumph of Guinea

Gonçalves' cargo was accepted at its real value as an earnest of future possibilities. That it came from the underpopulated sea-edge of the Sahara, and had therefore plain limitations, was considered irrelevant. The merchants of Lagos were as aware as Henry himself of the possibilities of a green and fecund country to the south of the Sahara. It was the constant gossip of Ceuta and they handled the Ceuta trade, such as it was.

Criticism of Henry's methods and purpose, long vocal and recently vociferous, altered abruptly.

The second leg of Nuno Tristão's voyage produced no fresh captives. It produced, on the other hand, important evidence as to the potentials of the caravel. Tristão's ship was handy and it was possible with her shoal draught to stand close in, investigate and get clear in situations where with traditional vessels it would have been necessary to anchor and use the ship's boat. When on one of these investigations Tristão sustained bottom damage, it proved equally possible to lay the ship ashore in a reasonably sheltered cove, careen her, make good the damage, and haul off: 'He kept his tides as if he were in the Tagus', said one account admiringly.

Moving well, he passed the Port of the Galley, discovered Cape Branco – the White Cape – where he landed, found footprints and abandoned nets but no life, and turned for home.

Both men were properly rewarded. Gonçalves became Henry's secretary. In his new capacity he must have been aware of Henry's correspondence with Pope Eugenius. Barros, the historian of the sixteenth century, wrote in the *Décadas de Ásia* that Henry asked Eugenius for a grant in perpetuity to the Crown '. . . of all the land that should be discovered over this our Ocean Sea, from Cape Bojador to the Indies'.

If Barros is correct, this is the earliest significant reference to the Indies. But Barros wrote a hundred years after the event in a period when Portugal's hold on India desperately needed strengthening and her claims to priority were of the first importance, and nothing in the Pope's reply dealt either with India or with the land grants. It offered only to '. . . all of those engaged in the said war, by Apostolic authority and by these letters, full remission of all those sins of which they shall be truly penitent at heart'.

Spiritually it was comforting, politically it was of doubtful significance. None the less, Barros had used the term 'Indies' and it is necessary to ascertain what the name meant to a fifteenth-century Portuguese.

Gonçalves himself supplies an important clue.

Adahu, 'the Cavalier' as he is occasionally called, had cooperated well in captivity in the role of West African expert. Henry got from him a substantial volume of information on the coast, the caravan routes, the Western Sahara

Henry hoped his sea-route would rival these caravan trails across the Sahara, shown on a map of 1563

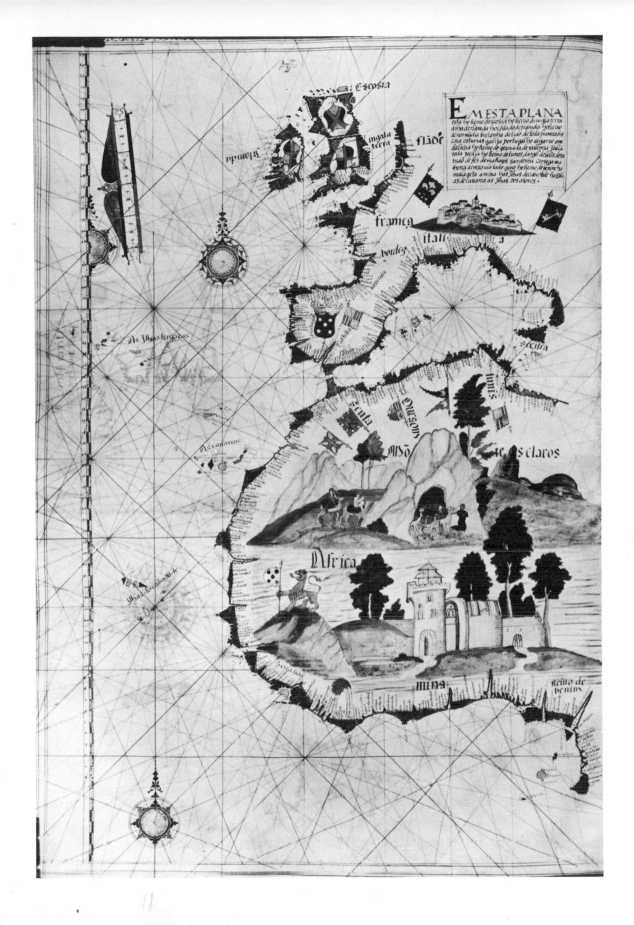

itself – and the slave trade. In due course he asked to be permitted, as a reward, to return home. If the two Azenegue youths with him were also sent back, he suggested, it would be possible to arrange an exchange. He estimated that the Portuguese could expect ten slaves in return.

Gonçalvcs pointed out, logically, that ten new souls for Christ were mathematically more acceptable than three, and that new information would come with them. Adahu said:

> ... the blacks could give him news of land much further distant, and he promised that when he spoke about the traffic with the natives he would find means to learn as much news as possible.
>
> The Infant answered all this and said that he was obliged by his offer, and that he not only desired to have knowledge of that land, but also of the Indies, and of the land of Prester John, if he could.

Henry's answer is vital to any understanding of his aim.

It is demonstrably the corner-stone of the tradition that Henry's most urgent purpose was the discovery of a sea route to India. It is authentic in that it rests on information supplied to Zurara in the course of his stay at Henry's house and is not, therefore, open to ordinary question. Its significance logically rests on the precise meaning of the word 'Indies'.

Los Indias in the fourteenth century – and for that matter later – was a broad term for the Orient. Specifically there were from remote antiquity two Indias: Nearer India and Further India or, alternatively, Greater India and Lesser India, and Nearer India was the coast of Abyssinia.

The usage is generic. It is a description rather than a name, and a parallel involving both it and Prester John appears as late as 1540, long after the actual discovery of India, in the narrative of the Portuguese embassy to Abyssinia entitled *Ho Presto Joam das indias* – Prester John of the Indies.

Much in support of the search for a sea route to India has been built on this single reference in Zurara, and the identity of 'the Indies' is obviously a matter of primary importance.

In classical times the term was employed to describe the coastal countries lying on the great northern curve of the Indian Ocean. They stretched from Taprobane – which was Ceylon – by way of the Gulf of Persia to the mouth of the Red Sea and on by Guardafui to the eastern shoulder of Africa. The Red Sea bisected this land mass, dividing Nearer India from Further India.

'Once on a time', says Cosmas Indicopleustes, the Nestorian Indian theologian who explored the Indian Ocean in the sixth century, 'when we sailed in these gulfs bound for Further India . . .' He was heading down the Red Sea towards Bab el Mandeb and goes on to describe a gale at the entrance to Ocean.

Ethiopia was a component of Nearer India but the general title of 'Indies' was itself capable of almost indefinite expansion. When Burma and the Malay peninsula were added to Western knowledge, the name Further India was transferred for a brief while to them, but when the great islands to the south were added, the whole by a general consensus came to be accepted as the East Indies. Half the world away when Columbus found the archipelago of the

'Presbyter John
– King of the Indies'

Caribbean that, seemingly inevitably, became known as the West Indies.

Much of the confusion as to the intentions attributed to Henry may be clarified by the simple assumption that his 'Indies' was the coast of Ethiopia.

Henry listed his *desiderata* carefully: knowledge of that land – which was Guinea; then knowledge of the Indies; and then knowledge of the Land of Prester John.

Prester John was the ally whose aid he proposed to enlist for his crusade from the south, and his contemporary identification is therefore also essential.

It is generally accepted that the Prester John legend had its origins in the notorious letter said by Alberic de Trois Fontaines to have been sent to Manuel Comnenus, Emperor of Byzantium, and to Frederick Barbarossa by 'Presbyter John – King of the Indies'

The letter is fictional, but the fiction created the legend of a Christian monarch of immense power who ruled in the East – in Persia or possibly in India – and who was at all times ready to aid Christendom against the Infidel.

A debunking process began in the middle of the thirteenth century when the Dominican, Jordan de Severac, went to India proper in search of him and found neither king, nor court, nor army available against the Infidel. But de Severac did find another legend, of a Priest King in Abyssinia, and with astonishing speed the Prester John legend translated itself into the mountains above Nearer India. The Negus – the Negusa Negasht – was cloaked in his robes. Abyssinia was the new power against Islam. The Land of Prester John 'where milk everywhere abounds and honey flows' was re-sited above the Horn of Africa.

All through Henry's policy-making runs one constant thread of hope: that his captains, in due time, would find a 'Christian Ruler' able to enter an alliance against Moslem Africa, and willing to attack from the south in conjunction with the Portuguese. It was to be as evident a generation after Henry's death in the elaboration of the plan for an exploratory pincer movement on Africa with Covilhão penetrating from Egypt in the east in conjunction with Bartolomeu Dias' attempt to round Africa from the South Atlantic.

Gonçalves himself headed south with Adahu and the youths in 1442. In one of the gorgeous low comedy episodes that at intervals enliven Henry's proceedings, he was accompanied by Balthasar, 'a gentleman of the court of the Emperor Frederick', who desired to experience a tempest at sea so that he could boast of it at home.

He did.

The ship, badly battered, was forced back to Lagos for repairs. At a second attempt Gonçalves reached the stretch of coast designated for him by Adahu, and, magnificently dressed in clothes provided by the Infante, the Azenegue was put ashore under promise to produce his ransom by a stated time. Comedy struck again. He disappeared – to almost English expressions of dismay that he could so have failed to play the game.

Stubbornly Gonçalves headed down to the Rio do Ouro and waited. One week later fate itself turned about. An emissary on a white camel appeared. An exchange was proposed and agreed for the following day and at the appointed time 100 men and women – slaves – were brought faithfully for inspection. Assisted by Henry's Ransomer of Prisoners, Gonçalves selected the agreed ten and was given – in token of good will – a shield of hide, a clutch of ostrich eggs – and a small quantity of gold dust!

The fate of Africa, the opening of the East, the solution of the mysteries of the ocean hung on that insignificant transaction. The arrival of the captives of Gonçalves' first voyage had stimulated a vivid interest in Henry's operations. The arrival of acknowledged slaves, obtained in peaceful barter, offered illimitable vistas. The arrival of gold – indisputable gold, however small its quantity – initiated a chain reaction!

Early in the season of 1443 Henry sent Nuno Tristão south again past Cape

The quayside at Lisbon, from the *Brevis Narratiosorum* by Lemoyne de Morgues

Branco. Before he reached it a consortium had been formed in Lagos for a private enterprise venture, headed by Lançarote, Almoxarifé of the Port, who had been brought up as a squire in the Infant's household.

Well to the south, at the feast of Corpus Christi, Tristão found a bay with islands. Twenty-five canoes were sighted, paddled in a new fashion, their crews using their legs to help them. He ran down one of them and picked up fourteen survivors, and went in to the island that was afterwards known as Arguim and took fifteen more. It had a great beauty with its 'infinity of Royal herons' (some called it the Isle of Herons), and in due course it became the first great centre of the slave trade.

By the time he returned to Lagos the Algarve was aflame with Lançarote's plans. With his fellow merchants he had raised funds to fit out six caravels – more than had started on any of Henry's ventures down the coast. He had Henry's consent and his effective blessing, and in 1444 he sailed with his ships wearing, by special consent, the banner of the Knights of Christ.

Henry had just been awarded by Pedro – acting as Regent – the 'Fifth and the Tenth' of the proceeds of all expeditions to the south, nominally the prerogative of the Crown, in consideration of the great expenses he had undertaken 'up to this point'. The banner of the Knights flew brilliantly over a profitable venture. In a series of ferocious attacks on Arguim and Tider, Lançarote took 235 persons, women and children and men in the first deliberate slaving foray on Africa. On the return to Lagos a selection of the best slaves was apportioned to the Church. For the remainder, a note to Henry said:

> . . . it would be well to order them to be taken out of the caravels at dawn, and to be placed in that field which lies outside the city gate, and there to be divided into five parts, according to custom, and that your Grace should come there and choose one of those parts whichever you prefer.

Zurara, writing twelve years after, was patently moved by eyewitness accounts of the event:

> . . . what heart could be so hard as not to be pierced with piteous feeling to see that company. For some kept their heads low and their faces bathed in tears . . . and it was needful to part father from son, husbands from wives, brothers from brothers . . . each fell where his lot took him.

Henry, 'mounted on a powerful steed', watched without emotion. His Fifth – forty-six men, women and children – was given away at once while he 'reflected with great pleasure upon the salvation of souls that before were lost'.

Plans for a new expedition were already in contemplation. The four years from the great sale at Lagos are the dynamic years of Henry's endeavour. Pedro was temporarily secure in the Regency. Portugal was quiet. Leonor was about to die in Spain; and though rumours of poison seeped into current gossip, the young King was not old enough and the Braganzas under Barcelos were not yet ready to make a take-over bid for power. Fresh expeditions were planned before their predecessors were complete. Stringent attempts were made to ensure the maximum possible advance with each new voyage.

Detail of a ship from *Landscape with the Fall of Icarus* by Pieter Breugel the Elder. Icarus has almost disappeared.

Gonçalo de Sintra, one of the two squires of the Rio do Ouro foray, was sent south with a caravel under positive injunction to sail direct to Guinea. At Cape Branco he called his crew together and proposed a slave raid *en route*, at Arguim. Against opposition he carried the meeting, and having made two captures only at Arguim and still intoxicated with possibilities of slaves and profit, went in again at the island of Naar. Recklessly crossing a creek at low tide and leaving his boat on the wrong side, he was cut off with five of his men, and killed.

Long before the survivors and his ship returned, three new caravels were heading south under Antão Gonçalves, Diogo Afonso (also a squire) and Diogo Pires, Captain of the Royal Galley. The entire coast was watchful when they reached it. Despite the obvious hostility, they left behind them a volunteer, João Fernandes, to make enquiries but returned empty-handed.

In the same year Nuno Tristão of the Rio do Ouro raid went south again to find the Green Country. His voyage ends the quarter of a century of parched advance down that bleak and most inhospitable coast. Along it the Sahara came close to the water's edge. Patches of scrub and small desperate streams – drainage from below the desert – fringed it at wide intervals. Its sparse tribes moved with the seasons. Now past it Tristão sighted a shore with palms and forest timber, beautiful to eyes wearied with the desert fringe. With a particular irony

A fleet of Portuguese carracks of the sixteenth century

the weather made a landing impossible, but Tristão went in close enough to see the natives on shore, and to judge that they were friendly.

His report on his return brought in a new name to the list of captains: a veteran this time, Dinis Dias, who had served under João I. Dias asked for a caravel to explore the new green country and was given one. His voyage has a refreshing absence of complexity. The record says that he never shortened sail until he had passed the Senegal. Beyond it men came out to him in dugouts but took fright, so he captured four of them, disdainfully, and went south again to a green headland which he christened the Cabo Verde. Beyond it the coast of Africa trended to the south-east. It was the western limit of the continent!

The succession of ships continued despite threats by the King of Granada against Ceuta. In 1445 Antão Gonçalves went down again with orders to recover Fernandes and, by what seems to be a miracle, did. He tried out a new route on the way down, replenishing with food and water at the Madeiras – the settlement was now productive.

Fernandes' exploit has been insufficiently acknowledged. Despite its casual, almost frivolous origin, it ranks as the first attempt to make a scientific examination of western Africa. He had an incredible courage and a lively mind. Making contact with the Azenegues and Berbers, veiled men, he moved with them on their seasonal migration. He described their nomadic life with clarity and understanding, he shocked Zurara with his description of their women, who covered their faces but left their bodies naked   which, as Zurara pointed out, is bestiality 'for if they had a particle of reason they would follow nature'. His account is one of the earliest sociological contributions to the Renaissance. To its zoology his gift is enormous: meticulous observations on the migration of the storks and swallows which come 'from Portugal' to winter in the south; on the antelopes and gazelles which endured the hostility of the desert.

His own survival was by no means the least of his achievements.

Gonçalo Pacheco, Treasurer at Ceuta, went next, raided *en route*, reached the Land of the Negroes in strong head winds and was blown back to Cape Branco. In an ill-planned landing his force was ambushed and seven men were killed. A report was spread that they had been eaten subsequently but, as Zurara says, only their livers were actually eaten – and that simply in vengeance.

Meanwhile, in the Algarve the death of Gonçalo de Sintra had already aroused a demand for counter-vengeance. Lançarote, backed by the Corporation of the town of Lagos, made an offer to Henry to take a major expedition down to the area and in a phrase sanctified in later days – teach the natives a lesson. Like other voyages in this period, the Lagos fleet had little if anything to do with original exploration. Fourteen caravels sailed from Lagos and the names of their captains are a roll of honour of the exploration. Ten more came from Lisbon under the veteran Dinis Dias, three from Madeira under Teixeira.

They sailed, with great simplicity, for revenge and plunder. The plan laid down a rendezvous at Cape Branco and the leading ships went on to the Isle of Herons (Arguim), where they met the returning vessels of Pacheco's expedition and persuaded them to turn back and join in an attack on the island of Tider. Pacheco's ships were short of food but they decided that it would be appropriate to throw half the slaves they had already taken overboard for the privilege and honour of joining in this prodigious essay in revenge.

A force of 278 men, divided in three 'battles', embarked in the ships' boats: footmen and lancers, crossbowmen and archers, men at arms. Closing the coast in the dark, the pilots misjudged their position and the beach was not reached until dawn. The enemy had withdrawn, and they were forced to make a nine-mile march in sand and heat. When the attack was launched, the enemy pulled back with skill – eight men were killed, only four prisoners taken.

Álvaro Fernandes, a nephew of Zarco, continuing south, reached as far as the hurricane-stripped palm trees of a headland that he called The Cape of Masts. This was a new 'farthest south', almost 2,000 miles from the Algarve.

In 1446 Nuno Tristão began a third voyage. Competition was very strong. He passed the mouth of the Gambia triumphantly, reached the river which was subsequently to be called the Rio Grande, and went upstream with two of the ships' boats and twenty-two men. In sight of a village the boats were attacked by a dozen native craft and a new weapon. Poisoned arrows killed Tristão himself and nineteen of his crew; four others survived, desperately close to death. Five ship's boys, all that were left, took the ship home 'guided by Divine grace' in one of the bravest of all the exploits of the voyages.

Not even poisoned arrows could quench the enthusiasm of Lagos. Nine ships sailed from Portugal in the next year and two from the Madeiras. Eight went to the Rio Grande – where five men were lost to fresh showers of poisoned arrows. The next three ships operated in known waters: Gomes Pires, Diogo Gil, who went to Messa in Morocco and established a profitable trading rate of one repatriated Moor for three Guinea men – plus a lion which for no obvious reason was sent to Galway in Ireland; and last of all Antão Gonçalves who drew

Grim Portuguese adventurers, grasping swords and spears, carved in ivory by a native of Benin

a blank at the Rio do Ouro. The whole coast was hostile.

One more venture must be listed in this period. Vallarte (Wollert), a Dane, and a courtier of Christopher III, asked for a caravel to go to Guinea. Henry's unquenchable belief that he would somewhere find Christian alliance against the Moors in the south reasserted itself. Vallarte was told that the ruler of the Cape Verde area was probably a Christian and possibly amenable. He was an indifferent seaman – the expedition took six months to reach Cape Verde – but as an ambassador he was a disaster and was promptly murdered with his boat's crew. His death marks the end of the vivid turbulent era that had opened with Antão Gonçalves' first captures at the Rio do Ouro, and had added, in eight years, 1,300 miles of new coastline to the *portolani*. It also brought 1,000 slaves to Lagos '. . . of which the greater part had been turned into the true way of salvation!'.

It is the last voyage recorded by Zurara in the *Crónica*. After it, for eight years, exploration was suspended.

In Portugal the affairs of the throne were approaching crisis. At the age of fourteen Afonso V reached his legal majority and Barcelos and the party of the young King engineered the end of the regency. Pedro withdrew to Coimbra, his standing in the country dramatically diminished; it was remembered that he had seized the regency, and though his rule, broadly, had advantaged Portugal, he had a talent for making enemies.

Henry, immersed in the affairs of the sea, made no attempt to support his brother.

The affairs of the sea, like those of the throne, were in a state of flux. At the height of what may be called the Guinea Rush, Henry had reopened his attempt

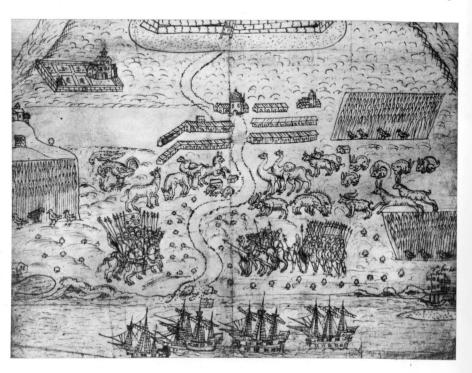

The island of Lanzarote, which Henry purchased

upon the Canaries. An expedition to Gomera had secured the submission of the Guanche chiefs of that island and with it, for the first time, a limited foothold in the group. Pedro – still regent then – had granted Henry a decree prohibiting ships from calling at the islands without authority. Finally in a complex deal Henry had purchased Lanzarote from Maciot de Béthencourt. Maciot had sold it previously to de la Casas and may have sold it elsewhere in the interim. Title was at least shaky. Henry gave the Captaincy to Antão Gonçalves – who was incontinently driven out by the natives!

The evidence is plain that the weight of enthusiasm had shifted from southerly exploration to a possibility of direct action against the Moors. Control of the off-shore islands was a desirable factor in the light of future operations.

In 1449 Barcelos, old now and full of venom, decided to destroy Pedro. Harassed into open revolt, Pedro made the mistake of abandoning his fortress at Coimbra. Henry left the Algarve too late to intervene – if indeed he ever had an intention of doing so. The revolt had one battle. At Alfarrobeira the King's forces made contact. According to a Belgian at the court of Afonso, '. . . a cross bow bolt struck Prince Pedro, the Duke of Coimbra, in the chest. He died of this wound within the hour. No other man was wounded in this affray, only the Duke.'

Charges of assassination were afterwards made; they were without effect, Pedro's death was the death of his faction. Thereafter the Braganzas controlled Portugal and the evidence is that Henry co-operated with the Braganzas. Within a year of his brother's death a new attempt was being made on the Canaries: it would have been impossible unless he had unreservedly accepted the new regime. The matter of finance is significant in this association. Though the Guinea Trade was at last beginning to show a return for expenditure – basically from slave sales – it is doubtful if it was yet self-supporting. Henry's private revenues were inadequate to cover the explorations. The revenues of the Order of Christ had been heavily drawn on for the extension of the Christian faith in Africa, Henry's annual subsidy from the Crown (sixteen contos) was consistently overdrawn, and he seems to have been substantially in debt – certainly to the Crown, possibly to the Monastery of Alcobaça, unquestionably to the Braganzas and the Jews.

Despite these difficulties, attempts on the Canaries continued: an attack in 1451; another, the seventh, in 1453. It is possible that the Crown participated in these but Henry's authority remained absolute. The Canaries were his prerogative. His influence at court is less easy to assess; it is, however, obvious at this time that policy began to move towards a resumption of the Western Crusade – Henry's unquenchable dream – and the relative merits of expeditions against Tangier, Rabat and Ksar es Seghir (Alcácer) were canvassed. No decision had been reached when Mohammed II launched the immense campaign that overwhelmed Constantinople, submerged the Peloponnese, swept east as far as Trebizond and was held only at the gates of Belgrade.

Portugal's standing was high in a nervous Mediterranean, and in the year after Constantinople fell Henry's achievement was handsomely acknowledged by a bull of Pope Nicholas V which recognized the rights of the Portuguese Crown to the conquest of western Africa from Capes Non and Bojador to Guinea and the southern shore.

When in 1456 Callixtus III, the new Borgia Pope, called Christendom to a General Crusade against the Turk, Portugal pledged herself and 12,000 men.

Christendom, as a whole, was unenthusiastic. Crusades were out of date. Portugal – lit by the hot flame of Henry's fervour – maintained her preparations.

The absence of references to exploration over this period has been attributed to the 'Policy of Secrecy'. A strong case unquestionably came into being for the formulation of such a policy a quarter of a century later when the quest for a sea route to India was in hot pursuit, but that it existed as early as 1454 is wholly questionable. The cessation of information can be attributed more simply, and at least as logically, to the cessation of the voyages themselves; Henry had reached his goal in Guinea, an increasing share of the Guinea Trade was coming into Portuguese hands, he had established his contacts and done, in plain terms, as his ambition had dictated '. . . by sea, what the King of Tunis for many years, had done by land'. The trading voyages continued, if sometimes erratically. Such secrecy as existed is inextricably mixed with the trading pattern and the problem of establishing full commercial exploitation. It was not exclusive. The participation of Alvise de ca' da Mosto makes the matter altogether plain.

Cadamosto, as he was known outside Venice, was the son of a wealthy and litigious merchant who had been banished from the Republic. Mending his own fortunes, he began a series of trading voyages which took him to Alexandria in the east and Flanders in the west. Shipping for the second time with the Flanders convoy in 1454, he was driven with it to take shelter from foul weather at Sagres. Henry was told of his arrival, and with commercial inspiration sent Antão Gonçalves – of the Rio do Ouro venture – to show him samples of dragon's blood resin, Madeira sugar, and ivory of the Senegal. The episode has an astonishingly modern flavour. Cadamosto, impressed by the 'samples', asked at once if permission to enter the Guinea trade was possible. Gonçalves, armed with figures and an assurance of Henry's 'special favour' towards the Venetians, claimed that not only was it possible but that, if he went, he could reasonably expect seven or even ten per cent return on his capital. An invitation ashore followed at once. Rapidly convinced by Henry, Cadamosto arranged for his ship's master to break bulk, and a caravel's load of trade goods was ferried ashore before the convoy sailed.

Until the spring Cadamosto lived at Henry's house. Preparations for fitting out a caravel were immediately put in hand. The terms of contract are interesting for the light they throw on the trading system. If Henry supplied the ship and Cadamosto the cargo, profits were to be shared equally. If Cadamosto supplied ship and cargo, Henry took twenty-five per cent only.

In the fifteenth century Venice and Genoa dominated the commercial Mediterranean. With the collapse of the Empire of the East inevitable restrictions were imposed on what had been the Byzantine trade. An urgent search for external markets began. In plain terms Venice and Genoa were Portugal's most

Embarkation in Venice, most powerful port of the Mediterranean; in the foreground, the travellers' subsequent adventures

dangerous potential rivals for the Africa monopoly. A policy of secrecy would have banned information to their merchants before all other nations. Cadamosto in fact lived on with Henry through the winter in company with the veterans of the Guinea trade. When he sailed in the spring he was as equipped with knowledge – and as certainly with *portolani* and sailing directions – as any other captain out of Sagres.

There can have been no Policy of Secrecy at that date. Henry operated under the guarantee of his papal grants and the rights awarded to him by the Portuguese Crown. At intervals there were interlopers in the Trade, but his confidence appears to have been justified.

Cadamosto went south-west first to the Madeiras, thence to the Canaries, and made his African landfall with precision at Cape Branco. He took with him the lively curiosity of a Renaissance mind. Fernandes had superbly created a tradition of African observation, Cadamosto translated it into terms of topographical science. The meticulous detail of his record is, outside Marco Polo, difficult to parallel. The customs of the natives, the government of kings, the incidence of elephants, the existence of the horse-fish (the hippopotamus), the sources of gold, the breast lengths of women – elongated for beauty's sake – were all important to him. Published ultimately in the *Paesi nuovamente ritrovati*, this is the textbook on emerging Africa. He was still seeking knowledge – and a tenfold return for capital – when his lookouts sighted two more caravels. The leading ship was captained by Antoniotto, a Genoese, the second

Dem geweltigen schiff im meer sein fart/
So sie Gott beyde nicht bewart.

Landfalls as accurate as Cadamosto's were rare: two sailors take sights with a cross-staff and a simple maritime astrolabe. Nocturnals, like the sixteenth-century Italian one below, also became available.

by one of Henry's customary squires. Both the Mediterranean powers had now been admitted to the Africa trade.

Neither of these voyages, nor their immediate successors of course, were missions of exploration in the oceanographic sense. None of the named voyages in this last phase went beyond limits established as far back as 1448 when it was known that the coast '. . . ran south with many promontories, and the Infant had it all added to the navigating charts'. They are, however, in many respects more important than a large proportion of the attempts at exploration, for they consolidated knowledge. Africa expanded with them from a coastline to a country with a hinterland.

Cadamosto's second voyage went south in 1456. He sailed from Lagos, direct this time for Cape Branco, made his landfall accurately, and ran into a gale from the south-west. He headed into the Atlantic to maintain sea-room and, on the third day, sighted two islands. He states that he made two landings, and there are no islands in the area save the Cape Verdes. The discovery was claimed later for Diogo Gomes and after him for Antonio da Noli. The dates are impossible to disentangle and the arguments rest largely on national bias.

From them Cadamosto went in to Cape Verde itself. The eleven-day passage up the Gambia which followed, the lead going all the way, is a minor masterpiece. His observations continued in perfection and he turned only when his men succumbed to fever. Afterwards he made a brief run down the coast past Cape Roxo to a river mouth so wide that they thought it was a gulf. None of the interpreters could understand the language of the natives here, and he discussed the matter with his men and decided to turn back for Portugal. 'God guiding them, they arrived safely.'

Diogo Gomes went south after them. Martin Behaim took down his narrative twenty years after in the Azores and it has some of the failures of memory and some of the errors of translation, for Behaim wrote it in the Azores in Latin and it was printed, eventually, by Valentim Fernandes in Lisbon. It lacks the omnivorous character of Cadamosto's work and its style is awkward, but it is a plain account of a voyage of great determination. Gomes went up the Gambia as far as the ancient trading focus of Cantor. From information given him by the natives he plotted the complex trade routes that met there: the slave routes from Timbuktu and Kukia and Geley, the camel routes that went north to Fez and Tunis, the gold routes to the region of Mount Gelu. Despite the onset of fever he made immense and successful efforts to win the confidence of the kings of the area, notably with the hostile Nomi Mansa south of the Gambia.

His survey completed, Gomes returned to Sagres. After which '. . . for two years no one went to Guinea'. Henry was preparing for the attack on Ksar es Seghir.

The assault on Alcácer, as the Portuguese called it, should logically have been the high peak of Henry's career. It was planned, originally, as the western arm of the double thrust of Pope Callixtus' crusade against the Turk, but Christianity, as has been indicated, had outworn crusades. Afonso V, young, ardent, impulsive, attacked alone. The Portuguese had raised a fleet of 280 sail and more than 20,000 men. It called magnificently to embark Henry at Sagres, made its

final rendezvous at Lagos, and waited for a wind off Tangier. On 17 October it went in to the assault. At midnight the Moors sent Henry a capitulation. Afonso gave them leave to go with their wives and their children and everything except their Christian slaves.

Henry's letter offering a donation to the Church of Our Lady in Ceuta in payment for Masses to be said for his soul

Ksar es Seghir was a small nut under a large hammer and it marks the end of Henry's lifetime crusade against the Moor. It was not the end of the attacks, other towns indeed were captured, but Henry had made his last move; and within a hundred years Morocco was in Moorish hands again and the dream of Christian empire ended.

Gomes stayed on with Henry. A deep relationship seems to have grown between the two men. But there were barely two years left,

> . . . in the year 1460 the Lord Infant Henry fell ill in his town of Cape St Vincent and died of the illness on 13 November of the same year, a Thursday . . . and the King Afonso was then in the city of Evora and he was very saddened, both he and his people by the death of so great a lord . . . .

At the end of the year Henry's body was taken to the great splendour of the perpendicular church of St Mary at Batalha and interred in the Capela Fundador.

His bequest to Portugal and to the world is immeasurable: Africa south of the Sahara, the magnificence of the East, the promise of the Americas, the possibilities of the Pacific are the *sequelae* of the conquest of Cape Bojador.

The paradox of his triumph is that it evolved from failure.

To assess either failure or success it is essential to understand his intention. Zurara's most valuable contribution to history is his analysis of Henry's motives. Begun in 1452 as has already been described, it is a work of the euphoric period in which voyage upon voyage followed Gil Eanes' conquest of what may be called the Bojador barrier. Earlier in this period he had stayed at Henry's house and discussed the operations with him. He wrote with the authority of a trusted chronicler, specifically directed by the King to record the achievements of an important era in the contemporary history of Portugal. In the nature of things his work must have been subject to inspection and revision either by Henry himself or by his professionals.

The six 'reasons' for the Conquest of Guinea are therefore to be accepted as Henry's personal explanation, communicated to Zurara after he had emerged from the black cloud of Tangier, had completed the effective survey of the Guinea coast, and was in the illusory mid-success of his Canary Island campaigns. They have an evident truth. In succession they declare that he was motivated by

> . . . a wish to know the land that lay beyond the isles of Canary and that Cape called Bojador, for that up to his time neither by writings, nor by the memory of man, was known with any certainty the nature of the land beyond that Cape.

> . . . the wish to find some population of Christians or some havens into which it would be possible to sail without peril for trade which would bring great profit to our country.

> . . . the belief that the power of the Moors was very much greater than was commonly supposed in that part of Africa and that it was necessary to ascertain its limits.

> . . . the fact that he had never found in thirty-one years a Christian King nor a lord outside this land who for the love of the Lord Jesus Christ would aid him in the said war.

> . . . the desire to make increase in the faith of our Lord Jesus Christ and to bring to Him all the souls that should be saved.

> . . . the inclination of the Heavenly Wheels [his horoscope] by which he was bound to engage in great and noble conquests and above all to attempt the discovery of things hidden from other men, and secret.

Dispassionately they constitute an outline plan for a military envelopment of Moroccan Africa. They set down a strategy which began with coastal reconnaisance, called for a determination of enemy strength and a definition of enemy territory, postulated the urgent necessity for the acquisition of new alliances, urged the development of trade – presumptively to pay for the war – made a strong gesture towards religion and acknowledged the fortunate intervention of the stars.

It is a blue print for an African crusade.

In the years after Ceuta it was Henry's obsession, but in the lifetime of his father it was beyond his grasp, and despite the temporary successes against the coast towns in after years, it was always shadowed with failure. The conquest of North Africa was beyond Portugal's effective resources.

The search for 'some population of Christians' which headed the list was equally a failure. Derived obviously from rumours of Ethiopia, it was impossible from the start.

The search for a Christian King, mixed with it, was outside the capabilities of the Portugal of Henry's day.

The ambition 'to make increase in the faith of Christ' had the possibilities at least of missions, but almost no Christian converts are reported except the pressurized converts of slavery. The only mission reported is that sent south to fulfil Gomes' personal promise to Nomi Mansa in the year of Henry's death.

A quasi success may perhaps be claimed for non-Christian trade, but for Henry that too was failure. With the west coast of Africa in his grasp he died in debt to the Crown, the Braganzas, the Monastery of Alcobaça, and the Order of Christ to the tune of 35,000 *dobras* (approximately 171,000 grammes of gold) having, according to Gomes, '. . . spent all his revenues and all he got from Guinea and in war in continual fleets at sea against the Saracens for the faith of Christ'.

The last entry in Zurara's list to require examination is the practical geographical result of the reconnaisance of the Guinea coast. Traditionally regarded as Henry's greatest triumph, it is without question an immense and seminal achievement. Divorced from its military framework, it constitutes the first magnificence of post-medieval exploration. The discovery of the Madeiras and the Azores, an expanded knowledge of the Canaries, the subsequent location of the Cape Verde Islands, are a small part only of its gain. It demolished the psychological bloc of Cape Bojador. Its captains plotted the western coastal bulge of Africa from headland to headland. Its outline was established – by bearing and distance – in precise increments as voyage succeeded voyage. It was added to the *portolani* in an authentic continuance of a superb tradition.

The Portuguese under Henry the Navigator. Between 1419 and 1456 the Portuguese established a foothold on the Atlantic islands and moved down the African coast as far as the Rio Grande.

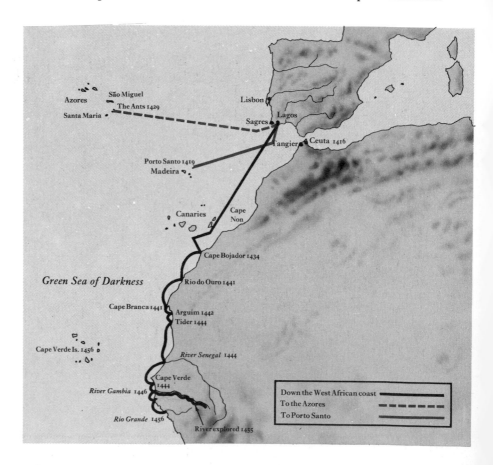

Zurara's catalogue of Henry's intentions is comprehensive, the outline of his account prodigious. It is, therefore, at least remarkable that the chief item in the Henrician legend – a search for a sea route to India – has no place in it at all.

Only one other contemporary reference of substance survives. Twenty years after Zurara's death Diogo Gomes dictated the story of his voyages to Martin Behaim, the globemaker. In this year of 1484, following Cão's two voyages, the search for India was at last nearing its zenith. Bartolomeu Dias indeed was fitting out his ships for the triumphant attempt to turn the southern point of Africa. Interest, despite any Policy of Secrecy, must have been at its height amongst the veterans of the Guinea voyages. Gomes himself may have been stimulated by knowledge. He told Behaim that 'an Indian named Jacob' had been attached to his expedition to act as interpreter 'in the event of our reaching India'.

Two questions once more present themselves. Did Gomes mean a man of Further India? Was Further India, by this casual suggestion, actually his destination?

No hard information as to the identity of Jacob is available, but it is extraordinarily difficult to accept that a man of Further India, bearing a Christian name, able to talk the language of the Guinea peoples and with prior experience of Alcuzet, Gelu and Timbuktu should have been available for the expedition.

The much-debated Laurentian *portolano*, showing the great extension of Africa to the south

It would be equally difficult to believe it of a man from Nearer India, but for two things. In 1452 an 'Embassy of Prester John', possibly of monks from the Coptic monastery at Jerusalem, was in Lisbon. It is at least plausible that a member of its entourage might have been retained to sail with Gomes. The date of the voyage is uncertain but it may have been as early as 1456. Moreover, in Afonso's reign it was discovered that the kings of Benin were under the ultimate authority of the Ogane of Ethiopia, who lived 'twenty moons' journey' to the east of Benin.

The second question is more important. Did Henry in reality believe that it would be possible for Gomes to reach Further India? Gomes makes no other reference to it in his text, nor does it appear that Henry's charge to him at his departure differed in any way from the customary '. . . proceed as far as you can.'

He made Cape Verde, carried on south-west to the Buba, and met the irregular current that runs between the islands and the coast. He seems to have abandoned at once any idea of progress to the East and went inland up the Gambia. This decision is highly improbable if his orders were in fact to attempt the India voyage. His flotilla of three ships, however, included no store ship and no extra equipment or supplies appear to have been carried. It is inconceivable that this lightly equipped expedition can have been planned for the gigantic leap into the unknown that was entailed in the goal of India.

Traditionally Henry is believed to have followed the Ptolemaic concept in relation to the shape of Africa. He may, by the time of Gomes' expedition, have moved to something nearer to the concept of the Laurentian *portolano*; his maps, his papers, most of the logs of his captains are lost. Removed from Sagres at his death, they were placed for safe-keeping in the Torre de Tombo at Lisbon. It is unlikely, at this date, that any special secrecy was applied to them but when after 1470 a formal policy of secrecy was adopted, they were effectively sealed with the flood of new documents. The loss of the Portuguese archives in the Lisbon earthquake of 1755 is one of the tragedies of history.

Absolute judgements as to Henry's decision making are impossible in their absence, yet enough is known by inference from the voyages themselves to judge his knowledge. In respect of Africa he had 'caused everything to be entered in the charts'. He was aware always of the points his ships had reached. He must have known the straight line distance from the Gambia to India if only by a rough calculation of longitude.

Ptolemy's Africa thrust down twenty degrees below the equator – and Henry's captains had not yet reached the equator. The Laurentian version is longer still. The straight line distance from the Gambia mouth to India along the tenth parallel is more than 5,500 miles. The rate of advance through the main phase of the explorations had by the most generous calculation averaged slightly less than 175 miles a season!

Gomes, when he reached Cape Roxo, just short of the farthest east of Henry's ventures, was, because of the bulge of Africa, still eight degrees west of his starting point at Sagres. Hard-bitten and practical, Gomes must have been at least as aware of this as his Royal master. That he would in the circumstances have consented to make the essay is not acceptable.

A fictitious battle between Ghengis Khan and Prester John, whose aid Henry hoped to enlist in the fight against Islam

Chapter VIII

The Cape of Good Hope

The triumphant survival of the vision of exploration in Portugal in the years that followed Henry's death is the first plain measure of his achievement.

Afonso, like his uncle in earlier days, had in 1460 two clear options: the Crusade of Africa, in which he had been involved almost since his childhood accession, and the assumption of his uncle's leadership in the opening of the unknown world.

Henry had attempted – with a variable success – to keep both options open. Afonso chose the Crusade.

Despite attempts to include him in the broad pattern of the Portuguese advance, his contribution is unimportant. Two voyages went south in the two years after Henry's death but both are to be considered as left-overs of the preceding regime. Gomes set out first, so soon that the voyage must at least have been in consideration at Henry's death. It was not a voyage of exploration, though that may have been the original intention. Gomes sailed in an administrative capacity, invested with authority over 'all the shores of that sea' and carrying a cargo of horses. He was charged to put down interlopers, to investigate conditions of trade and rates of exchange, to suppress the smuggling of weapons to the Africans. He sailed directly to the small beach town of Zaya in the territory of the Barbacini where he found two caravels, one under Gonçalo Ferreira of Oporto, one under a Genoese – Antonio de Noli – both authorized to trade in the area.

'The merchants had greatly damaged the traffic in those parts' and Gomes brusquely restored the old rate of twelve slaves for a horse. Then, learning that a richly laden interloper was expected, he ordered Ferreira to intercept her. She was found to be valuable, and Gomes sent her with her captain to Lisbon for jurisdiction.

No attempt was made to work to the eastward and he left Zaya finally with da Noli for Cape Verde. Standing out into the Atlantic across a head wind, he claimed the discovery of the Cape Verde Islands but da Noli, making better weather of the homeward passage, reached Lisbon first and claimed priority. Cadamosto had lodged a still earlier claim. The award is hardly important; they were indifferent islands. De Predo, the captain of the interloper, was 'martyrized in a cart, and flung into the fire alive with his sword and his gold'.

The second voyage was definitely exploratory. Its date is uncertain but it has the stamp of Henry's method. Pedro de Sintra was sent south 'to find new countries'.

He passed the eastern limit of Cadamosto's discoveries at the mouth of the Rio Grande, found a tree-covered headland and called it Sagres, went on to find the Rio Verde, and still holding to the south-east, named Cape Ledo – the Joyous Cape. Fifty miles on he sighted a ridge of mountains and named them the Sierra

The Cape of Good Hope, named by Dias 'Cape of Storms'

Leone, or Lion Mountain, 'on account', as de Sintra told Duarte Pecheco, 'of the wildness of the place'. In a careful, informative progress he named the islands of the Selvagens, the Roxo and Cape Masurado, and at the Bosque de Santa Maria he turned at last for home.

It is one of the most vigorous and technically one of the most effective of the West African voyages. It has, however, received less than its proper degree of recognition, possibly because of the abrupt diminution of interest in African exploration that followed Afonso's decision to concentrate on the crusade against the Moor. For seven years nothing went south except traders, steadily and busily acquiring slaves and ivory and gold.

The crusades were unsuccessful and, still worse, unprofitable, and the Guinea trade began to show diminishing returns. Henry's death had removed the driving force, and in 1469 Afonso commercialized the princely pursuit of exploration.

Fernão Gomes, a wealthy merchant of Lisbon, acquired the rights to the Guinea coast at a cost of 200 milreis per annum. The details are curious: ivory was held as a royal monopoly at the fixed price of 1,500 *reis* the quintal; Gomes was permitted one civet cat per annum – it had an inordinate value in the manufacture of perfume. In addition to these matters Gomes committed himself to the exploration of 100 leagues of new coast a year, beginning at the Sierra Leone!

The contract exposes the total neglect of exploration after de Sintra's impressive voyage. It argues also a singular absence of control after Henry's death, for the starting point laid down by the contract is the Sierra Leone, but de Sintra had reached the Bosque de Santa Maria, 100 leagues south-east of the Sierra Leone, seven years before. Gomes was in effect given a free head start of one year's exploring.

It is improbable that it made any difference to him. As a Lisbon merchant he unquestionably had experience in the English trade and in the Continental voyages to France and to the Low Country ports. Experience in the Mediterranean is certain, for that trade was increasing, and he had probably had previous contact with the Guinea coast under licence from Henry in his last years. It is abundantly evident that he was decisive, active and supremely efficient. Though the record lacks the ancillary material that attaches to the chronicles of kings and princes, sufficient is known of the explorations planned and subsidized by him to establish his place amongst the great controllers of exploration in history. He has been deplorably neglected by Portuguese geographers.

In the five years of his tenure of the coast of Guinea his captains, disregarding the stretch from Sierra Leone to the Bosque de Santa Maria, opened 2,000 miles of new coast – substantially more, that is, than Henry's captains had accomplished in forty-two.

The first recorded voyage is that of Soeiro da Costa to Axem on the Gold Coast, a prodigious effort of nearly 600 miles – the equivalent of two years' advance in the terms of the contract; the second, led by João de Santarém and Pero de Escolar, carried the survey to Mina. These destinations became the master points in the subsequent exploitation of the coast. Fernando Pó,

Afonso V

Opposite
Portolan chart of 1468: the West Coast headlands, including Cape Roxo and Cape Ledo, are meticulously named

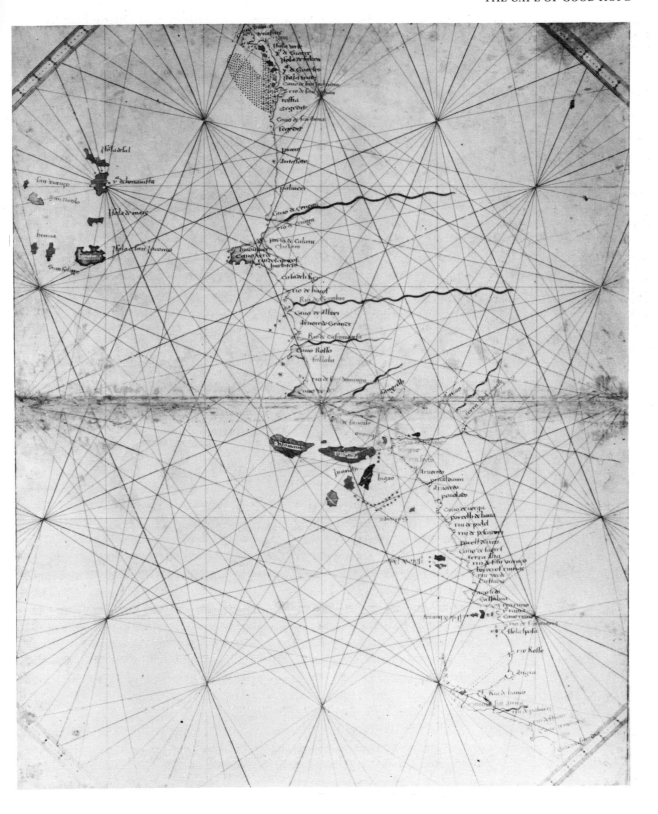

negotiating, or possibly by-passing the lamentable morass of the mouths of the Niger, determined the beginning of the southerly trend of Africa and discovered the high island that bears his name. Lopo Gonçalves, heading now almost due south, reached the equator below the Gabon river and crossed it. Ruy de Sequeira thrust past Cape Lopes and came to an anchor at Cape St Catherine in two degrees south latitude.

European man had established a presence in the southern hemisphere.

Simultaneously Afonso succeeded in establishing himself firmly in Moroccan Africa; crusade triumphed. Arzila, twenty-five miles south of Tangier along the coast, fell to a landing in heavy weather in which 300 men were drowned. High seas had made it impossible to get the heavy equipment ashore but two bombards, man-handled into the beach, brought down enough of the city wall

The thriving port of Lisbon, home of Gomes

for the Portuguese to carry it on St Bartholomew's Day. The bones of the Infante Fernando, a generation after the disaster at Tangier, were ransomed in exchange for two wives and a daughter of the King of Fez seized in the assault, and Tangier itself, isolated now between Ceuta and Portuguese-held Arzila, was evacuated by its people and passed to England in the eventual dower of Catherine of Braganza.

Spain challenged Portugal's extension of power in the endless involuted quarrels of the peninsula. Henry's West African monopoly had been for a generation a focus of envy and of friction; now interloping expanded into organized hostility. The men of Palos on the Rio Tinto, nearest Spanish port to the Algarve, sent a force of caravels south and lifted a chief of Guinea and all his family. Ferdinand of Aragon readied a fleet to challenge the Portuguese attempts on the Canaries. Fernão Gomes, with a businessman's realism, protested the annual payment of his lease in the absence of adequate protection and João, the heir apparent, newly invested with the rights that his uncle had held in Africa, decided against its renewal.

Gomes acquiesced in the decision – he had in fact made a solid profit from the operation – and now accepted the command of a fleet to convoy the season's accumulation of gold and ivory in the face of the Spanish threat. Relations with Spain had disintegrated swiftly; the death of Henrique IV of Castile had left a daughter, Joana, of doubtful legitimacy. Isabella of Castile, her aunt, proclaimed herself Queen of Castile, and Afonso, at the death-bed request of his brother-in-law, married his thirteen-year-old niece – and failed to obtain the necessary dispensation. In the war that inevitably developed he was defeated at Toro and went to France to seek aid of Louis XI. Cozened by Louis, he proceeded to Honfleur to embark for home, and at the last moment broke down and disappeared. He was found, disguised, in a village making preparations to spend the rest of his life 'in the service of God at Jerusalem'.

The psychological imbalance of the five sons of João I had finally transmitted itself to the tragic Afonso and his condition from this time deteriorated. He abdicated early in the crisis and João II was proclaimed King. Returned to Lisbon in what was palpably a withdrawal syndrome, Afonso resumed the crown but control was retained in the firm hands of João II. Four years later Afonso died, preparing once again to enter a monastery.

In the next year João II commissioned Diogo Cão to explore the coast of Africa south of St Catherine.

At his second accession he had initiated a far-reaching programme for the consolidation of the Guinea holding and for the acceleration of the India search. It has a great complexity.

Little more is known of the maps that João II used in planning than of those of Henry; the wide easy curve of Africa from Cape Verde to the Niger delta has at least a family resemblance to the sweeping curve of the reconstituted map of Hecateus – which without doubt was borrowed by Strabo for his later outline. Henry traditionally had relied on Ptolemy, and in his day the curve to the south-east may reasonably have been interpreted as the north shore of the

Sinus Hesperus, represented by him below the Fortunate Islands.

Gomes' captains at least were aware by experience that the vast curve swept actually from Cape Verde 2,000 miles to the Niger mouths. That Fernando Pó's report of its abrupt turn to the south beyond the Niger was regarded by them as 'a disappointment and a barrier on the way to India' is improbable. By this time they were completely conditioned to the theory illustrated by the Laurentian *portolano* that the mass of Northern Africa had a great projection to the south.

Scientifically João II's captains were better equipped than Henry's had been. He had assembled an advisory group quite as high-powered as Henry's: Master Rodrigo, Royal Physician and mathematician; Bishop Ortiz, the Royal Chaplain; the Jew José Vizinho, disciple of Zacuto of Salamanca, who himself was to come to Lisbon ten years later.

In 1482 when Cão sailed, they had completed the major elements of the work subsequently entitled *Regiment do Astrolabio e do Quadrante*. Though it was not printed before 1495, its list of latitudes begins at the equator, which places its completion in Cão's preparatory period and suggests that as João's chosen leader for the expedition, the conclusions of the group must have been made available to him. The manual comprised the Regiment of the North – for observation of the North Star – and noted that the star ceased to be visible at Mina. It propounded the Rule for Raising the Pole – which replaced the old Rule of the Martoloio; and it introduced the Rule of the Sun which listed the *alturas* from the equator northward.

The concept of a Sea Route to India – Further India, not the land of Prester John – may have evolved as early as 1471. It existed in practical terms in 1474 at João's take-over of Guinea and the explorations. It may have been conceived in the elation of victory at Arzila. Inevitably it was stimulated by the gathering speed of discovery under Fernão Gomes.

The quality of navigational instruments had increased proportionately. Cão

A reconstructed version of Strabo's world showing the curve of Africa

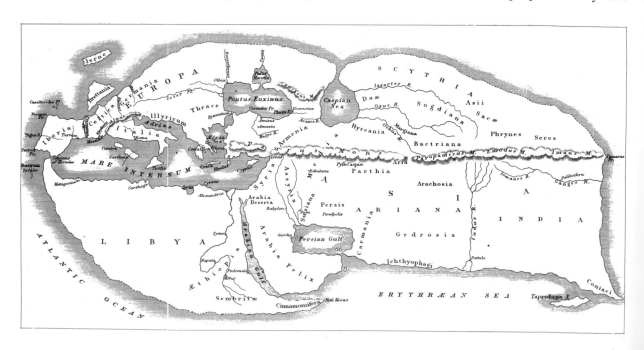

A German half-hour
sandglass of the sixteenth
century and a Portuguese
astrolabe

certainly had the quadrant; he probably had an astrolabe, though it may not
have been the simplified version for use with ships at sea; he possibly had an
early cross-staff. His compass was unquestionably improved and his sand-
glasses were more accurate and easier to operate.

These advances are implicit in Cão's decision to replenish at Mina, where
Diogo de Azambuja had just been appointed to build a castle at St Jorge as
Commander-in-Chief of Guinea. Amongst the officers at St Jorge were de
Aveiro and Bartolomeu Dias, seamen of note. Cão sailed after a prolonged
exchange of experience and, with a supreme confidence, laid a course direct to
Cape Lopo Gonçalves – 850 miles across open sea. Cock-crow coasting was
yielding to the new navigation.

From Cape Lopo he worked his way down to the limit of Gomes' discoveries,
St Catherine, and reached Luanda. In mid-August, marking headlands and
watering places on his running chart, he reached an area where, five miles out at
sea, they found the water fresh. Standing inshore, he opened the River Congo.

From Portugal he had brought with him stone pillars, which seamen called
padrões, quarried at Alcantara and capped with a cross on a cube of stone that

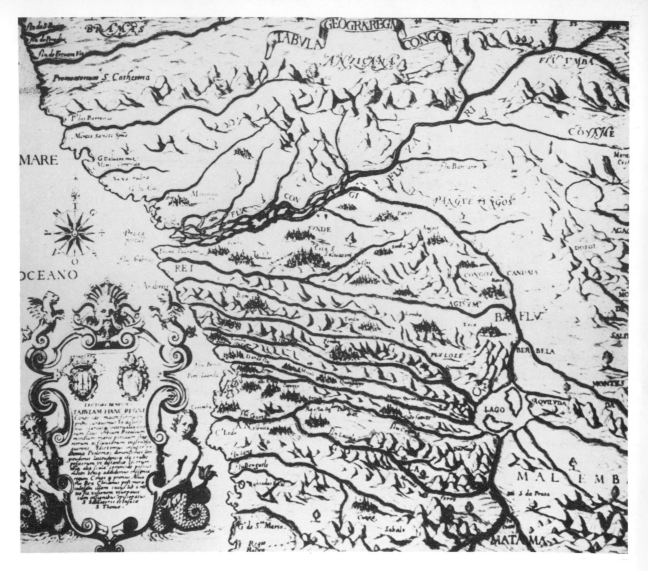

bore the Royal Arms. They were to mark the salient points of the new discoveries and he set up the first on the south bank of the Congo mouth.

The mouth of the Congo, reached by Cão in 1483

He made a long stay at the Congo, found the natives ready to trade, established communications with the King, and sent envoys. In March he went south again to a bay which he called the Castello d'Altar Pedroso because of its cliffs, and from there to a cape which he called Lobo (it was renamed later Santa Maria) where he set up his second cross.

The cross itself has gone, the cube and the column survived to be brought back to Lisbon in the nineteenth century. The inscription reads:

In the year 6681 from the Creation of the world and 1482 from the birth of Our Lord Jesus Christ, the most high, most excellent prince King João, second of Portugal, ordered this land to be discovered and these pillars to be put up by Diogo Cão, squire of his household.

From Santa Maria he headed back to the Congo, took hostages for men he

138

THE CAPE OF GOOD HOPE

had left behind, and returned to Portugal to an unprecedented reception. He was knighted on arrival, his Congolese hostages were elevated to the dignity of an embassy and taken into the King's Household. Public enthusiasm reached extraordinary levels.

The voyage was, in fact, valuable. Cão had added the Congo and almost 1,000 miles of new coast to the maps – but predecessors in Gomes' time had done as much without recognition. It has naturally a psychological importance as the first success of the reign of João II, but it is necessary to search elsewhere for the immediate and dramatic quality of the King's response.

Early in 1485 a rumour spread in Lisbon that Cão had not turned at Santa Maria, but had gone on to reach the Indian Ocean. Later in the year the rumour was current in Rome, whether before or after Cão's departure on his second voyage is uncertain.

In December the Portuguese Ambassador to the Holy See intimated that he had news of great importance to communicate. On 11 December he delivered an Address of Obedience to Innocent VIII and the College of Cardinals. In it he stated that Portuguese navigators had sailed 4,500 miles from Lisbon and 'had all but reached the Promontorium Prassim where begins the Persian Gulf'.

Ptolemy's map marks the Promontorium Prassim halfway up the East African coast, a little above Moçambique, and on almost precisely the latitude of Santa Maria on the other side of the continent. The importance of the claim is difficult to overestimate. It put the Portuguese at the jumping-off point for the crossing to India. After it lay one of the most used and best developed oceanic trade routes in the world.

It is inconceivable that the cautious João II would have made so blatant an attempt to deceive the Church. Diplomatic pressures on the Papacy achieved high levels at intervals, but Cão had already sailed on the second voyage and the possibility of imminent exposure would have been an absolute deterrent.

The logical alternative is that the King was himself deceived.

How?

It has been suggested that Cão, a highly experienced seaman, had determined that the coast trended sharply to the east below Santa Maria. In cool geographical fact it runs for twenty-seven miles due south – true, to the Bahia da Santa Marta and the small native town that became Lucira. At that point it makes an abrupt right-angled turn to the *west* and runs for seven miles to Cabo da Santa Marta where it turns sharply south-south-west for approximately 250 miles to the mouth of the Kunene river. There it trends slowly to the south-east and the Cape of Good Hope.

It lies in an area of high visibility, free of dust storms and of fog, with only heat haze as an occasional problem. The coast immediately below Santa Maria is steep, with a succession of 1,200-foot hills rising from the beaches and the 2,000-foot contour less than five miles inland. The right-angled stretch to Cabo da Santa Marta is backed by a 1,400-foot ridge. From the high ground where the cross was erected as a daymark on Cape Lobo, it must have looked like a wall.

Cão was expert in the 'headland to headland' technique of the navigators of his day as well as in open-water navigation. It is inconceivable that he could have

One of the *padrões* erected
Cão

Opposite
The *Ginea Portogalexe*

failed to note the coastal outline beyond the headland of the cross. It is still less conceivable that he could, as has been claimed, have mistaken the shallow indentation which came to be called the Lucira Grande, for the Indian Ocean.

A map or chart depicting this existed beyond question.

In 1485 the Venetian cartographer Cristofero Soligo had access to a Portuguese original of the coast from Benin southward. Then or shortly after – certainly before the return of the second voyage – he drew the remarkable chart known as the *Ginea Portogalexe*. Based primarily on the later voyages of the Gomes contract and the first voyage of Diogo Cão, it shows the coast in great clarity as far south as Cape Santa Maria. It has a superb delicacy. The sites of Cão's first *padrões* are marked by beautifully burnished crosses in heavy gold. It is a masterpiece of the cartographer's art.

At the Santa Maria cross the coast runs abruptly south-east, takes in a bay of size, runs for a little due east and then, by a series of capes, south-east to a great headland where it turns north and then north-east. The representation of the coastline is stylistically the same as the earlier coastline; it lacks, however, names for bays and headlands.

That Cão 'invented' this coastline is unacceptable. He must have known that he would be sent out, at once, to complete the survey – as indeed he was. That João II had it invented to deceive the Pope is at least equally unacceptable.

Yet that this nameless outline is the basis of the Ambassador's challenging assertion that they had 'all but reached the Promontorium Prassim' appears to be beyond reasonable doubt. That this claim is the basis of Portuguese assertions that their ships were operating in the Indian Ocean in the fifteenth century, and that Dias was in fact a rediscoverer, is equally beyond doubt. Its origins are therefore crucial.

Cão, returning to the Rio Poderoso (the Congo) seized hostages, as has been related. One of them, Caçuta, mastered Portuguese on the return passage to the point where he could be asked questions. It is logical that he would be asked, among the very first questions, the further direction of the coast. It is equally logical that, as a captive, moving towards an unknown land and an unguessable fate, he would answer the questions in the terms which he assumed his new masters required.

It is a situation that had been known in the previous history of exploration and was to be repeated endlessly in its future history. That Caçuta or one of the other hostages described a coast leading in the way in which his captors hoped it would lead is an aspect of human nature.

Cão as an explorer had to be an optimist. That he went south again believing in the possibility of the turn to the east is beyond reasonable doubt. He went briefly to the Congo with his four admirably-treated hostages, sent one with gifts and messages to the King, obtained the release of his own men and at once continued south. The record is painfully disjointed. He passed Santa Maria and reached Santa Marta, and must have found at once that there was no change of direction to the east. There is no reference to disappointment, no indication of chagrin. The coast held on first to the west of south, then a very little to the east of it, and careful professional survey continued.

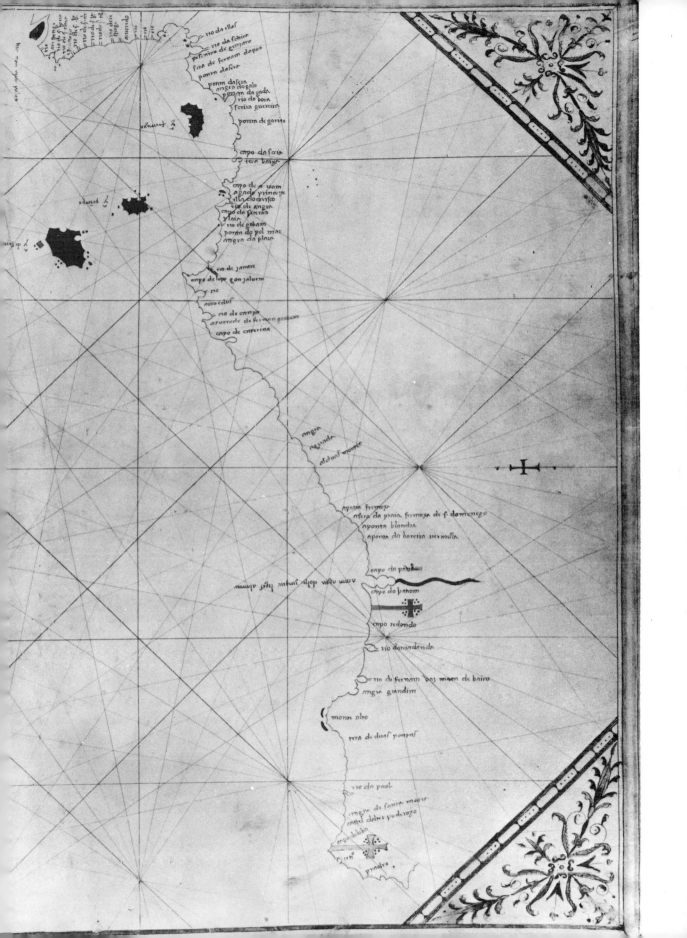

rio da illas
rio da fchira
pfmitio de pernaue
fira de fernam dapoo
ponta dafira

ponta dafira
angra dogalo
ponta da onda
rio da bora
feria gurrain

ponta de garito

cabo da fara
tun baixe

cabo de ã ioam
agade primago
illa elo cauisco
rio da angia
cabo da fierna
ylaia
rio de gabam
ponta do pol mai
angra da plaia

rio de janare
cabo de lope gonzaluem
rio
naro edtif
rio de campo
aruerede de fernan gomem
cabo de caterina

angra
rezinda
olduas montes

npiaia fremoza
nfira da piaia firmoza de f. domingo
aponta blancha
aponta da bareira vermelia

cabo do prado
cabo do banom
cabo redondo
rio damandamdre
rio de fernam baz maem de baixo
angra gamdim
monta alto
rra de duas pontas

rio da paul
angra de santa maria
caatel dalrey pudrozo
cnia dolobo
mõte
pindro

They had passed beyond the Congo forests now and they came to a scrub coast with thorn bushes and high grass. Beyond the mouth of the Kunene river it turned to semi-arid country and then to sand. Below the Ovityimbo country he planted his last cross on a promontory of the Namib desert.

Henricus Martellus in a note on his map of the world four years later ends with the words '*et hic moritur*'. Much ink has been spilt about them. Nothing is known of Cão's end; Barros in the *Décadas da Ásia* half a century later declared that he returned home. Nothing else survives. He has no known grave. His own times considered him a failure, but he ranks plainly with the greatest of the Portuguese explorers. There are no greater.

His failure – if it was a failure – was not permitted to check the sweep and vigour of the explorations. This is the wave-crest of the Portuguese enthusiasm. The final ten years of the reign of João II are the determining years in the opening of the world.

Fernão Dulmo had obtained royal permission to search for Antilia or Atlantis, the Island of the Seven Cities. A Genoese seaman named Cristoforo Colón had made application to the Court for backing for a voyage 'to discover and acquire islands and mainland in the ocean sea' – it was believed that he meant Cipangu and Cathay. João Afonso de Aveiro, returning from Benin,

Henricus Martellus' map of 1489. The scroll in the south-west corner ends '*et hic moritur*'.

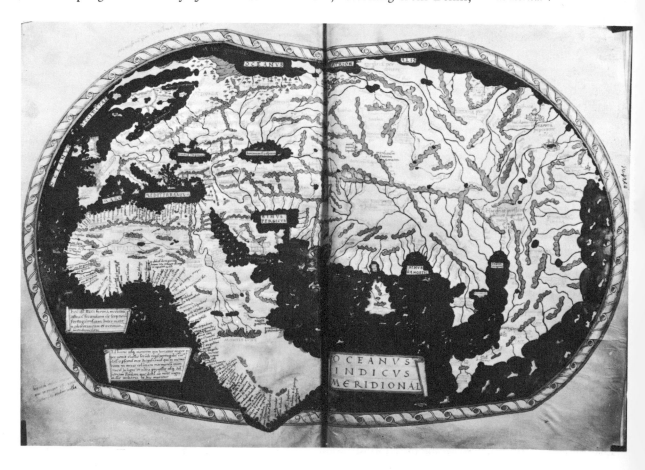

brought with him the first malaguetta pepper, and news of a Christian ruler, the Ogane, who lived 'twenty moons to the east of Benin' and was assumed to be Prester John.

Abruptly, King João terminated the recurring dynastic problems of his reign. The Duke of Braganza was tried and executed; the Duke of Viseu, pardoned in the same conspiracy by reason of his youth, was stabbed to death by João himself at a new revolt. The whole of his immense vitality could be devoted now to the furtherance of Henry's germinal quest.

João's committee considered Colón's proposition with more care than has generally been attributed to it, and turned it down in favour of a wider and more ambitious programme. The Dulmo proposition fades out of history after a limited search. Aveiro's proposition on a land route to Prester John was judged and rejected by the King himself (who decided that twenty moons' travel only meant 300 leagues). João's experts developed a plan of immense scope and ingenuity which involved a two-pronged assault on the Indian Ocean area.

Pedro de Covilhão, a Portuguese who had been squire to the Duke of Seville, was instructed to cross the Arab countries and make his way to India via the Persian Gulf. He spoke Arabic – he had been a spy at Fez and Tlemcen, and he had a remarkable record of adventure. He was to be accompanied by Afonso de Paiva as far as the Red Sea where de Paiva was to make his way to the Abyssinian highlands to seek out Prester John. Two priests were to undertake a separate journey to Jerusalem, presumably to communicate with representatives of the Coptic Church.

On 7 May 1487 the King received Covilhão and de Paiva in audience. They were given medallions inscribed in Chaldee (the name traditionally given to the Aramaic script of Abyssinia) with which to identify themselves, and a *carta de marear* prepared by Ortiz, the King's chaplain, and Master Moses. Their incredible journey began.

In their absence, Bartolomeu Dias sailed for the coast of Africa. He knew it, as far at least as Mina, from his earlier service with de Azambuja. Like Cão, he carried *padrões* with him and he would have had a version of Cão's map, corrected with the new additions to Cão's Cape Cross. He also carried two negroes whom Cão had brought to Portugal and four negresses whom he was instructed to land at appropriate places down the coast. They were to be well dressed in European clothes, and, astonishingly, equipped with 'samples' of trade goods, spices, silver and gold. It has a strong flavour of modern public relations and high pressure salesmanship.

As with Cão's voyages, little documentary evidence remains. The policy of secrecy had been in operation in varying degree from the time of Fernão Gomes. Now with a promise of solution imminent, the clamp down was total. Dias certainly called at points along the fertile coast but no record of these remains. He had two caravels and, following the close scrutiny of Cão's experience, a store ship had been added. The interminable desert coast offered no possibility anywhere of replenishment.

Dias put in in due course to an indentation about latitude twenty-seven

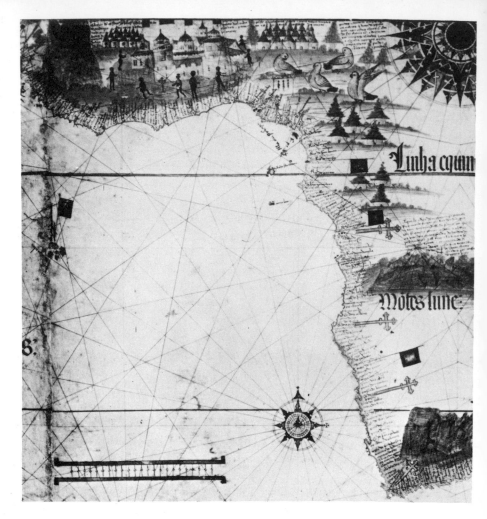

The 'Cantino' map of 1502 marks the *padrões* planted by Dias.

In the bay of Mina are a *nau* (right) and two caravels. Dias rounded the Cape in a caravel, but later designed a specially-modified *nau* for use on long-distance voyages.

degrees south which he called Angra Pequena, revictualled from his store ship, and left her at anchor with a small crew to await his return. A cross was erected on the headland known today as Dias Point and he stood south again.

He ran at once into head winds. Threshing backwards and forwards down the coast against the wind and the Agulhas current, he seems to have come to desperation but not to despair.

The provision of a store ship to act as an extended base is the first major technical development of the long-range voyages. Now, by *force majeure*, he arrived at the second. Cock-crow coasting had been abandoned by Cão in favour of the direct passage in known areas. Dias, baffled by the headwinds of the desert coast and the unremitting hostility of the current, came to a decision of immense courage. He stood out to sea across the wind. Gil Eanes had employed the manoeuvre on a small scale to defeat Cape Bojador half a century before. He had made a short leg out to sea and come in again below the Cape. Dias employed it to defeat a continent.

The accounts are vague and may not be entirely reliable, but there seems to be little question that he maintained a south-westerly course across a strong south-easter for thirteen days. 'With sails housed half way up the mast, when, the wind lessening they sought the land which they found ran eastward which hitherto had been in general north and south.'

The courage of the decision is immeasurable. He was 6,000 miles from Portugal, 3,000 from the nearest possible point of help at Mina. He faced an ocean that was totally unknown, that lacked even the comfort of legend like the North Atlantic or folk memory like the Greenland sea. He clawed off from a hot, desert coast and as he made ground to the south, it grew colder, and the seas higher, and the water chilled.

When he arrived at the decision to alter course is not known. It has been suggested that he reached a position forty degrees south and found the eternal westerlies, but it is more probable that somewhere about the latitude of Tristan d'Acunha, about thirty-seven degrees south, he found a westerly slant and turned thankfully to see if he had outrun Africa.

How he determined his longitude is nowhere stated. Dead-reckoning, immensely difficult in the circumstances of this most open ocean, gave him a painfully rough guide. Peter Perigrinus had failed to produce the perfectly shaped magnetic stone which would revolve in precise accord with the heavens. Robert the Englishman had voiced the requirement for a mechanical clock, and knocked it down as a 'vain notion'. On a simple human judgement Dias, finding no land on his new course, concluded he had defeated Africa and turned north.

He came, triumphantly, to a green and pleasant coast in a wide bay which they called Bahia dos Vaqueiros – the bay of the cattle herds – from the natives they saw pasturing their cattle behind the beaches. Courage and skill had been rewarded; without a sighting he had turned the Cape that was in due course to be called Good Hope, turned the jutting headlands beyond it, turned L'Agulhas which is the true southerly point of Africa.

The new coast ran from west to east.

Cautiously, before this new phenomenon, the natives drifted inland, Dias established no communication with them but assumed, wrongly, that they were the same as the natives of Guinea. They were, in fact, Hottentots, the nomadic Khoi Khoi, a brown people, not black, a nomadic wave of herdsmen and root gatherers who were driving the more primitive *Strandlooper* peoples into the southern sea.

Dias stood on to Algoa Bay at the eastern corner of South Africa and, still unknowing that it was the corner, erected a cross on the small islet of Santa Cruz. 'Here the crews complained greatly and wished to turn back, but the Captain Dias persuaded them to go on two or three days more and then return if they found nothing to induce them to continue.'

Much has been made of the incident. It was not, as it has too often been described, a mutiny. It was the custom of the time to consult in instances of disagreement. The smallness of the ships, the close and perpetual contact of all concerned made it essential and natural. Dias landed his officers and his leading hands, and they debated; then he drafted a document declaring their opinions, which they signed, and he asked them to carry on for one more stage.

Almost certainly the decision was correct. The store ship had made it possible for them to turn the south of Africa, but they had no information as to what lay ahead. They must already have been short of ordinary stores; the coast ahead of them, like the coast to the north-west, could well be desert. There was still the iron-hard journey home.

They stood past the pillar called St Gregory which they had set up on Cape Padrone, and almost at once and altogether incredibly, found that they had turned the other corner of Africa. The new coast trended north-east.

They found also that a steady current (afterwards it was called the Moçambique) flowed down it and promised a continuing obstacle. But they found, more importantly, that its water was warm. Dias at least was assured that it came from the matching tropics of the eastern coast and that the sea was clear to India.

Ptolemy was proved wrong. There was no landward link with the eastern world.

At the Great Fish river they went ashore for the last time – and turned for home. Well to the west they sighted at last the cape that Dias is said to have called the Cape of Storms, and João to have rechristened, with a more powerful optimism, the Cape of Good Hope.

The store ship was still at anchor when they returned to Angra Pequena, but only three of her men survived; the rest had died at the hands of the natives. They took on what was left of her cargo and burned her.

The end of the run was simple enough. They made a fast passage up Africa, called at Princes Island, found there Duarte Pacheo shipwrecked and stricken with fever, picked him up with his survivors and went on to Mina. There they took in the season's accumulated gold and arrived at Lisbon sixteen months and seventeen days from their departure.

They had reached the Indian Ocean. The sea route to India was clear. They had opened half the world.

Benin ivory of a Portuguese seaman in the crow's nest of a ship

COLOMBVS · LYGVR · NO
ORBIS · REPTO

Chapter IX

Otro Mondo

In the year 1451 the child Cristoforo Colombo was baptised in the city of Genoa.

In the same year 'the body of the Infante Henrique was taken in procession to the Monastery of Batalha, where the King awaited it'.

The coincidence is appropriate. Columbus was born into a world in which, under Henry, the germinal phase of oceanic exploration had been completed, Portuguese navigators had established the practical principles of discovery and the sea roads were effectively open to any man of vision. It is essential in any consideration of the achievement of the Genoese Columbus that his place in this, the main stream of exploration, should be assessed in relation to Portugal.

He was the son of a master-weaver, Domenico Colombo. His mother, Suzanna Fontanarossa, was Genoese. There is no acceptable foundation for the theory that they were Sephardic Jews, early detached from Spain and settled in Northern Italy. There is even less for the theory of their descent from the prestigious Roman family of Colonna. Hernando, his illegitimate son, in his life of the Admiral, rejects this with palpable regret, and opts for a still more exalted patronage,

> . . . believing that the Admiral was chosen for his great work by Our Lord, who desired him as His true Apostle to follow the example of others of His elect by publishing His name on distant seas and shore, not in cities and palaces, thereby imitating Our Lord Himself, who though his descent was from the blood royal of Jerusalem, yet was content to have His parentage from an obscure source.

Hernando's admiration for his father is demonstrably profound. It is, however, also of interest to note that at about the time he wrote this particular passage he was preparing the papers for the pleas in the family's law-suit against the Spanish throne.

Little documentary evidence exists in connection with Columbus' early life. It is claimed that he made a sea voyage at the age of ten, but in his account of the first transatlantic voyage he says that he '. . . took up navigation at the age of fourteen and followed it ever after'. In plain terms, he went to sea as a gromet – a ship's boy. Later, by his account in a letter to Ferdinand and Isabella, he served in one of the inconsequential wars of René of Anjou. That, as he suggests, he held a command in a cutting-out raid against a galleass at Tunis is entirely improbable but he made, unquestionably, at least one passage to Chios in the central Aegean. He had, in short, the basic experience of a Mediterranean seaman.

In 1476 he shipped out of Genoa with a convoy of cargo vessels carrying Chian products for Portugal, England and the Low Countries. Off Cape St Vincent it was attacked by French and possibly Portuguese ships. Accounts of the action are prodigiously confused, but the accepted version is that his ship, the *urca*

Columbus, a late portrait by an unknown artist

The port of Genoa in the fifteenth century

Bechalla, grappled with a great Venetian galley and was set on fire. The fire spread to the galley and, says Hernando,

> . . . there was no remedy for those on board save to leap in the water and die . . . But the Admiral, being an excellent swimmer and seeing land only a little more than two leagues away, seized an oar which fate offered him, and on which he could rest at times; and so it pleased God, who was preserving him for greater things, to give him the strength to reach the shore.

The story has all the attributes of miraculous intervention. The picture of Columbus staggering ashore on the beach close to – some versions say, below – the Infant's town at Sagres has overtones of destiny. Less ornamented versions of the incident maintain that the ships went in to Lisbon for refuge.

His brother Bartolomeu was possibly already at Lisbon in the establishment of a cartographer. Columbus remained there until the September when he shipped north either in one of the vessels of the convoy which had completed her repairs or, more probably, in a Portuguese merchantman. She called at Galway on the west coast of Ireland and went from there to 'Tile, whose northern part is in latitude seventy-three degrees north, and not sixty-three degrees as some affirm'.

Tile was Thule – Iceland. There was a substantial trade as early as the fifteenth century: woollens, wine and food-stuffs went north; salt cod came south. 'In the month of February 1477,' Columbus wrote in a note on sailing weather in the five zones, 'I sailed one hundred leagues beyond the island of Tile.'

The claim has not been seriously questioned, but it is at least reasonable to ask the motive for a passage of 300 miles inside the Arctic Circle in the impenetrable darkness of an Arctic February. Jan Mayen, the only land to the north of Iceland at approximately that distance, was barren, bleak, uninhabited, and at that date unacknowledged.

In any event Columbus was in Lisbon again in the summer and evidence suggests that he was at once accepted into a circle connected with charts and sailing directions, navigation and discovery. He may have made other voyages at this time, certainly in 1478 he made a deposition to a Genoese court in relation to money matters connected with the failure of a shipment of sugar from Madeira to Genoa.

In the following year he married.

Much of the background of this marriage lacks explanation. Hernando, in the *Life*, deals with it coolly. The bride, he says, 'was Dona Felipa Moniz, of noble birth and superior of the Convento dos Santos'.

Moniz was, in fact, her mother's family name. She was the daughter of Bartolomeu Perestrello, Captain Donatory of Porto Santo and leader of the final settlement. Described by Zurara as a 'young nobleman' of Henry's establishment at Sagres (the family came from Piacenza in Lombardy) he had been the central figure in the grimly hilarious episode of the pregnant rabbit. Her brother had succeeded, after litigation, to the Governorship of Porto Santo, and the family had social standing. Hernando's description of Dona Felipa as 'superior' of the Convento dos Santos is confusing. It does not imply that she was in religious orders, the convent at that time was a school for the daughters of Military Knights, but it does imply a status beyond her probable age. She was the child of Perestrello's third wife.

Columbus was twenty-eight. What induced a mature woman of considerable social and religious background to marry a brash adventurer of humble parentage, possibly younger than herself, of foreign extraction, and penniless to boot, is difficult to conceive.

What, on the other hand, induced Columbus to marry a woman caste-bound in the Portuguese tradition and clearly without money of her own is equally difficult to imagine. Hernando supplies one possible answer. The Admiral's mother-in-law, with whom they lived after the marriage, 'observing the Admiral's great interest in geography', told him her version of the voyages that had resulted in the discovery of Porto Santo and the Madeiras, and 'gave him the writings and sea-charts left by her husband. These things excited the Admiral still more; and he informed himself of the other voyages and navigations that the Portuguese were then making to Mina and down the coast to Guinea.'

The Perestrello Papers (unaccountably not in the possession of his son Bartolomeu) must to Columbus have represented a prize of inestimable significance – worth at the very least a marriage of convenience. But in addition, marriage into the family gave him an entrée to the social and moneyed world of Lisbon immensely removed from the strata of chart makers and scholar geographers and merchant seamen with whom he had previously circulated. Still

Overleaf
The Catalan Atlas
illustrates the exaggeration
of the length of Asia.
Columbus' theory extended
it still further.

153

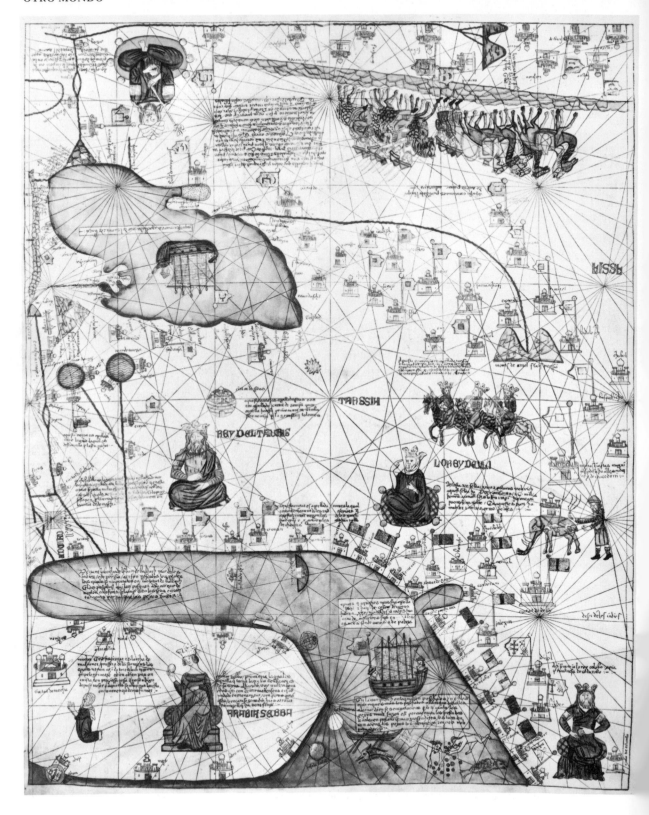

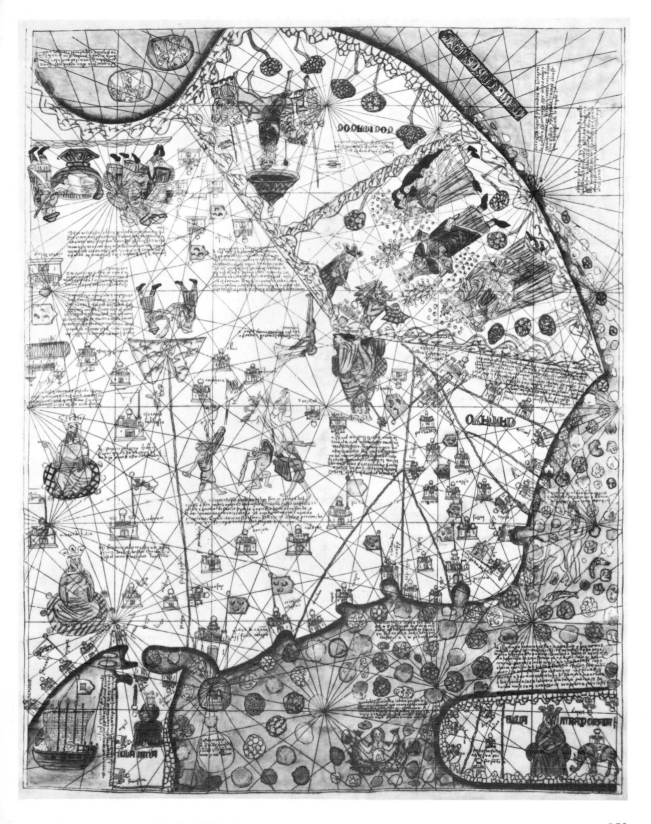

more importantly, it gave him access to the aristocratic command level of the leaders of expeditions and the governors of islands.

There is a remarkable acceleration in the formulation of his theories at this period. He read voluminously: Ptolemy, Strabo, Pliny, Marinus of Tyre, Marco Polo, Pierre d'Ailly – over and over – and the early Renaissance geographers. He had already established a fixed idea that the Asian land mass extended infinitely beyond previous calculations to the east. He found support for his theories in Lisbon, and he may have found further support at Porto Santo where, with his wife, he moved in due course to live with his brother-in-law, the Governor. Certainly at Porto Santo he began to acquire evidence beyond the legends of land to the west in eyewitness accounts of worked timbers sighted after prolonged westerly gales, of tropical seeds and vegetation, of floating bamboo. He inquired endlessly of men who had made searches to the westward, men who had been involved in the later discoveries of the Azores and in the African ventures. His voyage to Mina must almost certainly have been made at this period, though he himself gives no date for it. Porto Santo was a listening post in the ocean. To it came ships homeward-bound from Guinea and from searches for Antilia and St Brendan's Isle. The writ of the policy of secrecy did not run so far from Lisbon.

By the time he returned to the capital his concept of the land masses of the world had hardened into absolute certainty. Marco Polo, with his exaggerated estimates of the length of Asia, was partly responsible. D'Ailly in the *Imago Mundi* – his geographical bible – had declared categorically that the Atlantic was 'of no great width' between Morocco and the end of the eastern land mass. The second book of the prophet Esdras had stated with the authority of the Apocrypha that God had dried up six-sevenths of the globe, and there was left only one-seventh of the globe for Ocean.

Calculation of the precise width of the Atlantic depended in essence on estimates of the circumference of the globe. The convention was that the globe was divided into 360 degrees. The key to calculation was, therefore, the length of a degree at the latitude involved.

Columbus piled error on misconception. At some time very shortly after his return to Lisbon he obtained information, presumably at the level of his new circle, of a correspondence between Afonso V and the Florentine cosmographer and physician Paolo Toscanelli. The correspondence was at one time suspect but is now accepted. Towards the end of 1481 Columbus, according to Hernando, wrote to Toscanelli through Lorenco Girardi, a Florentine in Lisbon, outlining his theory and 'sending him a small sphere on which he showed his design'. Toscanelli – Paolo the Physician – answered: 'I perceive your noble and grand desire to go to the places where the spices grow; and I send you a copy of a letter which some time since I sent to a gentleman of the household of the most serene King of Portugal . . .'

With the letter was a copy of the chart which Toscanelli had drawn for Afonso to illustrate his theory. Twenty-six spaces were marked on the chart due west of Lisbon. Each of these, Toscanelli declared, represented 250 miles, making altogether a total of 6,500 miles to the 'very great and noble city of Quinsay', which was Hangchow. The airline distance to Hangchow is, in fact, approximately twice Toscanelli's figure west about.

Columbus's calculations are always intricate and often erroneous. Eratosthenes had arrived at a remarkably accurate figure of just under sixty miles for a degree at the equator; Columbus, however, preferred Alfragan. The Arabian had worked out a figure of a little under fifty-seven Arabic miles (approximately sixty-six nautical miles). Columbus, for ingenious reasons of his own, decided that Alfragan had meant the short Roman mile, not the Arabic, and concluded that the effective figure was forty-five nautical miles, thus producing a staggeringly over-optimistic estimate for the shorter degree at latitude twenty-eight north, where he proposed to attempt the crossing. So, taking into account Marco Polo's statement that Cipangu (Japan) was 1,000 miles east of Asia, he computed the distance to Cipangu at 2,400 miles.

Diogo Cão had just returned from planting the cross at Santa Maria, 3,500 miles to the south in the Atlantic – 2,400 miles of open sea to the west was well inside the potential of the day. Toscanelli's letter ended with a contagious enthusiasm:

> . . . it will be a voyage to powerful kingdoms and noble cities and rich provinces, abounding in all manner of spices and jewels in abundance . . . I do not wonder that you, who are of great courage, and the whole Portuguese nation, which has always distinguished itself in all great enterprises, are now inflamed with desire to undertake this voyage.

Columbus was – the Portuguese were not! João II had just given a series of grants (which cost him nothing) to a number of men of islands which they might discover to the westward, provided always that they were not in 'the parts of Guinea'. There was, however, no observable flame; the Portuguese were concentrating on the established tradition of the African route to India, and they were wholly convinced that it was now within their grasp.

At a moment that must have been incomparably unpropitious Columbus approached the King. Barros is understandably blunt: 'The King, as he observed this Christovão Colom to be a big talker and boastful in setting forth his accomplishments and full of fancy and imagination with his Isle Cypang than certain whereof he spoke, gave him small credit.'

He was, however, a cautious man. He referred him to his cosmographic committee: Diogo Ortiz, Bishop of Ceuta; Master Rodrigo, his Physician and a cosmographer of repute; Master Joseph, a cartographer – men who in due course briefed Covilhão prior to his departure for India overland.

Precise evidence as to the submissions of Columbus, and their decisions, is wanting. It is known only that they turned him down. He was 'boastful'; aggressive would be the modern term. His mathematics were deplorable. His demands for subsidy and reward were alike outrageous. More important than any of these things was their conviction that Portugal was on the very verge of success. Cão's second voyage began probably late in 1484 (one of the crosses bears that date) and Portugal had committed herself finally to the southern route. '. . . They all considered the words of Christovão Colombo as vain, simply

João II, who turned down Columbus: 'a big talker . . . and full of fancy and imagination'.

founded on imagination or things like that Isle Cypango of Marco Polo.'

They have been derided down the years for it. Yet they were right: Columbus's target was Japan; he was short of it by 7,000 miles.

Some time towards the middle of 1485, with his five-year-old son, he took passage for Palos on the Rio Tinto where the coast of Spain trends south towards Cadiz.

Hernando says that he did so in anger after João sent out a caravel to forestall his plan. It is possible that this was a later confusion with Dulmo's voyage in 1486; Dulmo had elected to search for the Island of the Seven Cities at his own expense. The accusation is hardly important, Hernando asserts simultaneously that he left on terms of friendship with the King.

Felipa, his wife, had 'meantime died'. She has no other epitaph. It is difficult to avoid the conclusion that she was a stepping-stone – used. But, largely because of her and the Perestrello family, Columbus left Portugal equipped as an explorer. He had been the associate of Portuguese navigators, the assistant of Portuguese cartographers, the irascible friend of Portuguese seamen. The Portuguese trade with Africa in the last decades of the fifteenth century was the only school of exploration in the Renaissance world. He was as much a product of the tradition of Sagres as Cão and Dias and da Gama.

Despite his qualifications, he arrived in the Rio Tinto penniless. The legend is that he walked to the monastery of the Rabido to place the small Diego in a place of safety and that an accidental meeting at the gate won him the friendship of Antonio de Marchena, *custodia* of the Franciscans in Seville and an astronomer. Antonio took the boy and gave his father an introduction to the Duke of Medina Sidonia.

Hope rose high, but Medina Sidonia brawled with the Duke of Seville and was barred the city, and Columbus – in Spain he took the Spanish spelling Colón – went to Cordoba, too late to make contact with the Catholic Sovereigns that winter.

In May he achieved an audience.

The story of the Spanish negotiations has been exhaustively examined. No two views of it correspond, but the commission which Ferdinand and Isabella appointed to consider the proposals lacked the expertise of the Portuguese commission, and Columbus in Spain was demonstrably more evasive and full of secret knowledge even than in Portugal. The published reasons for the first rejection in late 1490 – that the voyage would require three years, that the western ocean is endless, that St Augustine doubted if in fact there were Antipodes, and that if there was anything worth while to discover it would have been discovered already are not as witless as they have been made to appear. They represent much the standard of European thought at the time. Moreover, the commission almost certainly had additional reasons.

They may, for example, have known that in 1488 Columbus had applied to João II for a safe conduct (to avoid trouble over his Portuguese debts and consequential litigation) in order to begin a new approach to the Portuguese court, and that it had been shipwrecked in the triumph of the return of Bartolomeu Dias from the circumnavigation of the Cape of Good Hope.

They may, additionally, have learnt that he had sent his brother Bartolomeu to the English court to enlist the interest of Henry VII – with specific instructions to go on to France and Charles VIII if that failed. He was still accepting a subsistence allowance from the Spanish court at the time!

In Spain he had changed only the spelling of his name; he was still blusterous, a big talker, full of fancy. He can never have been lovable, and the Sovereigns were preoccupied with the war against Granada – Spain's particular crusade. In the late summer of 1491 he went back to La Rabida, defeated, to collect Diego and go himself to France.

Juan Perez, *Guardian* of La Rabida and a confessor to the Queen, volunteered to make one last approach. The Queen sent money for new clothes and a mule to bring Columbus back to court, and at court he reiterated his stupendous demands: Admiral of the Ocean Sea, Viceroy of the Indies, immense and overwhelming rights over land discovered, ten per cent of the revenues . . .

Granada fell. He walked in solemn procession up that formidable hill to see the end of the Moorish dream. Then he was summoned to an audience and finally and totally rejected.

Luis de Santángel's well-known intervention has the undertones of a song of the troubadors. Though persuaded to change her mind, the Queen did not pawn her jewels; Santángel, as Treasurer of Spain, underwrote the larger part of the necessary cost of the expedition with the funds of the Santa Hermandad, the rural security force; Columbus was intercepted by the Queen's messenger at Pinos Puente, and the Enterprise of the Indies was under way.

Palos was selected as the point of departure, not for his convenience but because, as the Sovereigns frugally pointed out to the authorities of the port, '. . . for certain things done and committed by you to our disservice you were condemned and obligated by our council to provide us for a twelvemonth with two equipped caravels at your own proper charge and expense . . .'.

The venture began, then, with certain acerbities. Yet it would have been impossible to select a more appropriate port from which to mount the expedition. Palos, effectively, was an extension of the Algarve. Its people were cut of the same timber, its ships were the same caravels that Portugal and this Atlantic coast had developed, its men trained by illicit intervention on the coast of Africa.

Columbus took the ships that were offered, the *Pinta* and the *Niña*, thankfully enough. The *Santa Maria* he paid for out of funds supplied, and cordially disliked. She was a Galician from the Biscay coast, heavy, slow and unhandy; they called her *La Gallega*. She was about 100 tons – the measurement derived from the *tonelada*, a cask holding two pipes of wine of about 2,000 lb weight. *Niña*, his favourite, was a *caravela latin* of sixty tons, roughly seventy feet in length, the counterpart of the small and lively ships that had solved the problems of the Portuguese coastwise exploration from the middle of Henry's operation. As Dias had just ascertained, this solution was not so useful for running before the trades in the open ocean. *Pinta* was a *caravela redonda*, square rigged on two masts. She may have been about fifty-five tons. They were not any of them cockle-shells. Despite nineteenth-century incomprehensions, they were well-found ships of a type hardened on scores of exploratory voyages. Ninety men sailed with them, forty in the *Santa Maria*, the rest equally divided between the caravels.

Columbus sailed in command of the expedition as captain of the *Santa Maria*. Vicente Yañez Pinzón sailed as captain of the *Niña*.

Before dawn on Friday 3 August 1492, Columbus, having taken Communion, boarded the *Santa Maria* and 'in the name of Jesus' ordered her to sea. At the hour of prime she drifted with the ebb past La Rabida and the sound of the singing of the monks came out to them. A little nearer to the open water, according to tradition, she passed the last ship of the new exodus of the Jews.

The passage to the Canary Islands was unremarkable except that *Pinta* had trouble with her rudder, which jumped the gudgeons. Columbus suspected sabotage. A jury rig gave further trouble, and Columbus left her to make Grand Canary while he pressed on to Gomera to see if he could charter a substitute through Doña Beatriz de Peraza y Bobadilla, the young and beautiful widow who governed Gomera for her small son.

They missed each other and he went back to Grand Canary where new fittings were forged, and *Niña*, displaying an excessive tendency to yaw in a following sea on the way down, was re-rigged as a *caravela redonda*.

A conjectural model of the *Santa Maria*, a clumsy Galician ship

Doña Beatriz entertained them when they called back at Gomera to fill up with stores and water. She was a strong-minded young woman. It is an island tradition that she hanged a man who had attempted her honour from a window of the tower of San Sebastian that still stands in Gomera. Island tradition also says that she was not so brusque with Columbus.

True or not, he did not overstay his welcome. Early on 6 September he said Mass again, and sailed in light airs. At nightfall on 9 September the expedition finally lost the Peak of Tenerife.

The weather served him; there was no heavy wind, and no flat calm. His track chart shows one brief alteration to the north-west about longitude forty-seven. On 22 September, less than two weeks out, Hernando records '. . . the grumbling, lamenting and plotting went on day after day; and at last the Admiral himself became aware of their faithlessness and wicked designs against him.'

There was little enough he could do about it except falsify the daily position – and he had done that from the start. There was a violent argument between the three ships about it in early October. *Pinta* claimed that they had made good 634 leagues, the pilot of the flagship said 578, *Niña* 540. The Admiral knew that the figure was 707 but he was anxious that the men should not know that they were so far from home. 'The Admiral', says Hernando pawkily, 'dissembled this error.'

Martin Alonso Pinzón,
captain of the *Pinta*

Right
Possibly the closest likeness
to Columbus in middle age

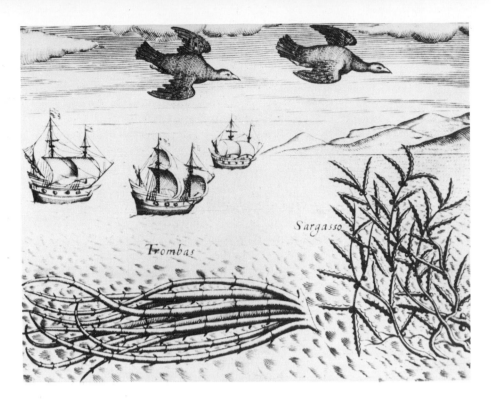

Sargasso weed found in
the Doldrums

Bird sightings comforted them. Pelicans, they maintained, were an indication
that they were close to land. The bosun bird, the *rabo de junco*, never went far
out to sea. Sargasso weed was interpreted as a sign of a coast.

On 25 September at sunset Martin Alonso Pinzón sighted an appearance of
land and they headed towards it – and found nothing!

On 7 October everybody sighted land and *Niña*, ahead of the fleet, actually
hoisted a flag and fired a gun. A prize of 10,000 *maravedis* had been promised by
the Sovereigns for whoever should sight it first.

Each time the 'illusion of land faded clean away' and they carried on, grumbling more acridly.

On 10 October the voyage balanced on the edge of mutiny. The evidence in
the famous lawsuit after the death of Columbus (which dragged on from 1514 to
1536) is contradictory to the point of outrage. That Martin Alonso offered to
string up half a dozen of the leaders represents one aspect; that Columbus lost
his nerve, the other.

It is probable that neither version was wholly true. What is equally uncertain
is that at ten o'clock on the night of the eleventh, with *Santa Maria* running hard
before a brisk gale in disregard of his stipulation that there should be no night
sailing close to land, Columbus sighted a light 'like a little wax candle, rising and
falling'. Gutierrez, the King's butler, backed him, but nothing more developed.
Four hours later, with the ship still crashing along before the wind, Rodrigo de
Triana, in the *Pinta* ahead of the rest of the fleet, sighted a bar of white sand and
the darkness of trees, and *Pinta* in her turn fired a gun.

Columbus claimed the reward for his light, though they were thirty-five miles
out at sea when he said he saw it, in a gale, in water 3,000 fathoms too deep for

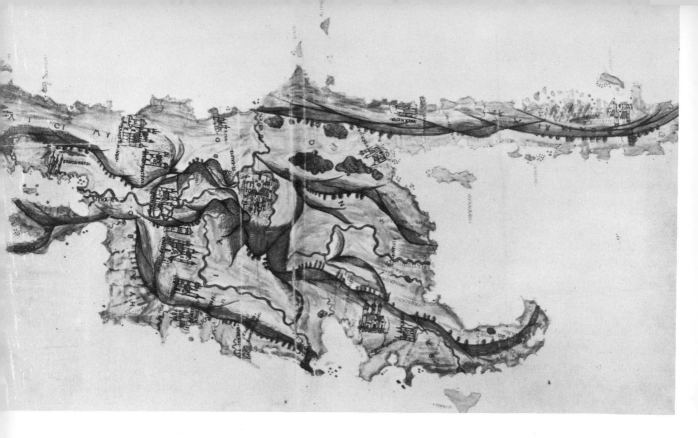

fishing. It signified, he said, 'the spiritual light with which he was to illuminate those parts'.

The accounts of the next morning are singularly unemotional.

> . . . at daybreak they saw an island about fifteen miles in length and very level, full of green trees and inhabited by a multitude of people . . . and the Admiral went ashore with an armed boat displaying the Royal Standard . . . the people had no jewels or metal objects except some gold pendants which they wear hanging from a hole made through the nostrils. Asked whence came that gold, they replied by signs, from the south, where lived a king who had many tiles and vessels of gold.

The shape of the Enterprise of the Indies is determined in that brief answer. Columbus had a manuscript copy of Marco Polo: '. . . the king of the Island (Cipango) hath a mighty palace all roofed with the finest gold . . . the floors of the halls are paved with gold plates . . . There are pearls in the greatest abundance.'

It is unfair to criticize Columbus for his credulity here – unless he deliberately misconstrued the 'signs'. In the first twenty-four hours he had been offered confirmation of a vision, and he headed away at once in the direction of Santa Maria de la Concepción – which is today Rum Cay – to begin the search for the tiles of gold.

In due course, and after inquiry, he learnt that the easiest source of gold was the island of Babeque – where it was gathered on the beach, by candle-light. He reached Cuba, coasted west, turned, coasted east, made a probe to the north for Babeque, missed it and turned back again for Cuba.

On 24 November Martin Alonso Pinzón, with fresh information about Babeque, deserted his admiral and disappeared. Columbus carried on with two ships. He wrote to the Sovereigns, 'this country, most serene Princes, is of such marvellous beauty that it surpasses all others as the day surpasses the night'.

Opposite above
An early map of Española
Opposite below
One of the first maps showing the discoveries of Columbus, dated 1506. North America is omitted

Below
Natives of Española: a European view of their customs and, right, an encounter with Columbus

He crossed at length to the harbour of St Nicholas Mole on Haiti, which he named Española because 'the land and the trees reminded him of Spain', and all through December he worked his way slowly towards the end of the Tortuga Channel, questioning Indians, establishing friendly relations, making gifts, asking for the Great Khan. In the Moustique Bay his people captured a young girl, naked except for a nose plug of gold, and they clothed her and sent her back with presents. The gesture paid dividends, they became disastrously popular. Their reputation carried past Tortuga and their popularity with it, and when they came to the exquisite bay of St Tomas, '. . . in the other places all the men try to conceal their women from the Christians out of jealousy, here they do not, and the women have very pretty bodies . . .'

Columbus calculated that in the two nights they lay in the bay a thousand natives came aboard the *Santa Maria* by canoe and another five hundred swam off. Nobody slept. In between other entertainment the men who were now interpreters questioned them in connection with gold, and Columbus wrote: '. . . Our Lord in his goodness guide me that I may find this gold, I mean their mine, for many here say they have knowledge of it.'

He had sent a boat down to the village of Guacanagari, the paramount chief of the area. It returned reporting safe passage and news of a place called Cybão, which was pronounced with the same lisp as that with which the Spaniard pronounced Cipangu or Japan. Clearly he was in sight of his goal! At sunrise on 24 December he cleared for Caracol Bay and the village of Guacanagari.

Once again the wind headed him – what there was of it. They made a long tack to seaward and gained nothing. At darkness they were barely a league beyond Cape Haitien in the silent night. At eleven o'clock the watch changed and Juan de la Cosa, the master, took over from the pilot. Columbus talked with him on deck for a while and went to bed. The new watch appears to have waited until he completed his prayers and then they drifted to quiet corners, and sleep. Juan de la Cosa ordered the helmsman to steer by a star – he must have been able to see one through a hatch – and turned in. The helmsman found a gromet still awake and gave him the big tiller, against all standing orders, and himself curled up and slept.

Elementary arithmetic suggests that out of 1,500 visitors there must have been a minimum of five complaisant women to every man on board the two ships, the gromets included. One bawdy maritime phrase covers it all: the *Santa Maria's* crew was shagged out.

Precisely at midnight of Christmas Eve the *Santa Maria* ghosted very gently on to the barrier reef, four miles to the eastward of Cape Haitien, spiked herself as the swell lifted her on to a spear of coral, and settled like a tired bird.

It is the sorrowful ending of the First Voyage.

It is the terrible beginning of a new human tragedy.

The fortress of the Navidad, built of the timbers of the *Santa Maria*, armed with her bombards is the engendering symbol of the rape of the Americas.

After Navidad the world altered.

The building of Navidad

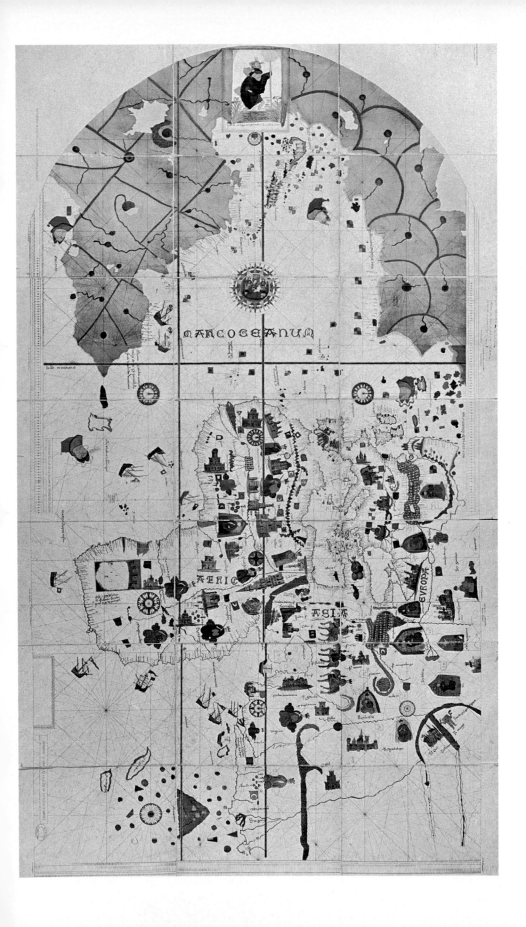

Dom Vasco da gama :- — 6º

Chapter x

India Achieved

In the name of God. Amen!

In the year 1497 King Dom Manuel, the first of his name in Portugal, dispatched four vessels to make discoveries and go in search of spices. Vasco da Gama was the captain-major of these vessels.

João the Perfect died in early middle age; prior to his death there was a protracted interruption in the stream of exploration that has not been adequately explained. Bartolomeu Dias, it will be remembered, had returned from the gateway to the Indian Ocean in December 1488. Da Gama, as the *Roteiro* declares in blunt and business-like prose, sailed after a delay of nine years – the years in which Columbus had made his first climactic voyages and a great expectancy had spread across the Western world.

To what extent did the origins of delay lie in Dias's checkmate at the Great Fish River?

Documentary evidence is altogether lacking, but it is at least probable that coming on the heels of Cão's aggravated failure in the second voyage, it represented to João – not himself in any sense a man of the sea – a powerful discouragement. The closing years of João's reign have an increasing turmoil. Maintenance of absolute monarchy in a country with a tradition of powerful aristocracies was in itself a continuing burden. The death of his only son immediately after a marriage that had been a triumph of policy, was a personal grief. Relations with Spain, always anxious, were deteriorating as the expulsion of the Moors moved towards the final splendour of Granada – and the knowledge that Spain would be free in due course to swallow Portugal. The painful onset of the uraemia which ultimately killed him must have affected judgement. The decision to follow up Dias's effective triumph was endlessly postponed.

One sound practical reason must also have stayed João's hand. He was still waiting for the results of the elaborately prepared reconnaissance of Covilhão and Paiva – who had set out in 1487 in search of the information that he needed on the Indian Ocean and Prester John.

Paiva was dead.

In 1491, when Covilhão's dispatches almost certainly reached João, Covilhão himself was in the last stages of his journey to Abyssinia.

The journey is among the most remarkable even in an age of astonishing journeys. The two men went first to Barcelona and then by Naples, assisted possibly by Lorenzo de' Medici, to Rhodes. From Rhodes they went with a cargo of honey to Alexandria, fell ill, lost most of their honey, but made their way with other merchandise to Cairo. From there, disguised probably as Arabs, they went south down the Red Sea with 'some Moghreby Moors' to Aden, where they separated.

Miniature portrait of Vasco da Gama

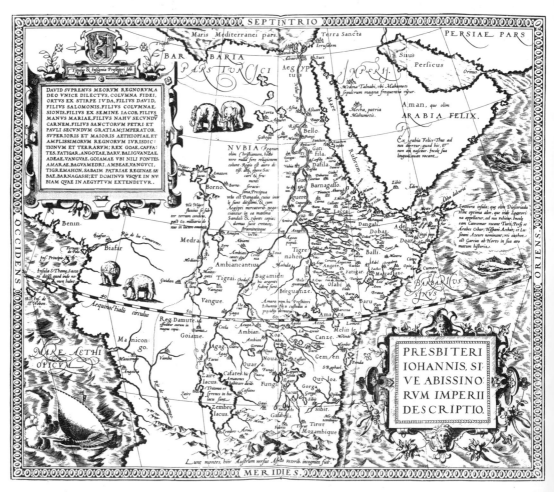

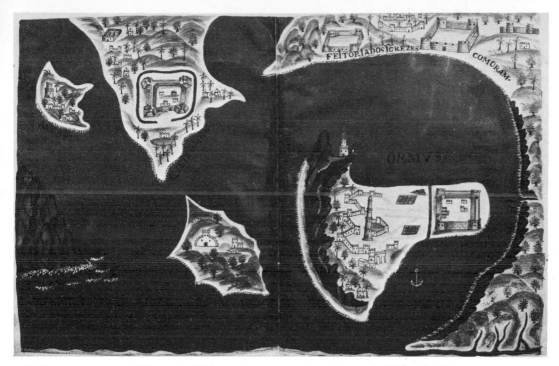

Paiva crossed to Africa. Covilhão took passage in a 'Mecca ship', possibly with a returning pilgrimage for India, and in about thirty days, learning the full significance of the monsoon in the eastern sea, reached Cananor on the Coromandel coast.

The route was ancient, established and covered jealously by the twin antagonisms of religion and a monopolistic trade. Covilhão's audacity is difficult to assess in an age of altered values. His intelligence work is at least at a comparable level. Da Gama's voyage shows in its certitude and its confident execution the quality of the information made available.

From Cananor Covilhão made his way to Calicut, the principal port of the coast, moved north to Goa and from there took ship west again to Hormuz at the entrance to the Persian Gulf.

It is a remarkable indication of the efficiency – and complexity – of the Indian oceanic trade that from Hormuz he was able to ship within a reasonable time to Sofala, the export head of the widely dispersed south central African gold trade, a little south of the modern town of Beira. From Sofala, somewhere in 1490, he got back to Cairo. Waiting for him he found two Jews of Spain – Joseph of Lamego, a shoemaker, and the Rabbi Abraham of Beja – sent by João to pick up his reports. He found also news of the death of Paiva.

His reports were sent back with Joseph of Lamego. Abraham had João's orders to go on to Hormuz, and Covilhão took him there and then, apparently for his private satisfaction, shaved his head, dressed himself in the white robes of a pilgrim and made his way to Mecca and Medina. In 1493, roughly about the time Columbus returned from Española, he made his way to Abyssinia and a life sentence of power and luxury as adviser to the Negus, with everything allowed him except his freedom.

Prester John had already faded from the Portuguese calculations. No one

An early map of Hormuz

Opposite
A carrack of the early sixteenth century leaving port before the wind and, below, the kingdom of the Negus of Abyssinia, 'Prester John'

believed in this day of a Christian thrust from the south against the expanded power of Islam.

Queen Isabella

Columbus, on his return, went first to João's court (removed to the country because of pestilence) and understandably incurred the displeasure of Queen Isabella thereby. It is impossible to dissect the thought processes of João at this pregnant moment. Whether he lamented his failure to take the possibility that Columbus had offered him, as the legend says, is at least uncertain. He made, however, no attempt to launch an immediate eastern voyage to circumvent Columbus's claims. Probably, knowing his man, he mistrusted the evidence. That islands had been discovered was unquestionable, that they were Indian islands was entirely a different matter. Politically it was, however, necessary to come to an arrangement with Spain. For the greater part of the next year he was involved in the preliminaries of the Treaty of Tordesillas.

In June 1494 the provisions emerged. The world was to be divided in two by a line drawn through a point 370 leagues to the westward of the Cape Verde Islands: Spain took the west of it, Portugal the east. It was neat and simple, except that no agreement was reached on the length of a league, that no one could establish longitude with accuracy, and that nobody had conceived the possibility of an unimagined southern continent with half its coastline to the east of the line of demarcation.

Columbus made his second crossing. João was already a desperately sick man and he had been defeated in his wish to put his bastard son on the throne by the opposition of the Queen and the court. He was in a slow retreat. Though he nominated da Gama for command of the follow-up expedition, and ordered the unhappy Dias to prepare it, he had lost the fire that once had flamed within him.

Nothing is recorded of the reactions of Dias. The evidence, such as it is, is that he accepted the decision loyally.

Da Gama was the son of the Alcaide-Mor of the little fishing town of Sines, midway between the Tagus and Cape St Vincent. He appears to have had a reasonable competence as a seaman but the only episode of his prior history that emerges in relation to the sea is that he had once been directed by João to seize a number of French ships in Portuguese ports in compensation for acts of piracy.

In 1495, with the venture still in early preparation, João died.

Manoel, his nephew, at his accession decided to put the matter to the Royal Council. The Council's view is not necessarily the measure of popular enthusiasm, but it is plain fact that the majority of members were opposed to any move to resume the attempt to reach India. Its effect on Venice (traditionally the monopolist of the India Trade), its possible effect on other trading nations, its immediate cost, and the ultimate cost of any attempt to conquer – or even to control – India influenced the Council and probably reflected opinion outside the Council. The gilt was no longer brilliant on the gingerbread of exploration.

Manoel, however, was not simply 'Fortunate'; he displayed, very early, a power of decision. Despite his councillors, he ended debate with an order to Dias to complete the preparations. The task required the best part of two years but by mid-1497 the ships were ready.

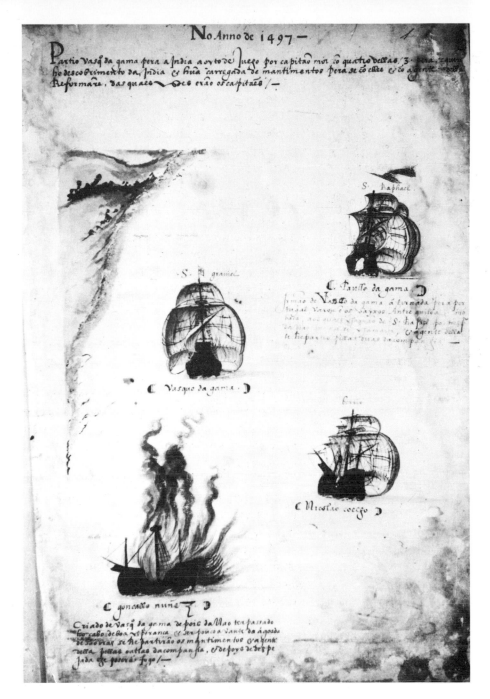

Da Gama's fleet *en route*
for India in 1497

Specially designed by Dias in the light of his oceanic experience, the *São Gabriel* and the *São Raphael* were *naus* of about 200 tons by modern measurement, their draught was less than that of normal commercial vessels and they were probably longer. They were, of course, square rigged. There was one caravel, the *Berrio*, and a store ship. They carried an armament of twenty guns described as *bombardes* – primitive breech loaders – and their ships' companies were supplied with armour, crossbows and the normal hand weapons of the day. In plain terms, this was an armed reconnaissance. Ortiz, of the scientific committee which turned Columbus down, supplied the necessary charts – presumably based on material derived from Covilhão and other sources. Abraham Zacuto, also of the committee, supplied the instruments, including the wooden astrolabe used by da Gama at St Helena Bay. Both the *naus* carried *padrões* as markers, and one had a priest.

At Montemor, in a solemn ceremony, da Gama was given the silken banner of the Knights of Christ. The vigil was held at the chapel of Belem which Henry had built for his people, and on 8 July the fleet sailed. Dias sailed in company, bound for Mina with a caravel. Eight days later they passed down the lee of Lanzarote in the Canaries and thirty-six hours after lay to, fishing, off the Terra Alta. The voyage to Cape Verde had become routine.

That night the fleet lost contact in fog and continued in sections for a pre-arranged rendezvous at Santiago in the Cape Verdes, where the ships replenished and took in water.

On 3 August it sailed again, keeping to the eastward. At some point not specified in the record Dias parted company and headed for Mina. It is possible only to speculate on his feelings at this moment. He had discovered the way. He had laid down the track for the India voyage, he had designed and built the ships – and he had been dropped. One account says that he was on his way to take up the post of Captain at El Mina, an important and lucrative office, as a belated reward. If this was the case, his term was brief. He was in Portugal again at the end of 1499 in time to take a post as captain of a caravel in Cabral's India voyage. Two years was scarcely long enough to line anyone's pocket.

Da Gama's passage south is unremarkable. He made a wide sweep to the westward once the line had been crossed, on a recommendation that can only have come from Dias; but the evidence suggests that it was indifferently executed though the *Roteiro*, unhappily, gives neither courses nor positions. He seems to have found the south-east trades at a relatively high latitude and he reached south-west across them until, far to the south, he found a westerly slant.

Not, however, far enough to the south! As he worked slowly across the South Atlantic, south-easterly winds headed him and, possibly through inexperience, he failed to make sufficient allowance for the fact. He sighted land 300 miles above the Cape of Good Hope (which he should have cleared), failed to identify the coast, and hauled out again to sea. At a second attempt he found a wide bay, stood in and anchored in good holding ground. 'At daybreak on Thursday 16 November, having careened our ships and taken in wood, we set sail. At that time we did not know how far we might be from the Cape of Good Hope.' They were in fact still 100 miles to the north and it took seven days bucking the south-east airs to round Cape Point.

On 25 November they made Mossel Bay. The natives were more friendly here, and they bought an ox and found it 'as toothsome as the beef of Portugal'. The stay was light-hearted, even da Gama unbent. 'The captain-major ordered the trumpets to be sounded and we in the boats danced, and the captain-major likewise . . . .'

On Saturday 10 December, 'we passed the last pillar . . .' – Dias's beacon on Cape Padrone – henceforth the water was unknown.

For four days they worked up the coast, laying-to at night, and on the Wednesday morning found themselves back at their starting point. They had failed to reckon with the Moçambique current. But by Christmas Day they had made good four degrees and 'God in His mercy was pleased to allow us to make headway'. They called the land that they were passing Natal.

A little to the north of this point they stood out to sea. From here there is an assurance about da Gama's proceedings that contrasts sharply with the rounding of the Cape. The succession of events makes it plain that he had information as to the Moçambique Channel and the coastline of central Africa. The thrust into deep water suggests that he knew the water ahead was clear, that the land was profitless, and that he would find the assistance that he needed well to the north. 'We now went so far out to sea, without touching any port, that drinking water began to fail us and our food had to be cooked with salt water.' Actually they were only fourteen days at sea but it is probable that they had not watered since leaving Mossel Bay, and da Gama was clearly holding on to make as much northing as possible. On Thursday 11 January they anchored in an open roadstead off a small village.

Two men were landed, there was an interchange of gifts and they spent the night ashore. For the next five days, helped by the natives, they ferried water out through the surf. The people here had copper in plenty and their hilts and their shearhs were of ivory – they had reached the civilization of Eastern Africa.

On 24 January they entered the Quelimane River. It was necessary to careen again, the warm Indian Ocean water had increased the rate of marine growth on the hulls. Many of the men were ill with scurvy. The mainmast of the *Raphael* needed repairs. Altogether they were at Quelimane thirty-two days, and they erected a pillar here and called it *São Raphael* after the ship that had carried it. They were past the mouth of the Zambesi river now, more than 200 miles north of Sofala; they had overlapped Covilhão and they were within the area of the Moslem trading monopoly. '. . . Two gentlemen of the country came to see us. They were very haughty and valued nothing which we gave them. One of them wore a *touca* with a fringe embroidered in silk . . . A young man in their company . . . had come from a distant country and had already seen big ships like ours.'

On 1 March they came to Moncobiquy – Moçambique. It had a Sultan '. . . so proud that he treated all we gave him with contempt, and asked for scarlet cloth, of which we had none'. But eventually they satisfied him, and he was invited to eat with them. In the course of the meal da Gama 'begged him for two pilots to go with us'.

The importance of pilots in this phase of the voyage is entirely understandable. The knowledge that a pilotage system existed is, in view of the endless language difficulty, less easy to understand and da Gama's insistence on pilots and his clear intention to go to any lengths to acquire them can only derive from Covilhão's instructions for the Indian Ocean crossing. At this first request da Gama was patently negotiating for an ocean pilot – the price offered, 'thirty *mitikals* in gold and two *marlotas*', was far above the figure that would have been offered for coastal pilotage.

The *mitikal* or *miskal* was a Moçambique weight equivalent to forty-one grammes of gold. The *marlota*, the make-weight, was a robe of silk.

An agreement was made subject to a condition that one of the two pilots always remained with the ships. It was foredoomed. One of them lived on an island outside Moncobiquy. They took the other and went to the island in search of him, having previously mounted bombards in the sterns of the ships' boats, and were challenged by boats from the island – six of them, 'armed with bows and long arrows and bucklers'.

Da Gama secured the pilot who was with him and opened fire.

These are the first shots in the 500-year war between the Far East and the West – a war that is not yet ended.

It is impossible to overestimate the importance of the episode. Prior to Moçambique da Gama was a moderate leader and an indifferent navigator. After Moçambique he shows a fire and a decision that alters the character of the voyage. Paulo da Gama, in the *Berrio*, made sail with commendable speed and came to their assistance, but the 'Moors' had already reached the land and da Gama boldly sent Coelho ashore. The 'lord of the place' taking them for Turks, they secured the second pilot – or another.

Light airs and the Moçambique current again played havoc with the passage. They drifted south, lost twelve days waiting for a wind, were forced back to Moçambique for water, and had their second skirmish. On 24 March, having been 'sneeringly' told that if they wanted water they would have to look for it,

A formalized view of the island of Quiloa, after colonization

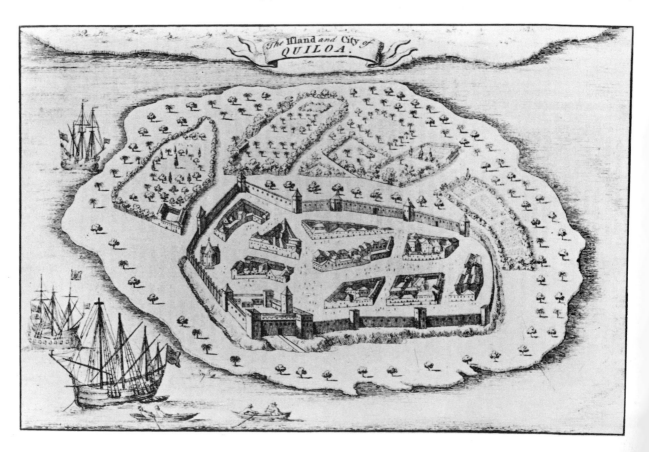

they went in in strength and, bombarding palisades that had been erected at the landing place, pursued and took a number of boats and captured prisoners.

Light airs continued. They made little headway until the end of the month. The pilots deceived them over the island of Quiloa which, they had been told, was occupied by Christians. Finally, they headed for Mombasa. As they ran parallel with the land in the final approach, *São Raphael* went aground on a shoal, six miles out. At low tide she was high and dry. They laid out anchors and when the tide rose again she floated and they kedged off.

On 7 March they ran past the island of Pemba and anchored off Mombasa, eager 'to go on land and hear mass jointly with the Christians reported to live there under their own Alcaide'.

There were no Christians. The pilots had misled them again. Visits were interchanged but there was an evident hostility. On the Tuesday when they weighed anchor to enter the port the *São Gabriel* was in collision and they anchored again. In the turmoil the Moçambique pilots jumped for it and were picked up by a *zavra*, a local boat, and so got clear.

That night da Gama put two of the remaining Moors on board to the question, 'dropping boiling oil upon their skin', and was informed that a plot had been made to take the ships as soon as they entered the port.

They remained, defiantly, until the Thursday when they moved eight miles and anchored again. At dawn they hunted two local boats and captured one of them to impress a pilot. At sunset they anchored off Malindi.

Their new prisoners told them that there were at Malindi four ships belonging 'to Christians from India' and that if they went in they would be able to get from them qualified pilots for the Indian Ocean passage.

The word Christians appears to have given rise to interminable misunderstanding. It is possible that there were on this coast a handful of Nestorian Christians – merchants from India – but the local people must have equated the Christians da Gama asked after with Hindus. There were no Christians at Malindi. There were, however, pilots.

Da Gama was fortunate. There was intense rivalry, hostility even, between Mombasa and Malindi at the time of his visit and messengers between the anchorage and the shore brought word that the King of Malindi 'would rejoice to make peace with him . . . .' Much more importantly, he would provide pilots.

Presents were interchanged and there were festivities. Warily da Gama refused to land, but the King came off and circled the ship and bombards were fired in salute – or demonstration. Ashore the Christian Indians shouted 'Christ, Christ' – or so the Portuguese held. It is more probable that they shouted 'Khrishna! Khrishna!'

On the Sunday the King sent aboard a confidential servant whom da Gama seized. An ultimatum was sent ashore demanding the pilots that he had been promised. 'The king, when he received this message, sent a Christian pilot.'

He sent, in fact, a Gujerati. Though the *Roteiro* does not name him, it is accepted that he was Ibn Mâdjid, the Mu'allim Kanaka – the pilot-astrologer – who produced the volume of rutters and sailing instructions that is known as *Al Muhet* between the years 1468 and 1489.

That da Gama made contact with Ibn Mâdjid at Malindi seems certain enough. Whether he made the crossing with him is not entirely clear. There are legitimate doubts as to whether a man of Ibn Mâdjid's standing would have accepted a post of this character in the circumstances in which it was offered. Not being a Christian there was, of course, no religious inducement. Pay is unlikely to have been an important factor. More significantly, he must have realized that the Portuguese were interlopers, patently forcing a way into a most jealously guarded monopoly.

That scientific curiosity, on the other hand, may have outweighed these things is possible. Ibn Mâdjid might have been so anxious to study European navigational methods and Portuguese achievement that he would sink reasonable doubts. A measure of uncertainty remains. Whether it was Mâdjid or another, the Portuguese sailed on Tuesday 24 April 1498 '. . . for a city called Qualecut with the pilot whom the King had given us'. A month later the fleet reached Calicut.

The *Roteiro's* account of the crossing of the Indian Ocean is disastrously inadequate. Three brief paragraphs complete it. The first says that the land to the north enclosed a huge bay, with a strait; that there were many large cities, including Quambay and 600 known islands, the Red Sea and the 'house' of Mecca. The second, that the North Star 'which we had not seen for a long time' was once again visible. The third, that after seeing no land for twenty-three days 'we sighted lofty mountains, and having sailed all this time before the wind we could not have made less than 600 leagues'.

The last paragraph ends: 'On Sunday we found ourselves close to some mountains, and when we were near enough for the pilot to recognise them he told us that we were above Calicut and that this was the country we desired to go to.'

That night they anchored two leagues from Calicut 'because our pilot mistook Capua, a town at that place, for Calicut'.

Would the author of *Al Muhet* in reality have mistaken Capua for Calicut?

Calicut: on the shore a dignitary, shielded by a parasol, is carried past boatbuilders and fishermen

CALECHVT CELEBERRIMVM INDIÆ EMPORIVM.

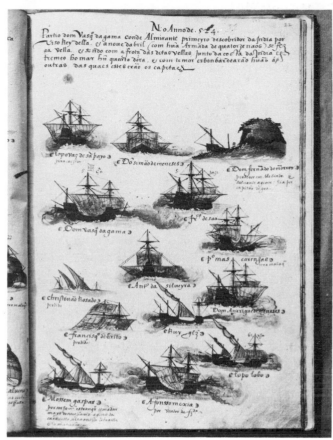

A year later, after an abortive attempt to set up a factory, da Gama returned to Portugal. He had not seen the last of Calicut. In 1502 he sailed again, this time as 'Admiral of India'. A massacre had occurred in his absence, and such was his ruthlessness in avenging it that he established, with extremely favourable trading terms, the foundations of the Portuguese empire in India.

Left
A respectful Da Gama greets the Samorin of Calicut
Right
Da Gama's fleet sailing for India in 1524.

Da Gama died in India, but his remains were taken back to the Church of the Jeronimos in Lisbon

Chapter XI

The Globe Encircled

6 September 1522, San Lucar

To the King's Most Exalted Majesty:
Your Most Exalted Majesty should know that we, eighteen men only, have reached here with one ship of the five which Your Majesty despatched to find the Spiceries under the command of Hernando de Magellanes, of glorious memory.

The opening paragraph of de Elcano's letter to the Emperor Charles V is a masterpiece of compression. In four brief lines it encapsulates three incredible years of mutiny, murder and wreck. Eighteen men came back with *Victoria* and a load of spices. *Santiago* was wrecked off the coast of Patagonia, *San Antonio* deserted, *Trinidad* surrendered to the Portuguese, *Concepción* burned. The venture cleared a profit of a little under £300.

It was, in addition, the first circumnavigation of the globe.

Fernão de Magalhãis – Magellan in the English rendering – who planned the voyage, was born into the fourth level of the Portuguese nobility, a *fidalgo*, at Sabrosa in the Trás-os-Montes. As a boy he was made a page to Queen Leonor. In 1485 he entered adult service with Manoel the Fortunate and in the custom of the time volunteered for the India service with Francisco de Almeida, the second Viceroy.

He was at the action at Cananor where he was wounded, and limped thereafter. From India he was sent, with a young and eager reputation, to help in the building of the fort at Sofala in Africa. In 1508 he was back in India where he took part in the decisive sea battle off Diu against the combined fleets of Egypt and India which gave de Almeida effective control of the Indian Ocean. Later he was in both the Malaccan ventures. In 1511 he sailed with d'Abreu in the remarkable voyage that located the southern spice islands in the Banda Sea below and to the east of the Moluccas.

He returned to Portugal a highly qualified Eastern expert, a seaman of reputation, and a soldier of courage. He had attained the rank of Captain, and he volunteered for the campaign against Azamor on the Moroccan coast, where he was again wounded. He was also accused, falsely according to his friends, of irregular conduct. It seems to have been 'trading with the enemy'.

He shrugged it off and, growing ambitious, applied to the King for a step in rank – which would also have meant a step in his emoluments.

Manoel brought up the matter of Azamor. Magellan waited a year and reintroduced the claim. Manoel, irritated at persistence, told him crisply that he could offer his services elsewhere.

He was living at the time in the closely knit maritime area of Lisbon, where Columbus had lived before him and where he would have heard early through the seamen's grapevine that Balboa, acting on Indian information, had crossed the narrow barrier of the isthmus of Panama and from a hilltop seen an illimitable

Cabral

ocean streaming west. Rumours of it had been current since Columbus's third voyage and a search for a strait through the land mass had been made – the belief that the Indies was an isolated archipelago was already in process of being adjusted – Bastidas and Ojeda, Balboa himself, and Cortés had all taken part.

In 1500 Pedro Álvares Cabral, appointed to succeed da Gama, had sailed from Lisbon with the thirteen ships of the Second Indian Voyage. On 22 April '. . . at the hour of vespers we sighted land, first a very high rounded mountain, then lower ranges of hills to the south . . . the Admiral named the country the Land of the True Cross.'

It is possible that Brazil had been discovered and the discovery suppressed during the prolonged battle of the Papal Bulls. It is, however, unimportant. Cabral had now established Portugal's claim to a vast share of the southern continental mass to the east of the Pope's dividing line, and there was no passage through to the real East here either. His destination was still India. Superficially the new country promised little except food for the two lesser stimulants to exploration – intellectual curiosity and sex. The importance of sex in the great sea ventures of the early Renaissance has never been precisely quantified. Pedro

Sex and the Spaniards in Brazil

Indians in Brazil chopping wood; a dragon lurks behind the bushes.

Vaz da Caminha's letter to the King on the discovery would provide an important piece of evidence for any assessment. With a singularly modern candour he says of the beach reception, 'There were three or four girls among them. These were very young and pretty, and had abundant long black hair down their backs. Their private parts were tightly knit, well raised, and half free from hairs; thus we were not at all ashamed to look at them.'

They looked, and sailed for India. It is one of the ironic contrasts of the explorations that a bare month after the halcyon episode of Brazil, four ships were lost in a gale near the Cape of Good Hope and with them that most splendid man Bartolomeu Dias de Novais.

Other men thrust in succession down the South American coast: Amerigo Vespucci, the Florentine banker from the House of the Medici, who went, certainly, as far as the Plate – and whose name was given to America by the humanist Waldseemüller when he reprinted Vespucci's journal of the four voyages; Nuno Manoel who reached Patagonia; Dias de Solis who examined the estuary of the Parana.

News of these ventures came inevitably to Lisbon. Magellan heard of them as he heard of the new Bull *Praecelsae Devotionis* which gave the Portuguese the right to anything they might find by sailing east. Out of step with his King, aggrieved and resentful, he began to develop a plan which would make it possible to circumvent the Bull. It appears to have been perfected in close association with the astronomer Ruy Faleiro, who had produced a book of longitudes, and its kernel was the assumption that the Spice Islands lay *not* in the Portuguese half of the world as defined by the Bulls but within the Spanish zone.

It involved, implicitly, a transfer of allegiance.

In October 1517 Magellan went to Seville where he married Beatriz Barboza, daughter of a senior official of the port. There he was joined by Ruy Faleiro and possibly by Ruy's brother Francisco, who subsequently published an important *Arte del Marear* in Castilian. In early 1518 he and the elder Faleiro went to the court at Valladolid.

By an elaborate exposition of longitude they proved to the satisfaction of King Charles that the Spiceries indeed lay within the Spanish sphere of influence. Magellan's draft plan for the voyage was approved. Instructions for the purchase of ships were issued to the *Casa de Contratación* at Seville.

Magellan and Faleiro were in grievous error. Amerigo Vespucci, who had been appointed Pilot Major to the *Casa de Contratación* after his fourth voyage, might have argued the matter, but he had been dead for five years. In plain geographical fact the islands lay well within the Portuguese hemisphere, but Magellan and Faleiro (the latter at the point of a mental breakdown) were appointed joint Captains General and the immense work of preparation began.

Five ships were purchased. Four of them were sound, one elderly. Magellan's flagship, the *Trinidad*, was 110 tons, *San Antonio* – the elderly one – 120, *Concepción* 90, *Victoria* 85, *Santiago* 75. All were square rigged, all had a lateen mizzen, all had the clumsy after-castles of the time.

The recruiting of officers and crews presented a major problem. Basic pay scales were low, the rewards of success high but demonstrably problematical.

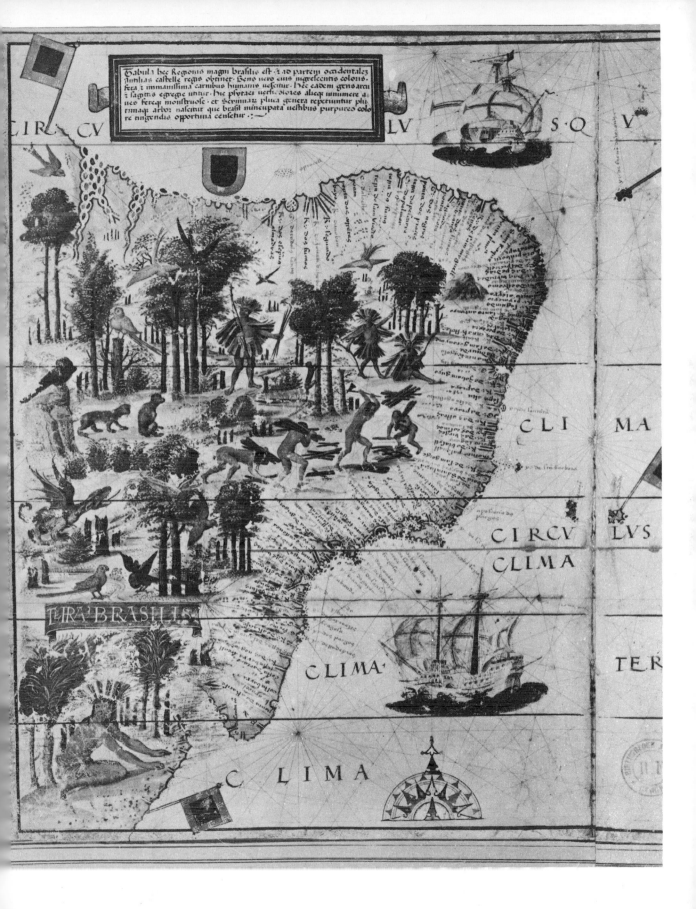

First efforts in Seville met with a limited response, and recruiting agents went to Malaga and Cadiz. The sea has traditionally a high degree of internationality: few fleets, however, can have sailed so inextricably intermingled as this. There were 102 Spaniards, 40 Basques, 25 Italians, 17 French, 6 Greeks, 5 Flemish, 2 Irish, 6 coloured men, a Mallorcan, an Açorean, and Master Andrew of Bristol, gunner.

Juan Sebastian de Elcano (the spellings vary) was among the Basques recruited. Born in the fishing village of Gueteria in the province of Guipuzcoa on the iron-hard coast of the Biscay, he had been conditioned to the sea in early boyhood. At twenty-two he was master of a small vessel in the armada that Jimenes de Cisneros, the hard-bitten Cardinal Archbishop of Toledo, led against the Barbary corsairs in 1509.

In the spring of 1518 he was in substantial legal trouble. Heavily in debt, he had sold an armed ship to the Savoyards against draconian regulations. Because of this, though he had been master of his own ship, he accepted the petty officer's appointment of *contramaestre* (bosun) of the *Concepción*. He was, according to his own statement, about thirty-two.

The ships lay along the mole of the Royal Dockyard at Triana, across the Guadalquivir from the *Torre del Oro* and Seville.

Fitting out took the better part of five months. The time is not exceptional; the process of getting equipment, sails, rigging, bombards and smaller guns was by tradition leisurely and by temperament liable to interruption. With Magellan's expedition a new factor intervened: an intense nationalism was engendered between Spanish and Portuguese factions which, on at least one occasion, broke out into open rioting along the quays. Simultaneously, Portuguese diplomatic action began in an attempt to have the expedition cancelled.

The mental breakdown of Faleiro unquestionably aggravated the situation. He had to be removed from his shared Captain Generalship, the command structure was simplified and commands in individual ships were changed. De Elcano was promoted master of the *Concepción* after one such shuffle.

Magellan's wife gave him a son. It is doubtful if he saw much of him under the ordinary administrative pressures and the exacerbating strain of nationalist friction. The trouble at last culminated in an inquiry ordered by the King. De Elcano's testimony is of importance. The Captain General, he said, was 'a discreet and virtuous man and careful of his honour'.

The inquiry produced little more. It did nothing to disabuse Charles of his view that the King of Portugal was energetically attempting to wreck the expedition. It did equally little to assure Magellan of the loyalty of his subordinates.

On the following day the fleet, still only partly stored, was moved down river to San Lucar.

On 20 September 1419 it cleared for the Moluccas.

It is important to recognize that the destination *was* the Moluccas. No scintilla of evidence survives to prove that Magellan proposed a circumnavigation of the globe. His plan was to discover and define an east-west route to the Moluccas in

Portrait of Magellan, now in the Uffizi, Florence

FERDINAN: MAGAGLIANES

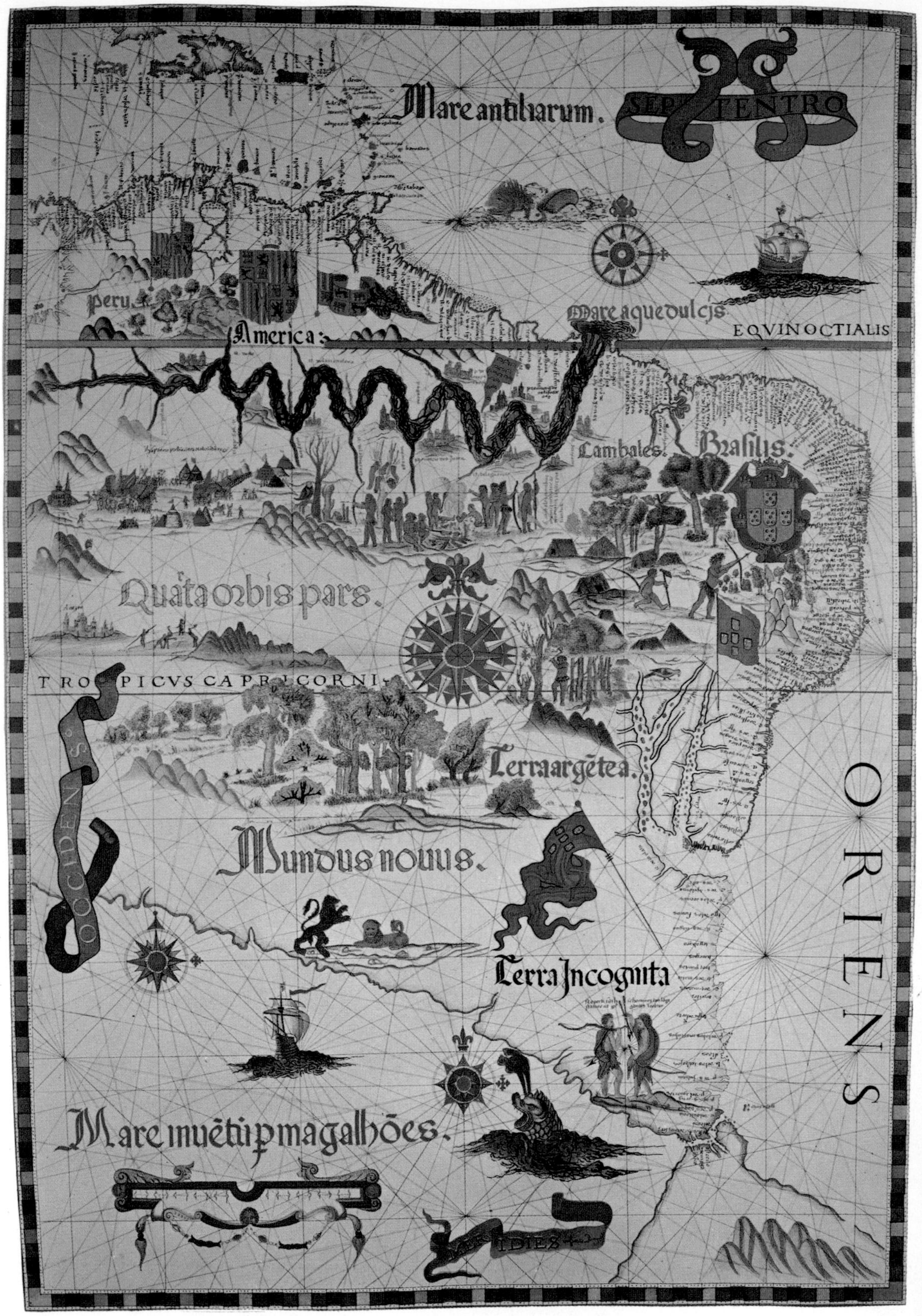

Mare antiliarum.
SEPTENTRO
Peru
America:
Mare aque dulcis
EQVINOCTIALIS
Cambales.
Brasilus.
Quarta orbis pars.
TROPICVS CAPRICORNI
Terra argetea.
ORIENS
OCCIDENS
Mundus nouus.
Terra Incognita
Mare inuetu p magalhões.

the East Indies, to determine – if possible – their longitude, to ascertain if they were in the Portuguese hemisphere or not, and to find other spice islands – possibly beyond the islands of the Banda Sea which he had already visited.

This completed, he must, logically, have visualized a passage home by the same strait as he had used for the outward journey but using a different wind. Such a route would be outside the practical possibility of Portuguese interference. Economic realities were a first consideration.

The passage from Cadiz to the Canaries was straightforward – a simple, necessary, shake-down cruise. On 30 September all five ships were loading pitch at the southern end of Tenerife for the inevitable necessities of the voyage. On 1 October a caravel made contact with them carrying an urgent message to the Captain General from his father-in-law. It informed him that before his departure certain of his captains had declared that 'if they had trouble with Magellan they would kill him'. The trouble that had begun on the mole at Triana and that had developed in the chancelleries had followed him to sea.

Despite this, the passage south is featureless save for a nerve-end-touching calm off the African coast, and a furious reaction to an alteration of course made by Magellan without consultation with his captains. The Royal Instructions laid down that he should do this, but he was in fact Captain General: command at sea is individual. Juan de Cartagena's violent outburst was made not in the interests of navigation but of the anti-Portuguese element in the personnel of the expedition. It had all the arrogance of the Spaniard.

On 19 December Magellan's course brought them to the staggeringly beautiful bay they called Santa Lucia, and that today is Rio de Janeiro. They kept their Christmas there and revictualled as best they could, and on 26 December they sailed again.

The search for a westward passage began at the Plate. It had been visited before, but Magellan was still unsatisfied. The wide shallows to the west, he felt, might yet conceal a passage. Early in February they knew they did not.

On Saturday 31 March 1520 they reached the shelter of the great harbour of San Julian in Patagonia, which Nuno Manoel was said to have discovered, and anchored on the eve of Easter.

Magellan, anxious about his stores, had ordered the fleet to be put on half rations; the fury over his autocracy as to the change of course was exacerbated. On the morning of Easter Sunday de Elcano told Elorriaga, master of the *San Antonio* and a fellow Guipuzcoan, that Cartagena, captain of the *San Antonio*, and Quesada, captain of his own *Concepción*, planned to petition Magellan to give them the intended course at sea in conformity with the King's instructions.

Nothing further developed in the course of the day. No information of possible trouble seems to have reached Magellan.

At midnight Quesada and de Elcano left the *Concepción* with an armed boat and rowed in silence to the *San Antonio*. Elorriaga, who must have rejected de Elcano's attempt to implicate him, resisted and was killed by Quesada with a dagger. The ship was seized by the crew of the *Concepción*'s boat and Cartagena's followers, and mutiny flourished.

Above
Though this map was drawn five years after Magellan's voyage, the continent of South America ceases at the Plate

Right
Magellan's arrival at Rio de Janeiro

Magellan's reaction was swift and ruthless. With his own boats he took the *Victoria*, her captain was killed, and Magellan ordered him to be hung head downward from the yardarm.

The *Santiago*, the smallest ship of the fleet, had remained loyal. With the captured *Victoria*, Magellan had the balance of force. The surrender of the *San*

Antonio came swiftly, followed by that of *Concepción*.

Luis de Mendoza of the *Victoria* was cut down, drawn and quartered; Quesada was executed by his servant on a promise of pardon. Cartagena and a priest who had supported him were marooned in Patagonia.

Grimly Magellan re-officered his ships with Portuguese. De Elcano and forty others were sentenced to death. Magellan reconsidered the sentences when it was clear that the mutiny was suppressed. Instead they were put in chains.

Inevitably there were heavy delays, but while he waited Magellan sent the smaller ships south to look for the strait that had established itself in his mind as a fixed idea.

Santiago was wrecked searching for it south of Santa Cruz, and the fleet was reduced to four.

At the end of August, almost a year out, Magellan left San Julian and anchored again in the Rio Santa Cruz. The mutineers were released from their chains. Magellan judged it possible now to send two of the big ships south to carry on with the search.

Two degrees south of Santa Cruz the ships sighted a cape which they called Las Virgines. Beyond it the coast fell sharply away in a wide channel. They returned, reporting that they had examined it for five days and a channel continued on, unbarred by land.

Magellan is said to have wept.

There was still much to do. *Concepción* and *San Antonio* were sent to make an extended survey, and lost contact. *Concepción*, docile now under a Portuguese

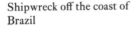

Shipwreck off the coast of Brazil

captain, returned to report the loss. *San Antonio* had deserted, mutiny was not yet dead. The search was maintained for as long as Magellan dared but on 28 October, having surveyed the strait with boats, he decided that he could wait no longer.

On 28 November, after astonishing luck with the normally frustrating winds of the strait, *Trinidad*, *Concepción* and *Victoria* headed into the Pacific.

He called the last headland Deseado – the headland that all men had desired – and in light airs headed north up the coast that today is Chile. For three weeks light airs held them against the land; then, a little before their second Christmas, he found a wind and began the crossing. On 24 January they sighted an island, almost certainly Puka Puka in the Tuamotus, but they could not make it and carried on.

The wind held light. The sea was very calm. Food ran short first, afterwards water. The first month passed and there was no sign of land – the Pacific is scattered with islands but their route took them clear of everything. The second month passed,

The Magellan Straits, from a sixteenth-century map. In the Tierra del Fuego an idyllic family group sits among rheas, penguins and geese while the warriors go hunting.

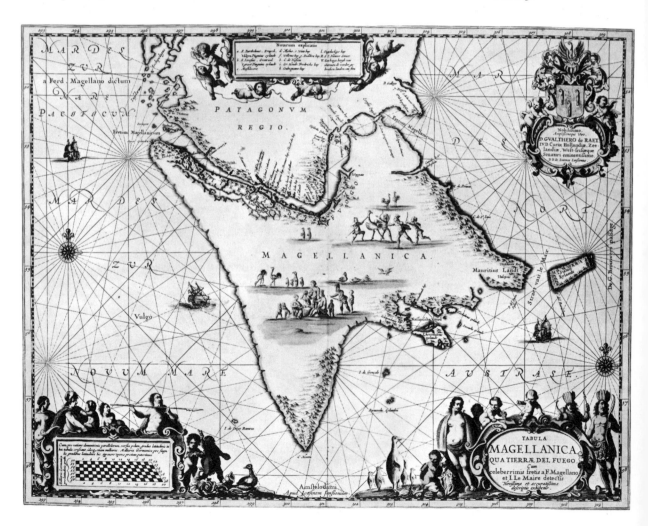

. . . we ate only old biscuit turned to powder, all full of worms and stinking of the
urine that the rats had made on it . . . we drank water impure and yellow. We ate
also oxhides which were very hard because of the sun, the rain and the wind. And
we left them four or five days in the sea, then laid them for a short time on the
embers and so we ate them. And of the rats that were sold for half an ecu apiece
some of us could not get enough.

Antonio Pigafetta, from whose *Relation*, the best and most human account of
the voyage, this passage is taken, is commendably realistic on the subject of
Magellan's captaincy; only a great leader could have brought them through the
attrition of that hundred days. On 6 March they made the landfall that saved
them – the island of Guam, in the Ladrones. Natives came out to them with
food for barter, and the long hunger ended.

But Guam could solve their problem only partially, they needed complete
re-supply. Magellan lay off Guam long enough to take in food and water to see
him through the final leg of the journey, and sailed at once. There were three
options open. Had he sailed south, the shortest passage, he would have made
New Guinea, 1,100 miles from Guam. Had he sailed a little west of north, he
would have reached Cipangu – Japan – the country which Columbus had
sought so vehemently a quarter of a century earlier.

He chose the third possibility – due west; and 1,200 miles on he reached the
Philippines.

Unquestionably he acted on information made available at Guam and
translated by the youth Henrique, the personal slave who had been with him
since his sojourn in the Indies. The passage was made in light winds. At some
point in it the ships crossed the longitude of 130 degrees east.

Twelve hundred miles south it passes through the Banda Islands. Magellan
had reached 130 degrees east in the complex adventures of his first voyage. This

day he reached it for the second time – west about.

It is improbable that he was himself aware of his achievement. He had no means of establishing longitude. At most he may have concluded that he was very close to his destination, though he must have known that he was well to the north; Guam would have enabled him to establish a latitude, only dead-reckoning could have fixed his position, and after more than a hundred days at sea dead-reckoning was scarcely as much an approximation as an act of faith.

He was not aware that he had just fifty-three days to live.

The landfall was made at the island of Humunu. On Easter Sunday he heard mass on shore at Massava. Early in April he reached Cebu, the entrepôt of the central Philippines.

Cebu handled trade with China and the south, and possibly also with Japan. It was one of the economic centres of the primitive Philippines, and he set himself to negotiate an alliance with its ruler. Precisely how the complex European concept of alliance was transmitted to Cebu by the youth Henrique is not known, but an understanding was reached. Whether in the course of it Magellan was inveigled into local power politics is a matter of opinion. Certainly the chief of Mactan, the islet lying off the entrance to the port of Cebu, refused to enter the alliance or to pay his share of the tribute.

Magellan was an intransigent man: it was a first necessity in exploration. In the common form of expansionism it was necessary that a lesson should be administered. On 27 April he landed on Mactan with forty-nine men while a rearguard of eleven Spaniards and 1,000 of his allies of Cebu lay off in boats.

Lapu Lapu, chief of Mactan, overwhelmed him. He died in the shallows, and the greater part of his landing force died with him. De Elcano took no part in the landing.

The consequences to the expedition of the loss of leadership were immediate and tragic. No obvious successor was apparent. Remarkably, despite the anti-Portuguese agitation of St Julian's harbour, a vote appointed João Serrão of the *Concepción* and Duarte Barbosa as joint Captains General. Both men were Portuguese. It is unimportant. Barbosa had at some time mis-treated Henrique. A new plot was hatched with astonishing speed. Henrique, who had the ear of the ruler of Cebu, warned him, falsely, of danger. Notwithstanding the massacre at Mactan, a feast was laid on. Both Captains accepted invitations. Both were murdered, and twenty-five of their men with them. De Elcano was not at the feast.

The fleet cleared Cebu in something understandably approaching panic. It was desperately short of senior officers now. Four had gone in the troubles at the strait, three more in the Philippines. Andres de San Martin, the cosmographer, had been lost on Mactan. Hastily they appointed the other pilot, the Portuguese Carvalho, as Captain General. De Elcano, for the first time since St Julian, returned to the limelight as captain of the *Concepción*.

It lasted barely a day. He reported her as unseaworthy and they burnt her, transferring her trade goods and her fittings to the other two ships. De Elcano was made master of the *Victoria*. The fleet headed for Borneo.

Carvalho was ineffective and without decision. The ships moved irresolutely through the islands, and in Borneo lapsed once more into trouble with the Sultan, which involved Carvalho's small son whom de Elcano was supposed to guard on a visit to the Sultan's child. The boy was kidnapped and two men with him. At the end of July Carvalho was deposed after a meeting in which he was strongly attacked by de Elcano. Gomez de Espinosa, the Master at Arms, was made leader in his place. De Elcano was appointed captain of the *Victoria*.

On 6 November, seven months after Magellan's death, the disintegrating remnants of a fleet reached the Moluccas.

At Tidor they found spices, and a Sultan anxious to play off Spain against Portugal. When the ships loaded, however, *Trinidad* was found to be unsound.

Whether any agreement was reached to separate or whether de Elcano made a unilateral decision, is not recorded. The matter is elided in his letter to Charles. On 21 December he cleared for Timor, leaving behind him sixty men and a worm-eaten ship. From this point forward he is altogether ruthless.

At Timor he replenished the *Victoria* with great care. He had no intention whatever of experimenting with Magellan's idea of a return journey through the Spanish hemisphere. He had a full cargo of spices and he planned to use the tried Portuguese return route via the Cape of Good Hope. He proposed, however, to keep well south of the normal track to avoid contact with his own people.

He went south as far as Amsterdam Island and he is credited with its discovery. From Amsterdam he swung north-west to clear the Cape of Good Hope, but his navigation was at fault and he made land at the Great Fish River with the Cape of Good Hope still to clear. Somewhere in the interim *Victoria* had sprung her foremast. Unable to carry foresails save in light airs, she limped across the equator in early June. On 11 July de Elcano's grim authority for the first time faltered. He put it to the vote of his crew whether they should put into Africa or the Cape Verde Islands – both of them firmly in Portuguese hands. Spain's Canaries were still more than 700 miles to the north, and they had been at sea for 150 days. De Elcano's letter says, 'on this course twenty-two men died from hunger.'

Attempts to bluff the Portuguese authorities failed; their boats and thirteen men were seized, and he made sail and ran. 'It so fell to us, overstrained at the pumps, working at them by day and by night, and more exhausted than men have ever been before, that with the help of God and the Blessed Virgin Mary, we continued under sail . . .'

They made their landfall at Cape St Vincent. The record is superb, even in that bold and stoic age. Yet the character of de Elcano remains utterly equivocal. The end of the first paragraph of his letter to the Emperor announcing his triumphant return sticks in the throat: '. . . Magellanes of glorious memory'. Magellanes whom he had betrayed.

He was one of the first leaders of the mutiny against Magellan. His roles at Cebu, at Mactan, at Tidor were obscure and involuted. From every crisis he emerged with advantages, having, apparently, played no part. He was the man behind the arras.

Charles gave him a grant of arms. Its motto ran *Primus circumdedisti me* – 'You first encircled me.' The arrival of the *Victoria* at Lucar was beyond question the finish of the first continuous voyage around the globe. That Magellan had already achieved it in separate ventures in no way detracts from it.

The Emperor did not give de Elcano the knighthood that he wanted.

Magellan

Chapter XII

Elizabethans

The intricate and explosive pattern of exploration that had its first reward in the accidental discovery of Porto Santo, completed its splendid outline with the track-chart of the *Victoria*. Africa, India, North and South America, the archipelagos of the western and eastern seas had, in a single century, been added to man's knowledge. Trade had been expanded over four oceans. The authority of Portugal and Spain was extended, by the right of prior discovery, across two-thirds of the habitable globe. Immeasurable sociological changes had begun their ferment.

England established her place in this noble expansion on a basis of simple hijacking.

Hawkins and the Elizabethans have been defended with scholarship and skill, special pleading has been reinforced by national pride, but the kernel of the matter lies quite simply in a plea for damages lodged following an attack on a ship belonging to Blasius de Veiga of Santiago in the Cape Verde Islands: '... and the said Blasius and other Portuguese, overwhelmed with many insults and tortures and despoiled of their goods, were cast out upon the bank of the River Mitombi in Sierra Leone.'

John Hawkins of Plymouth cast them out – and got away with 200 slaves and 15,000 ducats worth of goods, and that is plain hijacking by any standards. He took the ship too, though he seems later to have restored her because, according to the evidence, he had taken a larger and more useful vessel with even more slaves on board. Queen Elizabeth was not a partner in the syndicate which underwrote that venture (though Winter, her Surveyor of the Navy, was) but she was active in Hawkins's second voyage. The first had been profitable.

To understand the episode it is necessary to go back to origins. England's contribution to the exploration of the Atlantic was belated and, except for a limited area in the extreme north, insignificant. Her participation in the profitable practice of interloping was equally belated but, in its ultimate development, decisive in the battle for the freedom of the seas.

The record of exploration is lamentably clear. If legendary figures like St Brendan, who was Irish, and Madoc, who was Welsh, and Machin the lovelorn man of Bristol, are disregarded, the story of English exploration begins with Giovanni Caboto, of Genoa.

John Cabot, as the English reshaped his name, was born within a year of his fellow Genoese, Cristoforo Colombo. He went to Venice in 1476, the year in which Columbus reached Portugal following the attack off Cape St Vincent. When Columbus was turned down by João II and went to Spain, Cabot went to London, having failed to arouse interest in Venice in his theory that a short route to India lay across the Atlantic on latitude sixty degrees north.

Henry VIII, by Holbein the Younger

He had acquired a high level of navigational expertise, he had substantial Mediterranean experience, he knew the Red Sea, and he claimed to have been to Mecca.

Little documentary evidence exists as to his early years in London but he moved, presumably for business reasons, to Bristol and in 1496, when Henry VII made a progress through the West Country, he had a sufficient standing to meet the King. It is clear that he persuaded Henry. On 5 March letters patent were issued to Cabot and his sons authorizing them to search for unknown lands and to bring whatever goods they obtained to Bristol. There was no subsidy; the parallels with Columbus did not extend into England.

The tremendous achievement of Columbus was already known across Europe and in March he was absent on his second voyage. The knowledge seems to have had little effect on the Merchants of Bristol. When Cabot asked for backing, the response was meagre. He sailed in June with a single small ship, the *Matthew*, and eighteen men. The number indicates that she would have been between forty and sixty tons.

Almost no factual details of the voyage remain. He cleared Ireland, and though his course appears to have been roughly north-west, there seems to have been no serious attempt to reach sixty degrees north. On 24 June he made a landfall on a coast which he described as 'temperate', claiming that pau-brasil (the valuable red dye-wood) and silk were probably attainable here, and noting that the sea in the area was alive with fish.

There was no dye-wood, nor was there silk, but he had located the vast fisheries of the Newfoundland Banks and, as he pointed out optimistically, it would end England's dependence on the Iceland grounds, which was incorrect. The land itself was, he claimed, Cathay.

There was sufficient enthusiasm on his return to fit him out with five ships. He proposed to go back to his temperate coast and to work along it to the north-west until he reached Cipangu, which was Japan. That fixation he also shared with Columbus.

The second voyage ran into trouble early despite or, possibly, because of its size. He failed to make Newfoundland and fetched up instead against the wild east coast of Greenland. In sixty-seven degrees north he met ice and when he searched for a way through, mutiny developed. It was resolutely handled, but he abandoned the Greenland coast, worked round Cape Farewell, carried out a swift reconnaissance of part of Davis Strait and headed south after making contact with natives along the coast of Labrador.

A description of Cape Cod exists, but little more. He sailed down the Viking tract past the site of Leif's huts and the *Skraeling* country, and turned at the Chesapeake for England. It is an astonishing voyage, executed with skill and courage and equal to the finest of the Portuguese attempts before Dias.

It seems, however, to have aroused singularly little excitement and there was no effort to promote a third voyage. Cabot had been given a pension by Henry after the first: he drew it in 1499 – and died.

Sebastian, his son, emerged in 1512 as Cartographer to Henry VIII, who sent him with the English army to aid Ferdinand of Aragon against the French.

The movement of Renaissance 'experts' is subtle and incessant. He appeared next as Pilot Major of Spain and a member of the *Consejo de las Neuvas Indias*, the governing body of the new Empire. Two years later he was back in England where he was offered command of an expedition to Newfoundland – and turned it down. In 1525 he sailed, from Spain, under instructions to rationalize trade relations with the East. It is said that he had information of an immense treasure in the estuary of the River Plate but later evidence suggests that he spent three years searching for a land route to Peru, and its yet greater treasure, by way of the rivers that converge in the estuary.

On his return to Spain he was sentenced to banishment for failure, then pardoned by Charles V – Pizarro in the interim had been authorized to attack Peru from the north – and finally he was re-appointed Pilot Major. For twenty years he had no overt contact with England.

England herself continued oblivious to the possibilities of exploration. A third of his way through his reign Henry was suddenly impelled to suggest that the Merchants of London should set up a company to finance discovery, but the suggestion was barren. Ten years after this, an ambitious scheme to colonize the Pacific by way of a north-west passage was published, and failed to achieve any support whatever. England's merchants were making solid profits out of Continental alliances. English seamen were making even more solid profits out of Channel piracy. The vision of empire was dim.

Plymouth men burnished it.

William Hawkins (he spelt his name Hawkyns originally) traded out of Plymouth to Atlantic ports. He handled salt and olive oil and sugar and hides and wine. Some of it came from the Canaries where alliance had let the English in and he had access to the gossip of the ocean. He must have known, as a circumstance affecting trade, that the French had reached the coast of Brazil barely four years after Cabral, and in 1530 he would have learnt promptly that they had sacked the stark new fort at Pernambuco. In that year he fitted out the ship *Paul* of 250 tons and took departure for the River Sestos in the heart of the malaguetta pepper coast – the Grain Coast – in Guinea.

Only the outline of the story is known, but he made the coast without interference, traded and ran across the Atlantic to Brazil. Probably he loaded 'brasil wood' there: it fetched £10 a ton in England at that time. Romantic detail is altogether lacking – any detail is lacking, though this is one of the significant voyages of British history. It opened, very quietly, an era.

In 1531 he sailed again in the *Paul*. Things ran so easily this time that he left Martin Cockeram of Plymouth behind as hostage and brought home a 'heathen king' to show to the court in London. Between voyages he had found time to father a son. John Hawkins was born in 1532 as the *Paul* went south and west for the third time.

Other ships cut into the Brazil trade – from Bristol, from Southampton, from Portsmouth. John Pudsey, with consummate effrontery, built a fort on the coast below Bahia. John Philips with the *Barbara*, of London, made the direct passage without calling at Guinea. He became involved in hostilities with the natives and suffered damage, and snatched a Spanish ship in the Caribbean with

The prosperous port of Plymouth in the sixteenth century

a cargo of hides and sugar on the grounds that his own was leaking too badly for the passage home. He was not unnaturally arrested on return on a charge of piracy lodged by the Spanish Ambassador.

In February of 1540 the *Paul* made her final voyage for William Hawkins. The Plymouth Customs Ledgers declare that she returned with 'one dosen olyfantes tethe', which indicates that she had been to Guinea, and ninety-two tons of brasil wood, which proves that she went to South America. Thereafter old William Hawkins appears to have concentrated on the rich rewards of privateering in the Channel and the south-west approaches between official duties as Mayor of his native city and Member of the Parliament.

Letters of marque are as old as Edward I. Henry VIII modernized them with a flexible system of licences, fundamentally directed against French vessels, but adjusted according to the policy of a particular period. The licences were in time extended to cover French goods in foreign bottoms, which the Plymouth men took with a splendid literalness. Hawkins was in trouble over this and spent a spell in prison for contempt. It seems to have done him no particular disservice.

Henry's death made little difference to the position in the Channel, but there was, almost at once, a marked advance in interest in distant water ventures. Sebastian Cabot returned.

There are, as always, degrees of mystery about his movements. It is recorded that he left Spain without the permission of the Emperor, Charles V. Whether he had in fact fallen out with Henry prior to his acceptance of his Spanish appointments is not recorded, but he was in London again within little more than a year of Henry's death and moved at once into his old office.

His influence on maritime thinking from this time forward is rapidly discernible. Early in 1551 a London consortium headed by Sir John Lutterell was formed to open a trade with the Atlantic ports of Morocco. A leading member was Henry Ostrich, who had married Cabot's daughter. Command of the expedition was given to James Alday, who was in Cabot's employment.

Lutterell and Ostrich died in an epidemic which swept London, Alday was desperately ill, and the command passed to Thomas Wyndham. Cabot must have primed him with recent information about the Moorish ports; the expedition was eminently successful and Wyndham was commissioned immediately on his return to make a second voyage.

Simultaneously with this voyage Northumberland proposed the formation of a major company to undertake exploration – an echo possibly of the scheme which Henry had put forward early in his reign. Cecil headed it. Great merchants like Gresham, with Howard, the Lord Admiral, took shares in it. Sebastian Cabot was appointed Governor! Its object was to discover a north-east passage to India, and it followed closely on a proposition he had put to Northumberland for an attempt on Peru using the Amazon as an approach road.

Amazons in battle, by Jacques Thevet, 1558

Cabot seems to have changed direction as easily as he changed allegiance. He claimed to have discovered the North-West Passage in his early days, and he may possibly have found the channel into Hudson's Bay. Now he accepted the control of the new company with energy. In 1553 The Merchants Adventurers of England for the Discovery of Lands, Territories, Isles, Dominions and Seignories Unknown dispatched three ships under a soldier, Sir Hugh Willoughby, with a seaman, Richard Chancellor, as pilot to the expedition.

They lost contact in a great gale off northern Norway. Willoughby went on with two ships, rounded the North Cape and was swept across the Barents Sea to Novaya Zemlaya. With the approach of better weather he groped his way back to Lappland to winter there. Chancellor, the professional seaman, worked up to the agreed rendezvous at Vardo at the extreme tip of north-eastern Norway, waited, and when Willoughby failed to arrive, felt his way into the White Sea and moored for the winter at Archangel from which small town he made his way by land to Moscow and a climactic meeting with Ivan the Terrible. In the spring fishermen found Willoughby's ships at anchor – silent.

No north-east passage was discovered though one existed. It required giant ice-breakers, however, to keep it open. A north-west passage also existed, although only for enormous tankers at inordinate expense.

But Chancellor's embassy to Ivan established the Moscovy Company.

In the year that Willoughby sailed, Wyndham, with two voyages to the Gold Coast to his credit, sailed again. This time he took with him a renegade Portuguese pilot named Antonio Pinteado. Whether Cabot recruited him for the venture is not known, but he was a man of reputation.

They sailed four weeks after the death of Edward VI with three ships, two of them supplied by the Navy. The plan provided for a direct attempt on the Gold Coast. It was an important element of the English attitude that Portugal was entitled only to rights of effective settlement. Wyndham traded deliberately east and west of the now ageing castle of Mina. It was, apart from Arguim, the oldest established settlement on the West African coast. Having ascertained the limitations of Portuguese occupation – and gathered the gold available – Wyndham headed, against Pinteado's protests, for Benin and pepper.

It was too late in the season. In the appalling fever trap of the delta of the Niger Wyndham died and half his men with him. One of the ships was abandoned, but Pinteado brought out the other two and died in his turn. Forty men, desperately sick – among them a boy, Martin Frobisher – got back to England.

The profits, however, were enormous.

John Lok, as a consequence, followed Wyndham's track the next year and came away with a valuable cargo and 400 lb of gold. Portugal dispatched the inevitable angry Ambassador and Philip of Spain was in London with his English Queen. The writing on the walls of Seville was plain for any seaman to read: after Africa, the Indies. Despite the protests of the seamen, the merchants, the courts and the Privy Council, it was made plain that the raids had to cease.

Sir John Hawkins in 1591

Whether John Hawkins (William's second son) was knighted by Philip of

ÆTATIS SVÆ LVIII
Anno Dñi 1591

SIC PARVIS MAGNA

1591

Spain or not is one of the more engaging mysteries of the English maritime record. This claim is made but no documentary proof, unhappily, exists. He had without the knighthood, however, a sufficient social standing. He was the son of a long-time Member of Parliament, a prosperous Mayor of Plymouth, and a venturer of importance. In 1559 he married Katherine, daughter of Elizabeth's Treasurer of the Navy, and in the following year transferred his operations to London. He was at once involved in the promotion of a syndicate of remarkable authority: Sir William Winter, Surveyor to the Navy; Benjamin Gonson, Treasurer to the Navy – his father-in-law; Thomas Lodge and Lionel Ducket, Knights, City magnates and experts in the nascent – and illegitimate – trade with Africa. Since Cabot's second voyage companies had steadily acquired status and prestige. Two aspects of this new venture are, however, unique. It was proposed, from the outset, to take slaves from the Guinea Coast; more outrageously, it was the intention to sell them in the Spanish sector of the New World.

In simple terms, a private trading organization under senior officials of the Naval Administration proposed to defy Spain and Portugal simultaneously.

Elements of the international situation made it perhaps a degree less dangerous than it appears. Portugal in the second half of the sixteenth century was immensely preoccupied with her original spices and with her expansion into the China trade. Macao had been acquired barely five years before. Resources were heavily strained. Philip of Spain had just ended a futile war with France and had declared a moratorium on 2,000,000 ducats of inherited debt. Both countries were on the defensive in the Atlantic. Winter and Gonson must have been vividly aware of this.

Slaving had never been conspicuously an English pastime, though possibly only because England had never secured control of a profitable slaving area. It carried no sociological stigma. Las Casas' tragic battle a generation before had been fought on behalf of the Indians of Española, not on behalf of slaves in ordinary.

The circumstances of the new association are none the less remarkable. Hawkins sailed in October for the Canaries, Spanish territory, and it is clear that the scheme had been matured in advance. Pedro de Ponte, a Spanish merchant (the suggestion that he was an Englishman named Briggs is at least improbable) had a pilot waiting and at once sent confidential information to Española of Hawkins's intentions.

Hawkins himself went south with the minimum of delay, passed the Cape Verdes and headed for the Caces river. There he took the ship belonging to the unhappy Blasius de Viega and sailed her, in prize, to the River Mitombi where, with due lack of ceremony, 'they were cast out.'

In the Mitombi he found and took two other ships, then two more a little farther south, and finally, at Sierra Leone, a 'great ship' belonging to the official contractors for the slave trade and carrying, according to subsequent charges, 500 slaves.

Sending one of his own vessels back to England with ivory, spices and gold 'obtained in trade' – but possibly in piracy as well – he readied the 'great ship',

Philip of Spain

Sir Francis Drake, painted by Marc Gheeraerts in 1580

re-stowed his slaves and stood out from the coast of Sierra Leone in search of the north-east trades. Various estimates exist as to his total haul. The Portuguese figures give 200 slaves for de Viega's ship, 140 for the two vessels taken in the Mitombi, 70 from the next one captured, 'many' from the fifth, and 500 for the 'great ship' – 1,000 in all. An estimate made in Española says 400. Hawkins says blandly 'at least 300 . . . partly by the sword and partly by other means'.

He had, patently, no licence to trade. Goods by Spanish law had to be documented through Seville for sale in the new colonies. Slaves were handled by special contractual arrangements. To ease his way across these first hurdles Hawkins went not to the Capital of San Domingo but to Puerto de Plata on the north-east coast, 175 forbidding miles across the island from San Domingo, where a rendezvous seems to have been arranged by de Ponte. There he met planters and, possibly because of official attempts at interference, moved hurriedly to Isabela, a minor port. Trading began.

The accounts of subsequent proceedings have a splendour of mendacity, with both sides perjured to the gullet. The English version is that the unfortunate colonists, neglected by their mother country, welcomed the arrival of needed goods and fresh and vigorous slaves. Subject to reasonable understandings, they were willing to defy governmental restrictions and in the interests of a nascent society evade restrictive laws. Local officials were urgently anxious to be bribed.

The Spanish version is that Hawkins went in under cover of his guns, forced his stolen slaves and his unquestionably illegal goods on an innocent and undefended colonial community. It has the pathos of rape. The Portuguese version is that Hawkins was a bastard from any point of vantage.

All three views are, in some measure, correct. What is not possible to accept is, firstly, the implication that de Ponte, operating remotely from across the Atlantic, could have suborned six ships, operating on different rivers in Africa 1,500 miles from the Canaries at an indeterminate date, to be ready, loaded, and willing to make a mock submission to unpointed guns. Secondly, that he could fit this into a timetable which required the simultaneous corruption of a widely dispersed island administration across 3,000 miles of ocean, in a conjoined enterprise of bullying, bribery and barter.

The loose ends are innumerable. Acknowledging island venality and Elizabethan probity, only one thing could have brought all the loose ends together – the threat of superior force.

The aftermath of the operation is still inadequately explained. Hawkins sent the *Sancto Amarco*, the 'great ship', with a locally chartered caravel back to Spain. They were of course certain to be seized. The *Sancto Amarco* in fact went in to Lisbon, the caravel to Seville. The diplomatic and legal battles that followed are spectacular. Queen Elizabeth herself participated. The ships did not in law belong to Hawkins; their cargoes, mainly hides, were not significant. They were sent for highly devious reasons, knowing that they would be seized. The reasons remain obscure. They may have been meant to provide a smoke-screen for the real success of the expedition. They may have been intended to provide a *casus belli* for the next expedition. They may have been intended to arouse Elizabeth's personal indignation by exposing her to a snub from Philip, which

was in fact duly administered.

Elizabeth took a share in the next voyage!

The syndicate for this was prodigious. The Queen herself supplied the flagship, the *Jesus of Lubeck*. The newly created Earl of Leicester, the Earl of Pembroke, William Cecil, Clinton the new Lord Admiral, and the old hands Winter and Gonson headed the syndicate. Hawkins fitted out three ships in addition to the *Jesus* – the *Solomon* of 130 tons, the *Tiger* 50, and a new *Swallow* 30 – crews and landsmen together added up to 170.

They sailed in company with ships going south to the Guinea coast for gold and were wind-bound for some time at Ferrol where, unaccountably, they were not interfered with by the Spaniards. A call was again made at Tenerife for a conference with de Ponte.

The slaving was not as easy as it had been on the first voyage. With the advent of the gold ships the tribes had moved inland. Hawkins went to the island of Sambula and captured men already enslaved to the Samboses and then, leaving his big ships on the coast, went twenty leagues up the Callousas river and

On the left, Hawkins' flagship, the *Jesus of Lubeck*, from the Anthony Roll

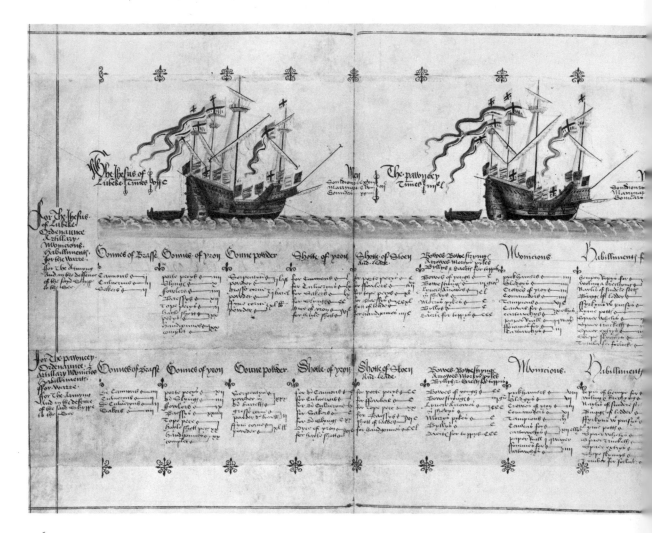

returned with two caravels full of negroes. Whether these were directly captured is uncertain. The Portuguese charged him subsequently with piracy, but at a small town named Bymba he found them cooperative and joined them in a night attack. In the darkness he lost control, and the attack was beaten back to the ships with the captain of the *Solomon* and six men dead and twenty-seven wounded. '. . . We returned back somewhat discomforted although the Captain in a singular manner carried himself, with countenance very cheerful outwardly, as though he did little weigh the death of his men, although his heart inwardly was broken in pieces for it.'

Subsequently the Portuguese depositions in the complaint to London said that altogether Hawkins had attacked sixteen ships, taken 600 slaves, and ivory and gold in addition. Hawkins says he traded.

By early March the fleet was watering boldly at the dangerous Carib island of Dominica. In mid-March it was at Margarita, the pearl island. At the end of the month Hawkins was on the Spanish Main at Cumana.

The Governor of Margarita, reasonably enough, had been hostile and refused a pilot. Hawkins was indignant, but overcame the problem by himself taking a pinnace into the shallows while the deep-draught ships maintained position on him in the open water. In April he was at Borburata on the Main, for whose Governor he had a letter from his nephew Lorenzo Bernaldez, the accommodating Governor of Santo Domingo. Bernaldez was away. Hawkins insisted on permission to sell sickly negroes before they died, but found few buyers. When Bernaldez on his return also hesitated, Hawkins said bluntly that what he was not granted he would take, and trade began.

When it was done, Hawkins threaded his way across the Caribbean. He had vestigial charts only. The sea was studded with islets and reefs, he had no information as to the currents, but he found his way to Florida, smelling out de Laudonnière's efforts to find the fabulous Florida treasure.

De Laudonnière had failed, the colony he founded was to be massacred a few weeks later. Hawkins went on, working up the coast to the Grand Banks, replenished with fish from the Newfoundland fishing fleet, and crossed to England.

Navigationally it was a brilliant voyage. Politically it was less effective. Profits, however, were sixty per cent.

Through the winter he rested. Incredibly he struck up a friendship with Guzman de Silva, the Spanish Ambassador, and was given the offer of a Spanish command in the Mediterranean. The fitting out of four ships began. It is impossible to decide who was bluffing. In the upshot Philip failed to make up his mind, and Hawkins went on fitting out his ships. De Silva concluded that they were being set up for another slaving venture and protested, loudly. Hawkins was haled before the Admiralty Court and ordered to enter bond of £500 to guarantee that he would not go himself or send ships to the Indies.

Two renegade Portuguese, Homem and Luis – rams caught in a peculiar thicket – chose this moment to offer Winter a new Treasure: this time it was a gold-mine in Africa with an output of £300,000 a year. Hawkins was brought into the picture. A substitute employment for the four ships fitting out was instantly available. De Silva, perennially suspicious, had an audience with the

Queen and asked her point-blank for the second time if Hawkins was going west. The Queen said no. Being a cautious man, de Silva asked Cecil the same question, and Cecil swore 'with a great oath' that Hawkins was not. De Silva knew that Hawkins was loading his ships with beans – slave rations. What de Silva did not know was that a venture under Hawkins's aegis was already in the Indies. The episode has all the delicate intricacy of a madrigal.

John Lovell had sailed in 1566 with three of Hawkins's ships – not, this time, on a semi-state venture but on a purely private foray. With him sailed the young Francis Drake. On the outward passage and on the West African coast they took five ships, not without bloodshed; afterwards they followed Hawkins's tracks as far as the Rio de la Hacha, made Española from there and 'did much damage'. It was on the whole a botched voyage. Profits were indifferent.

Drake was back in Devon in time to ship with Hawkins in the *Jesus* and he was at Plymouth when a Flemish fleet under Spanish colours sailed into the Cattewater without saluting. Hawkins opened fire testily, and there was an international incident. The *ritornello* of the madrigal was reached when Homem and Luis, having squeezed all that was possible out of everybody, bolted for France.

Hawkins reported to the Queen, and, 'The queen's majesty gave new commandments that our general should, seeing the Portugals were gone, make his voyage towards Guinea, and there making slaves negroes, with them to sail over from that coast to the West or Spanish Indies.'

Early in October he sailed. He had two Queen's ships – the *Jesus of Lubeck*, patched up since the last voyage but unquestionably rotten, and the *Minion* – and four armed merchantmen.

The African voyage was unsatisfactory. Portuguese defences had stiffened; an English ship had actually been sunk the previous season and another captured Hawkins got only 150 slaves by his normal methods, too few for a profitable voyage, and he promptly organized an alliance with the King of Sierra Leone to attack the town of Conga.

The action was militarily successful. In a sharp night raid the town was taken, but to Hawkins's chagrin his allies incontinently massacred the majority of the inhabitants – a deplorable waste of good slaves. He was left with 260 only, and headed west eventually with a total of 500.

The passage along the Main was normal: a mixture of naked force and bribery. At the Rio de la Hacha the young Drake came into prominence. He had a score to pay off from Lovell's voyage. Promoted to the command of the *Judith*, he went in alone, put two shots through the house of the Treasurer, captured a Spanish caravel, and lay off waiting for the Admiral. Hawkins seems to have approved, grimly, and they went on to Cartagena.

Cartagena was one of the handful of defended ports in the Indies. Hawkins tested the Governor's resolution with a few shots, made no impression and prudently withdrew; the hurricane season was approaching and he was anxious to get clear. With his original ships and the captured caravels he headed for Cabo San Antonio at the western extremity of Cuba in search of the Gulf Stream.

Light airs and head winds betrayed him. After three weeks he had still not made the Cape and when he did, they ran into hard weather. One ship lost contact and the *Jesus*, old, rotten and patched, worked badly. It was little more than a moderate gale but the *Jesus'* seams began to open up and Hawkins had to ease her away until she was running before the wind. He made a landfall on the coast of Florida. There was no harbour available and while he fought to hold her off, the wind changed suddenly into the north and blew, hard! The *Jesus* was carried across the gulf, desperately close to sinking, and the only port possible was San Juan de Ulua, terminal of the silver route from Mexico. He had the information from a Spanish ship and with it a warning that the *flota* – one of the two great annual convoys from Spain – was almost due!

San Juan de Ulua was scarcely more than an anchorage. A shingle bank 'a bow shot long' protected it and the Spaniards had mounted a battery on the shingle. Hawkins hauled down the St George's cross under which he habitually sailed, hoisted a faded Royal Standard in its place, and bluffed his way in. The Spaniards, assuming his ships to be the forerunners of the *flota*, joyously fired a salute.

He had nine ships: his own four, two that he had captured on the Main, and four that he had picked up in the last few days and held lest they get ahead and give warning. By the time they were recognized they were inside the harbour, and the guns' crews bolted.

The *flota* was expected at the end of the month. This was the seventeenth; there was just time to make the desperately needed repairs to the *Jesus*. Work began at once.

At sunrise the next morning the *flota* was in sight on the horizon.

The *Jesus* was already dismasted. Flight was impossible. Moreover, being Hawkins, he had already landed guns to strengthen the captured battery. He decided to play for time. He needed it desperately. The *Jesus* was hardly more than a wreck, '. . . for in her stern on either side of the sternpost the planks did open and shut with every sea, and the leaks so big as the thickness of a man's arm, the living fish did swim upon the ballast . . .'.

The *flota* had brought with it a new Viceroy, Don Martin Enriquez. Barred by a head wind from any attempt to force the narrow entrance, Enriquez anchored. Negotiations began. In the end a compromise was reached: Hawkins would hold on to the batteries, Enriquez would enter, Hawkins would complete essential repairs and go. There was an interchange of hostages.

The foul wind held until the twenty-first, then it came clear and Enriquez entered the grotesquely overcrowded harbour and took stock. At once he began plans to break the truce.

Early on the morning of 23 September it became clear that trouble was making. Hawkins sent an emissary to Enriquez to protest, and ate in preparation for action. Enriquez acted.

As Barret, the emissary, returned to the *Jesus* with a fulsome denial of treachery, a trumpet blew. Instantly working parties ashore produced weapons, men dropped from the bows of the moored ships that overhung the shingle, the guns were rushed and taken before they could be fired, and the Spaniards began to warp a big merchantman up to the *Jesus* to use her as a fire ship.

As the Spaniards reached the *Jesus*, Hawkins ordered the bow lines of the *Minion* cut and she hauled into deep water with men of the *Jesus* boarding her. In bitter and formless actions both ships were cleared of the enemy and the hard fighting began.

The Spanish flagship was sunk in shallow water, the Vice-Admiral's ship burned out, a merchantman sunk. The shore batteries were ineffective, but Hawkins lost the *Angel*, the *Swallow* and the captured caravels were taken, the *Grace of God* lost her mainmast and was set on fire. The *Judith*, under Drake, got clear and anchored outside. Hawkins abandoned the *Jesus* as fire ships moved in and in the *Minion*, hopelessly overcrowded with 200 men, followed him. They lay at anchor for the night, certain that the Spaniards had no stomach for pursuit. Hawkins, recounting it later, said, '. . . with the Minion only and the Judith (a small bark of 59 tons) we escaped, which bark the same night forsook us in our great misery'.

The battle of San Juan was small and moderately murderous. Neither side came out of it with credit. The English said that Enriquez forfeited his honour by breaking his word. Nobody said anything about Elizabeth's word – or Cecil's 'great oath' in confirmation. Hawkins's failure to make certain that his guns ashore were adequately defended is hardly to be forgiven. Drake's desertion – he did not lose contact in the night, both ships were at anchor – has fostered argument for four hundred years.

Not until the Armada would Hawkins sail with him again.

Hawkins put half his men ashore on the coast of Mexico to the north of modern Tampico and well clear of the Spanish settlement, '. . . our people, being forced with hunger desired to be set on land, whereunto I consented.'

They died at the hands of the Indians, they died of starvation, they surrendered to the Spaniards, they fell into the hands of the Inquisition. Three got back to England. Hawkins, with his hundred, living on the shredded hides of their cargo, defied the Atlantic. De Silva says that he reached Mounts Bay with fourteen men. Drake had arrived five days earlier.

St Juan de Ulua marks the end of the inchoate relationship of Spain and England that had begun with Philip's marriage to Mary Tudor. Suspicion and enmity thereafter moved on to hatred.

Drake's attack on Nombre de Dios underscores it. Bribery, pressurizing were done with; this was a tough, unequivocal attack, an invasion aimed at Spain's most vulnerable point, the aorta of the flow of gold and silver from Peru.

He made a reconnaissance in 1571 with the connivance if not with the backing of Hawkins and Winter, and attacked in the following season. He misjudged his timing. The gold had not yet arrived, and he decided to lay an ambush on the Isthmus of Panama itself – and on his way to it he climbed a tall tree and, as Balboa before him, saw the limitless Pacific. The ambush was betrayed by accident – or drink – and he set another, so close that they could hear the caulkers working on the waiting Plate fleet. This time he triumphed, the haul was £40,000. What was more significant was its insolence.

Theoretically Spain was still at peace with England, yet Noble, Humphrey Gilbert, Grenville, Ralegh, Andrew Barker, Horsley, Oxenham, Lok, Frobisher and many others raided from Africa to Mexico, from the Main to Brazil in an unceasing aggression. They were successful or they failed, but the cumulative result was the Elizabethan concept of sea power.

John Hawkins stayed ashore because he had a mind on greater things. He was Member of Parliament for Plymouth two years after the return from San Juan. Five years later he wrote a thunderous attack on William Winter and corruption at the Admiralty. It is listed, dryly, under the title 'Abuses in the Admiralty touching Her Majesty's Navy, exhibited by Mr Hawkins'.

In November 1577 he was appointed joint Treasurer with his father-in-law. Within ten days Gonson was dead and a series of reforms was already in being.

He had time for other projects. The possibility of a settlement in the south in a great southern continent compounded of Lochac and Magellan's Tierra del

The Southern Continent, shown on a 1562 map of the New World: in the monster-ridden Atlantic Da Gama crosses the Line as Neptune approaches the Caribbean.

Fuego and rumours of the Solomons expanded into a dream of empire. John Deed, the geographer, coined the name British Empire about this time, not being, as a good Welshman, content with an English designation.

Richard Grenville, working with William Hawkins the younger, made himself leader of the project. They collected backing enough for the issue of a licence to find new land 'having the pole antarctic elevate' to be approached, preferably, by the Straits of Magellan. For political reasons the project was quashed.

In the year of John Hawkins's elevation to the Treasurership of the Navy it was revived and a syndicate including Leicester, Walsingham, Lincoln the Lord Admiral, the Winters, Hawkins and Drake backed it. Grenville was dropped; Drake was appointed captain of the expedition – he had put £10,000 into the syndicate – and his instructions initially were to pass through the Straits of Magellan and proceed 'along the coast' to a point about thirty degrees south to discover places for trade, and to make friends with the natives.

The instructions are ambiguous: 'the coast' may logically have meant the coast of Chile; as logically, the coast of *Terra Australis Incognita*. Drake declared subsequently that he had an interview with Elizabeth in which the Queen said, 'Drake! So it is that I would gladly be revenged on the King of Spain for divers injuries . . .' There is no documentary evidence that the interview took place, but Drake sailed with five ships in December 1577: the *Pelican* (120 tons), the *Elizabeth, Marigold, Benedict,* and the store-ship *Swan.* In a fascinating repetition of history he headed for San Julian and he arrived, as had Magellan, with mutiny on his shoulder. Like Magellan, he executed his second in command, Thomas Doughty, the chief conspirator – taking communion with him before the execution.

The passage of the Straits of Magellan was exemplary. The squadron had now been reduced to three ships and his flagship had been rechristened, prophetically, the *Golden Hind.*

He passed the gateway to the Pacific and turned north – patently he had never entertained the notion of a colony in *Terra Australis* – but off the heads the gales hit him and he was forced down to the south below the Horn. He lost the *Marigold* in darkness and heavy seas, the *Elizabeth* parted company, the *Golden Hind* found a slant in the wind and went north again.

Logically Drake's goal was Panama. Before he left England John Oxenham had sailed for the Isthmus, and Drake may have made a secret arrangement to cooperate with Oxenham in a plan to cross the isthmus and seize a base on the Pacific coast in alliance with the Cimmaroons and cut the treasure route. Politically it would have been of advantage to Elizabeth at that time. No record, however, survives. Drake passed north of the small village of Valparaiso, turned back to take a look at it and found a ship with 25,000 gold pesos on board. The incredible foray had begun.

North of the port he found a harbour in which he could careen the *Hind,* and got up his heavy guns from the hold. Simultaneously he built a pinnace of prefabricated sections which he had brought from England. Outside Callao he took a local craft and learnt that *Nuestra Senora de la Concepción* (her crew called her, irreverently, the *Cacafuego*) had just sailed, loaded with silver. He chased and took her. She had no guns, for the Spaniards still believed guns to be unnecessary in the remote Pacific. Her silver filled his hold. He got from her also the news that Oxenham had failed and was a prisoner at Lima, and he sent back the *Cacafuego* with a blunt warning to the Viceroy not to execute his prisoners.

He still held north but clear now of the isthmus area, and off Nicaragua took another small ship with two Pacific pilots aboard. He failed to persuade them – the word has a variety of connotations – to act with him. Instead he seized their charts and sailing directions and went up the known coast of southern California to the unknown. Somewhere near modern San Francisco he went ashore, built a hutted camp, emptied his ship and cleaned her and recaulked her seams. Then he put to sea again, still heading north. It has been suggested that he was searching for a route home by the North-West Passage, but it is hard to substantiate it; he was a highly sceptical man.

About the latitude of Seattle he turned and made a masterly passage of the Pacific – two months to his first island, one month from that to the Moluccas. At the Moluccas, playing off the English against the Portuguese, he extracted a treaty from the Sultan giving the English exclusive rights to the spice trade. He loaded six tons of cloves as an earnest of its possibilities and sailed for the Indian Ocean, the first of all English ships to sight it.

At the very edge of accomplishment he ran aground with a following wind.

Everything that the ship could spare was thrown over the side to lighten her. The rock held. Drake jettisoned guns. The rock still held. He put three tons of cloves over, and still it held. It is not possible to assess his desperation.

Then the wind dropped, suddenly, and the *Golden Hind* slipped slowly stern first into deep water.

His navigation after this is brilliant. He passed close in to the Cape of Good Hope – '. . . a very stately thing and the most beautiful cape we saw in our whole circumference of the Globe'. He watered truculently at Sierra Leone where Henry of Portugal's men had watered just after the Prince's death, and he made Plymouth at the end of September 1580.

The profits of the voyage are assessed as £500,000.

When Burghley heard, by way of Seville, of Drake's achievement off Peru he ordered Hawkins to prepare plans for the use of the fleet in war.

Whether Drake's circumnavigation is to be considered according to the strict canon as exploration is a matter of interpretation.

Militarily it was audacious, its seamanship was superb, in terms of profit it was triumphant – but Magellan *had* been that way before. Hawkins included, the early English voyages, other than those of the Cabots, discovered little that was unknown, less that was geographically significant. Their importance is in real terms political. They explored new facets of the progress of the Renaissance. They formed a massive inquiry not so much into a New World as into a new way of life.

They were the framework of the augmentation not of the Indies but of Britain as a world power.

Chapter XIII

Genocide

The consequences of action are in a practical sense often more important than its motives. Prince Henry of Portugal, sending Zarco and Texeira to reconnoitre the possibilities of a relatively limited Guinea trade, triggered the chain reaction which produced the Americas.

In the course of this, occurred four separate acts of genocide.

Genocide is a shock word of the mid-twentieth century. Raphael Lemkin coined it to define the destruction of national, ethnic, racial and religious groups. The act itself, before he coined the word, had an immeasurable antiquity. In the time of Christopher Columbus it was an accepted facet of life.

The motives of Columbus were simple, and sufficiently naïve: he wished to discover a sea route to India and he died convinced that he had done so. Genocide had no place in his plan – or in his necessity. When he landed on the beach of the island of Guanahani he wrote that it was '. . . inhabited by a gentle, peaceful and very simple people'.

From Guanahani he went in search of gold to the lush, high island which he named *la isola Española*, and his estimate of its population was 250,000.

Twenty years later it was 20,000. In 1548 Oviedo wrote that it was doubtful if 500 Indians of pure stock remained.

These are statistics of genocide.

Columbus had singular faults, but a wanton cruelty was not among them. The embryo *colonia* of Navidad was planned after the loss of the *Santa Maria* in a crisis situation; none the less he provided it with every reasonable safeguard. He sailed for Spain and assistance, leaving behind him, he believed, a secure community. He returned eleven months later with seventeen ships and settlers enough to plant a formal colony. At Monte Cristi, landing to investigate a possible site for it, they discovered two bearded bodies on the shore. He went on grimly, '. . . at the hour of vespers the Admiral moved his fleet in front of the town of Navidad and found it burned to the ground. That day they saw nobody in the vicinity of the town.'

He landed with a small force the following morning and saw wreckage only. A boat passage up the neighbouring river sighted nothing. On its return 'the bodies of eight Christians' were found 'in the fields near the town'.

Contact with the household of the local Cacique secured the bones of the disaster. The men of Navidad had quarrelled among themselves, and one had been killed. Malcontents broke away from the settlement and went inland, taking women with them to the 'mines'. Women were ritually objectionable in gold gathering and the Cacique Caonabo killed the Spaniards and descended on Navidad, burning it and driving the survivors into the sea. In the character of the time there was cause here, if not for genocide, at least for punitive action. Columbus simply abandoned Navidad and along the coast, 'at a suitable site for

Title-page illustration of 1601 telling the story of Navidad, with roundel portraits of Ferdinand, Isabella, Columbus and (*bottom right*) his brother Bartolomeu

Rey de Castilla y de Leon • Don Hernando V. el Catolico

La cara de Ysabel Rey. Por.ro de Cast. y Leon q. emendio el descub.o d. las india+

El Almirante sala de el alor villa del Conde de Miranda a descubrir

El Alm.e descubre las yslas de los Lucayos que fueron las primeras d. Indias

El Alm.te se despide del Rey Guacanagari Edificada la torre de Nauidad

La Gran batalla q. tubo el Alm.te con el Rey Guarinoex y cien mil ynaios en la vega Real

Buelue el Alm.te y hallo quemada la torre d. Nauidad y los Castellanos muertos

Las yndios procuran derribar y quemar la Cruz de la vega y el Adelan. pelea con ellos y los vence

HISTORIA GENE
RAL DE LOS HECHs
DELOS CASTELLANOS
ENLAS ISLAS I TIERRA FI
RME DEL MAR OCEANO ES
RITA POR ANTONIO DE
HERRERA CORONISTA
MAYOR DE SV M.d DLAS
INDIAS Y SV CORONIS-
TA DE CASTILLA
En quatro Decadas desde el Año de
1492. hasta el de 1531.
De Cada primera

Al Rey Nu.ro Señor

Primera Almirante de las Indias • Don X.poual Colon

El Alm.te descubro la ysla de la Nauidad y la tierra firme

del Prete Laguna

EN MA. EN LA EMPLENTA REAL 1601.

El Alm.te descubre con grandes tormentas la costa de Veragua

2.o Almirante y Adelantado d. las Indi.d Don Barr.me Colon Hermano

Indians panning for gold, demanded in payment of taxes

a fortress' built a new settlement which he called Isabela, after the Queen.

His forbearance is in that day astonishing. For the best part of two months he remained engaged in constructing Isabela, in laying on a water supply, in building a grist mill. Subsequently he was ill. Finally, in mid-March, he led an expedition inland and built a fort to cover the area where gold was available. Here he positioned a garrison of fifty-six men, afterwards reinforced, and organized a patrol system to prevent any recrudescence of the Navidad disaster.

Later in the year, leaving his brother Diego in charge at Isabela, he made a prolonged voyage of exploration to Cuba and Jamaica. Returning desperately ill, he '. . . found the island in a pitiful state, with most of the Christians committing innumerable outrages for which they were mortally hated by the Indians. The kings and caciques of the island were united in refusing to serve the Christians.'

The honeymoon was over.

To this point casualties among the Indians were remarkably low. Now Guacanagarí, who had maintained his support of the settlement, asked for help against the harassment of Caonabo. A joint campaign was agreed. According to Columbus's estimate the hostile Caciques had assembled 100,000 men but the figure is almost certainly an exaggeration. He himself had 200 men, twenty horses, as many hounds, and Guacanagarí's tribal levy.

Tactically it was a model action. A two-pronged attack sufficed together with the noise of the arquebuses, the terror of the horses and the accuracy of the crossbows to rout the Caciques.

The Admiral ascribed this to the favour of God and the good fortune of the Catholic Sovereigns, else it would have been impossible for two hundred poorly armed men, half of them sick, to subdue such a multitude. But the Lord wished to punish the Indians, and so visited them with such shortage of food and such a variety of plagues that he reduced their numbers by two thirds.

'Such a variety of plagues' is a strictly contemporary viewpoint. Epidemic disease was customarily acknowledged as a visitation. Smallpox, measles, possibly – even as early as this – malaria and diseases of the respiratory tract found no built-in resistance. The population graph of the Caribbean begins, at this point, its terrifying downward curve.

Military casualties were by comparison small. The slow reload rate of contemporary firearms, shortage of ammunition and the physical limitations of sword play in tropical heat restricted them, but in the aftermath of the punitive raids dogs were used to harass villages, communities were driven to refuge in the hills, limited agriculture broke down and starvation set in.

Taxes had to be paid in gold. When it was not forthcoming, pressure was applied. Forced labour was crudely handled and added to mortality. The gold areas became killers.

Ultimately the simple balanced economy of the area disintegrated, first around the 'mines' of the Cibao, then east from Isabela through the island.

The Arawak nation, the gentle Tainos of Columbus's first experience, was in the final throes of extinction.

Nothing in the history of the Aztecs suggests they be described as a gentle people. Yet, in the first meeting of Cortés and the Emperor Moçtezuma, there is an all but incredible *politesse*: '. . . the captain and the soldiers were given gifts, garlands, wreaths, strings of flowers to encircle their breasts, chaplets for their heads.'

Moçtezuma, who had been carried to the meeting in a litter under a pallium made of the green and iridescent feathers of the *quetzal*, against all custom put his

Columbus in the West Indies; in the background, the fortress of Isabela

Right
The meeting of Moçtczuma and Cortés represented in a Mexican codex

Tenochtitlan.

feet to the ground, approached Cortés and said, '. . . Lord you have reached your destination. You have arrived at your city of Tenochtitlán, you have come to take possession of your house.'

Hernán Cortés was born in the hard province of Extremadura. He was a University of Salamanca drop out. Four years after Columbus was sent back by Bobadilla, he landed in Española, scorned the future proferred by a small *encomienda,* and in the scarcity of lettered men in the Indies contrived to have himself made *Escriban Publico* (notary) of the small town of Azua.

He moved to Cuba as one of the 300 men of Diego Velasquez' expedition, achieved the post of King's Treasurer, and immersed himself in women trouble. After two spells of sanctuary in local churches, he extricated himself and was deputed to lead an expedition promoted (and in large part paid for) by Velasquez, who had developed a profound thirst for gold. Its object was to extend the results of a previous venture by Juan de Grijalva. Cortés put his entire savings into the expedition, subtly acquired an increasing authority, and finally slipped out of Velasquez' control with 11 ships, 508 soldiers, 100 seamen, 16 horses, 10 bronze guns, 4 falconets and 13 fowling pieces.

The march to Tenochtitlán is in the category of the historic military-geographical achievements: Alexander's advance to the Hydaspes, Xenophon's withdrawal to the Black Sea, Hannibal's crossing of the Alps. But Alexander retreated, Xenophon from the start was on the run, Hannibal pulled out tamely in a ship from the toe of Italy. The Spaniards stayed.

The cost is incalculable.

Contrary to accepted belief, military casualties were still low – even with the Aztecs. Despite the difficulties of the first stage across the foetid jungle of the coast, and the incipient resistance of the outlying nations, Cortés in the first five weeks of the march lost fifty-five men only. That this was one in eight of his initial force was tactically important, but as a casualty figure it is insignificant.

The first hard figure of enemy casualties was recorded by Cortés himself in a letter to the Emperor after the massacre at Cholula a few weeks later, when he wrote 'in two hours more than 3,000 died'.

Disproportionate conclusions have been drawn from it. The extent of the casualties was due to the fact that his new Tlaxcalan allies got out of hand, and the figure is not to be used as a yardstick for the expedition as a whole. Cortés went on and over the elevated pass between the great volcano of Popocatapetl and his wife Itzaccihuatl, paused – while, with a ridiculously English gesture, Diego de Ordás asked for time to climb the 18,000-foot cone – had his Pisgah-like view of the city of Tenochtitlán and began the long descent to the meeting with Moçtezuma.

None of the records suggest that the casualties of the march reached 10,000, counting both sides.

Even the death of Moçtezuma, himself struck down by sling stones flung by his own people, was not the climactic moment of the conquest of Mexico. The fate of the Aztecs had been decided three months earlier. Cortés, racing to Cempoala to deal with Velasquez' attempt to depose him, found that de Narvaez' ships had brought smallpox from Cuba. Cempoala on the coast was in the

Cortés' march to Tenochtitlan, 1519: (A) the Spaniards sink their ships; (B) they set out; (C) sandstorms; (D) Indian priests and their idols; (E) a skirmish with the Indians, (F) who make peace with the Spaniards, (G) and serve them a meal; (H) some Indians are baptised; (I) spies have their hands cut off; (J) the Spaniards reduced to eating dog flesh.

DON P̊. Z ZÅS.

terror of epidemic. From Cempoala it spread. *La noche triste* – the apocalyptic retreat over the causeway from Tenochtitlán after the death of Moçtezuma – killed its thousands, gold hunting expeditions killed tens of thousands, the breakdown of a tight and competent administration killed, in the long run, hundreds of thousands – but disease killed millions.

The pre-Cortés population of Mexico by general assessment stood at 25,000,000. In 1538 the population of Cortés' New Spain of the Ocean Sea was 6,300,000. In 1580 it was less than 2,000,000. An Empire of absolute power, a remarkable technical civilization, a religion of inconceivably splendid barbarity, an astonishing art form, had broken in the hands of a few hundred adventurers.

There is a grim and monstrous humour in the fact that the first instalment of the Emperor's share of the conquest, the Royal Fifth, was captured in transit on its way to Spain by the French buccaneer Jean Florin.

Within five years of the rape of Mexico a new factor was imposed on calculation. Epidemic disease struck in Peru even before the conquistador. At Quito in the extreme north Huayna Capac, the eleventh Inca, died of an unknown sickness that may have been measles or scarlet fever – in any event, a white man's sickness which had acquired its own volition and been passed, probably on land from village to village or possibly in local boats, without benefit of Spaniard.

Before he died he had been uneasy because of tales of pale-skinned men, bearded, who floated on the sea to the north.

Ninan Cuyoche, his declared successor, died in the terror of the new sickness before he could be installed. Thousands died; there are no statistics, only the ennumeration – thousands. Huascar, the remaining legitimate son, succeeded. Atahualpa, a son not born of a sister in the Inca custom and therefore illegitimate, was left in control of the Inca army to face the unknown.

Francisco Pizarro, who embodied it, was in his childhood a swineherd, born illegitimate in desperate poverty at Trujillo in the province of Extremadura. He had reached Española in early middle age and went with Ojeda's expedition to Uraba on the Tierra Firme. Cortés should have sailed with Ojeda but was ill.

At a later date Pizarro crossed the Isthmus with Balboa and shared with him the first sight of the Pacific.

His early record as an explorer has an aggressive determination. After a series of failures, he secured the backing of Hernando de Luque, Vicar of Panama, and went south in company with Diego de Almagro on a harsh and fruitless survey of the coast below the Isthmus. Funds for a second attempt were hard to come by but eventually, still with de Almagro, he worked as far south as the Inca coast town of Atacames.

While de Almagro went back for support, Pizarro elected to wait on the arid island of Gallo, and when after inordinate delays a single small vessel was sent to bring him back, he took it boldly south of the equator to a position level with Chimbote.

He returned to Panama with a careful and considered appreciation of the Inca empire.

The discovery was too important to be dealt with – or financed – in Panama,

D. FRAN.co PIZARRO.

and he went back to Spain. After the customary royal delays, he enlisted the help of the Queen and secured the notorious Capitulation of Toledo, which awarded him the prospective Vice-Royalty of Peru. It also earned him the fatal enmity of his partner de Almagro.

The disintegration of the Inca civilization had begun while he was on Gallo. Intrigue in the Andes had expanded into civil war before he sailed clandestinely from San Lucar, having been unable to meet the Spanish Queen's conditions as to the strength of his force. By the time he built the village of San Miguel to serve as an operational base, Huascar, the Inca, had already been defeated by his half-brother Atahualpa and was in prison. Pizarro struck over the Cordilleras into a dangerously divided country.

Atahualpa waited for him at the city of Cajamarca, pulled out of it as he approached, and occupied a strong tactical position with a force of 5,000 men. Pizarro sent an embassy on horseback to invite him to a meeting, and occupied Cajamarca.

Recklessly, contemptuously even, Atahualpa accepted the invitation, moved forces secretly to cut off any possibility of Pizarro's retreat, and entered Cajamarca. Neither side acted in good faith; Pizarro had prepared an elaborate ambush in the town, falconets had been hauled to the summit of a tower, cavalry were concealed in the arcades of the principal buildings, crossbowmen dominated the streets.

A successful gold hunting expedition

Left
Francisco Pizarro, conqueror of Peru. The codex shows Indian women kneeling before him

Vicente de Valverde, the Dominican friar who marched with Pizarro, was instructed to offer the new Inca Christianity. Atahualpa listened patiently and then rejected the offer, flinging the Bible to the ground. Pizarro sprang his ambush. The cavalry charged, the falconets were fired, Atahualpa was captured as his litter fell, and the massacre began.

The destruction of life in the military phases of the Peruvian conquest is impossible to assess. Spanish casualties against the enemy were relatively low; against each other they were savage. Factional fighting, revolt, the treachery of the divided conquistadors was unlimited. The casualties of the divided Incas in the civil wars of Atahualpa were possibly statistically greater. They were, in the upshot, decisive. The ten years from 1525 to 1535 were a decade of death. Within it the civilization of the Incas collapsed.

It was not, by a strict chronology, ancient – the first Inca reigned a little after the Norman Conquest of England – but it had developed into a sound economy. Its civil engineering was brilliant, its animal husbandry sound, its agriculture more than adequate. Peru at the conquest had more than 3,000 miles of good roads, most of them through atrocious mountain country. It is doubtful if there were 1,500 in the England of that day. Enormous blocks of stone were quarried for temples and for fortresses and moved with astonishing facility. Multi-faceted blocks were cut with superlative precision to make earthquake-proof structures. Metal work had reached a high level of excellence, weaving was a brilliant art form, astronomy had been perfected.

Everything collapsed with the judicial murder of Atahualpa, garotted as soon as he had filled the Room of Gold that had been accepted as the price of his freedom.

Fighting over the remainder of the spoils endured amongst the Spaniards for a quarter of a century, and to the dispassionate eye there is a rough justice in Pizarro's execution of his partner de Almagro without trial, and his own murder in succession by de Almagro's partisans.

It was a bloody age.

Slavery, if the flowers brought back from the beach at Bojador be excepted, is the earliest of all the effective consequences of the Renaissance explorations – the first to yield an economic reward.

Whether it is to be considered at a level with genocide is a matter, fundamentally, of definition. Genocide, it is laid down, is the destruction of ethnic or racial groups. So also is slavery. Cold estimates suggest that 14,000,000 slaves were landed live in the Americas in the four and a half centuries of the traffic, that twenty per cent of the number originally shipped on the coast of Africa died in the horrors of the Middle Passage, that a number equal to the sum of both of these died in the slave wars that flared across Guinea at the opening of every slaving season, in the breakdown of communal life that followed, in the increased incidence of disease and starvation, and in the terrible mortality of the slave marches to the coast.

No formal statistics exist; but the estimates are based, dispassionately, on the numbers of ships known to have been engaged in the trade, the recognized voyages, acknowledged ship capacities, general figures for slave populations in the Americas, and hard assumptions as to casualties. In 1790, for example, it is recorded that British ships carried 38,000, French 20,000, Portuguese 10,000, Dutch 4,000 and Danish 2,000. A total of 74,000 in human livestock for one year.

It is necessary to stress again that these overall figures are estimates. Some of them no doubt derive from assumptions made in the fervour of abolitionism, some from national animosities, but they should be read in conjunction with the figures for growth in wealth and population of ports like Liverpool and Bristol, and for that matter London, all of which were sustained in varying degrees in their post-Elizabethan development by the trade. They may be read with equal instruction in the light of the phenomenal expansion of Central America on a slave sustained economy.

Slavery is itself a disease of civilization. It was unknown in the hunting, and unproductive in the food-gathering economies. It became inevitable only when late Neolithic man descended to river valleys with wide cultivable areas and inherent possibilities of food surpluses. With the simultaneous appearance of transportation systems capable of handling such surpluses the appearance of an exchange economy was virtually automatic. As automatically, labour was elevated into a problem.

It is probable that the process began in the Nile valley. As early at least as 2600 B.C. debt slavery (self-sale into servitude) and child slavery existed in Egypt. Possibly it existed as early on the Euphrates. Ur countenanced it. It carried over from civilization to civilization. Even the intellectualism of the Greeks accepted it, though the Cynics disapproved and Aristotle pointed out

The lure of gold: a Peruvian whistling vase; *right* an Indian goldsmith at work polishing; *below* Pizarro watches the gathering of Atahualpa's treasures while an Indian receives a Christian baptism.

acidly that few men even had the necessary qualities of soul for a proper appreciation of freedom.

The Romans brought it to a customary callous perfection when they combined the expropriation of the traditional peasantry with the surplus of labour produced by endemic colonial wars to begin the dangerously efficient experiment of the *latifundio*. Christianity at all times exercised towards it a careful casuistry. Islam employed it as an appropriate punishment for unbelievers. Europe as a whole, despite the efforts of the Rus, emerged slowly from acceptance of it by way of a series of variations on the theme of serfdom. Spain and Portugal, because of their continuous contact with the Moslem invasion and the slow rate of the re-conquest, were, broadly speaking, the last of its exponents within the Western European framework.

At the beginning of Henry the Navigator's operations the supply of descendants of captured Moors had diminished sharply. Only Castile and Aragon still had direct contact with Granada and the hoped for rewards of a final conquest. Portugal was, understandably, unlikely to have moral or economic objections to a slave import from a new source.

None the less Gonçalves' intuition and Tristão's specific orders at the Rio do Ouro were not concerned with prisoners as slaves. Henry's requirement at this period was still quintessentially for information. He lacked all-important details of people, places and situations in the south. He needed, urgently, to be able to interrogate 'prisoners of war'.

This relatively simple necessity became grotesquely complicated by the nature of the captures of the second night. The man Adahu was an Azenegue – a Berber – of standing. Two of the youths were of a comparable class. The remainder were black Africans, themselves almost certainly slaves of the Azenegues.

Adahu's Machiavellian proposal for a ransom deal was made wholly on the basis of a known availability of African slaves for exchange. The value that he placed on his own person was a clear indication of price scales prevailing: the transaction as a whole was a revelation of the extent and existing professionalism of the slave system in Guinea prior to the discoveries. Its spread to this, the farthest north-west corner of the area, was the index of its general acceptance.

The raids at the Rio do Ouro did not therefore in any sense initiate African slavery. Henry of Portugal and the explorers were the catalysts only of its extension into Europe.

Remarkably that extension remained small. It is improbable that importation into metropolitan Portugal averaged significantly more than 500 or 600 a year, though a relatively high slave density was in time established in the Algarve. Despite the considerable attention that has been paid to Lançarote's first triumphant voyage and the sorrowful market that celebrated it outside Lagos, Portugal never found more than a marginal need for African labour.

There was a gap of sixty years before the first market opened in the New World.

Slavery was a fundamental factor in the advance of each of the successive Central American cultures. Long before the *Santa Maria* took departure from

Palos the Maya, the Aztec and the Inca civilizations incorporated it in their way of life. Cortés' description of the market place at Tlaltelolco is plain evidence of its condition at the conquest.

Afro-American slavery, on the other hand, is the consequence of Christopher Columbus.

It is one of the sharper ironies of modern history that his initial intention was to establish a traffic in the opposite direction. Clear evidence indicates that he conceived the possibility of an export of 'Indians' to Spain in the very earliest days of the reconnaissance of the Bahamas. At Cuba '. . . the Admiral decided to leave the Rio de Mares and ordered some of the people of that island made captives; for he intended to take some persons from each island to Spain in order that they might give information about their country.'

The parallel between his decision and the action of Gonçalves and Tristão at the Rio do Ouro is inescapable: both were made in the interests of 'information', each led with tragic speed to an organized slave traffic.

Even after the disaster to the *Santa Maria* Columbus still carried back with him in the overcrowded *Niña* a substantial sample of Indians. Ten at least survived the grim rigours of that passage. Six reached the Court at Barcelona.

The reception of Columbus at his first return has aspects of a Roman Triumph. His popularity was instant for the promise he brought with him was illimitable. None the less he returned to the Indies without any agreed arrangement to implement his ideas for a slave trade. Isabella's disapproval appears to have manifested itself early.

Despite disapproval he pursued the possibilities. Late in 1493 a scheme was drawn up and de Torres, taking back the ships of the first great fleet of re-inforcement, carried a 'Memorandum' to the Catholic Sovereigns. It included an outline of the proposals. Columbus informed them that he was already building a fleet of *fustas* for the colonial service. It would be able to take action against the Caribs 'who are the mortal enemies of your Highnesses' new subjects, the Tainos'. Caribs taken captive were to be shipped to Europe and sold on the basis of a regular trade to provide money for supplies, particularly of cattle, until the new gold mines came into production. Privately Columbus was convinced that the Caribs would make vigorous slaves in contrast to the indolent Tainos with their distressing tendency to die under pressure.

The recommendation is annotated cautiously by the court '. . . this subject has been postponed for the present, until another voyage has come thence and let the Admiral write what he thinks about it.'

The Admiral did not write, he took action. Deserters from his miniscule armed forces had harassed the inland villages; natural retaliation followed. Columbus sent in a punitive expedition to punish not the deserters, who could not have been located anyway, but the villages: 1,500 Tainos – men, women, children – were driven down to Isabela with horses and dogs; 500, 'the best males and females', were selected and herded on to the ships of the return fleet of 1495. Michele de Cuneo wrote: '. . . about two hundred of these Indians died, I believe because of the unaccustomed air, colder than theirs. We cast them into the sea. At Cadiz half of them were sick . . . for your information they are not

working people, nor have they long life.'

By 1496 Española was officially deemed pacified. Disease, violence, the breakdown of communal organization and consequential starvation had, according to the estimates of the time, killed off 100,000 at this date. Pacification and death were synonymous. Genocide was in flood.

The record of Columbus as an administrator is one of unmitigated disaster. In the small world of a ship he was brilliant; in the larger context of a colony, painfully incompetent. In March he sailed for Spain with a report – whatever gloss he put upon it – of failure. The position with regard to gold was increasingly unsatisfactory. The site of Isabela was unhealthy and useless for trade. Sugar grew but had not yet produced a surplus. Colonists were slipping away to new areas. The European population had shrunk to 630.

His brother Bartolomeu was left to establish a new capital, and Columbus went back to Spain to land in a gale of criticism. With his power of absolute

Indians on Española attempt to repulse invaders

conviction he talked his way through the gale and into a Third Voyage. Keeping masterfully south, he discovered Trinidad, found the passage into the Gulf of Paria, explored its further coast and passed out through the Boca del Dragón, satisfied that it was just another island. Then, on the Feast of the Assumption, direct inspiration told him that it was a Continent – *que son otro mundo* – an Other World!

Just two years later he was taken aboard the caravel *La Gorda* in chains by order of the Commissioner of the Catholic Kings, Francisco de Bobadilla.

At some period between this and the inception of his fourth and last voyage (politics in the Caribbean were always stimulating) he is stated to have recommended the introduction of African slavery as a solution to the problem of the vanishing Indian. It is entirely possible: he had had experience of Guinea as a young man; at the beginning of his Third Voyage he had called at Boavista in the Cape Verdes and must have refreshed his memory as to the qualities of the Negro. But by the time the first moves were made he had ceased to exercise his authority as *Virrey* – Viceroy of the Indies. In 1503 a small ship sailed from Lisbon with slaves recruited from owners in the Peninsula. Other groups were shipped subsequently with individual ships but no official steps were taken until in 1517 letters patent were issued over the seal of Charles V for the import of Africans to Española – on payment of dues to the Royal Treasury!

It is the culminating irony of the Spanish colonization of the Caribbean that the decision was made in response to the passionate appeals of the humanist Bartolomé de las Casas, the Apostle of the Indies, in the interest of the Taino people to whom he had devoted pity and a transcendent humanity.

A generation later, as has been said, there were barely 500 Tainos remaining, and the Negro had inherited the Caribbean.

A Taino funeral procession: the feathers imitate a native bird with a mournful cry

Chapter XIV

The Rise of the English

Gold, slavery and genocide, then, were the earliest consequences of the splendid adventure of the explorations. The consequences of the second phase are more complex; in it the intrusion of new nations, the exploitation of fresh territories, the explosion of international rivalries combined to produce a pattern of infinite change, indefinitely extended, and it is simplest to consider it by a brief examination of the consequences for each of the individual nations which imposed the pattern.

It is a finite period. The domination of Portugal and Spain lasted 100 years from the sailing of Columbus to the dispatch of the Armada. In that century England and Holland evolved as dynamic maritime powers. In it Portugal raped a third of Africa, seized the western third of South America and, like Venice, 'held the gorgeous east in fee'. In it, at last, unable to sustain the vast commitments of her achievement and simultaneously to provide an adequate home defence, she was compelled to submit in 1581 to the quasi-amalgamation with Spain which endured for sixty distressful years.

Her weakness had two causes. The first, that at the start of Henry's expansionism she was in relative terms a poor country. It has been suggested that she was bled white by the explorations. She was not. The early voyages were run on the proverbial shoestring: Henry's debts were for the most part accumulated in the profitless attempts to grab the Canaries and in futile attacks against the Moor. Even before his death the discoveries were beginning to produce a modest profit in national terms, though the real potentials of Africa had still to be recognised.

The second weakness was manpower. It was intractable. Portugal's normal population was small; cultivation was primitive; the plague which struck the preparations for the attack on Ceuta weakened her substantially; the necessity to maintain a strong garrison at Ceuta was a constant drain thereafter. Throughout the history of the expansion she lacked men to exploit the vast new territories that accrued to her. In a sense she still does.

When, for example, with the destruction of the Tainos, the demand for African slaves in Spain's new Indies flared, Portugal's establishment on the Guinea Coast was inadequate to handle it and to protect her monopoly. Arguim, Henry's single strongpoint, was too small; Mina, João II's foundation, was limited and unhealthy. The smaller settlements were insignificant, so that long stretches of coast remained outside effective sovereignty – or even maritime control. The same factor inhibited penetration or even exploration inland, which left the slave trade, as it grew, wholly in the hands of native dealers and the Arabs. They purchased slaves in the interior – or took them in ruthless raiding – and brought them to the coast for sale. The Portuguese were the middlemen and the transport agents only, and the high profits of the trade had to be shared

Albuquerque's unsuccessful attempt to take Aden and complete his stranglehold on the spice trade

with the Arab and native entrepreneurs while the Portuguese bore the losses of the transhipment. Against that background the trade from the first was open to interlopers – English, Spanish, Dutch and French.

In the east the problems were possibly even less capable of solution. Albuquerque as conquistador never had more than 4,000 men under command, his fleet was small, his sovereignty stretched 4,500 miles from the coast of Malabar to China, his strongpoints were separated by wholly unrealistic distances. The profits of Portugal's entry into the Spice trade, which he enforced, were by tradition prodigious – though clear balance sheets are not available. They were in degree counterbalanced by the continuing losses on profitless overseas possessions: Ceuta, Tangier – and for a long time, Brazil. Ship losses, consequential shipbuilding, and ship-manning were in addition a heavy drain on slender national resources.

Very simply, Portugal was under-capitalized both in men and cash for the immensity of her ambitions, and the Spanish take-over only increased her problems.

Spain herself won fantastic profits in the early decades of the discoveries – the gold of the Indies, the loot of the Aztecs, the treasure of the Incas. Basically, however, the economic platform from which Spain launched her incredible

A native pays homage to
Albuquerque on board
his ship

conquests was even less stable than that of Portugal. Geographically she was, of course, the bigger country and she had just added to her stature by the conquest of Granada, but her manpower base, at 5,300,000, was in the light of her internal requirements scarcely an improvement on that of Portugal. She was suffering still from the long drain of the re-conquest, her industry was minimal, her peasantry poverty-stricken, and her principal productive trade (handled from Barcelona by the Grand Catalan Company) had collapsed with the incursion of the Turks into the western basin of the Mediterranean. Her agriculture was primitive and climatically restricted. Castile was a man-made desert, its fertility destroyed by the biannual movement of sheep across its enormous plains from summer to winter pastures and back in the operations of the *Mesta*, the inordinately powerful shepherds' guild. That power rested on the blunt fact that the *Mesta* produced the wool which constituted Spain's only alternative trade – that with the cloth producers of Flanders.

Further to complicate her predicament, Spain, poised on the entry into the New World, compounded her basic weaknesses by uprooting the foundation of her commercial structure – the Jews. Columbus, dropping downstream from Palos in the first hour of the First Voyage, saw, it will be remembered, the last ship of that new Exodus making ready to sail.

A quarter of a century later, as the wealth of the Indies began to flow, Spain

acquired, involuntarily, the final disastrous drain on her financial structure – the Emperor Charles V.

In 1517 Charles, son of the Hapsburg Philip the Handsome, came obliquely to the Spanish throne – not yet either Roman or significantly Holy. Two years later he left for Germany, having triumphantly extracted a grant of funds from the reluctant Cortés. In 1520, bribing the Electors of the Empire to the tune of rather more than 800,000 florins, he defeated the King of France and was elected Holy Roman Emperor.

Magellan's voyage, dispatched about this time, sharply illustrates his difficulties. The voyage had to be subsidized at Charles' personal arrangement by the Fuggers of the Lily, the cadet branch of the inconceivably arcane banking house of the Fuggers of Augsburg who also financed and arranged his bribes for his election as Holy Roman Emperor. That it was necessary to use them for Magellan's venture is a significant measure of Spain's weakness. She could provide neither money nor trade goods for the five small ships which comprised the expedition: Jakob II, of the Fuggers, could.

Charles himself had a peculiar financial genius. He fought wars, subsidized revolutions, broke kingdoms on a system of short-term loans borrowed at twelve-and-a-half per cent which he paid off with new-borrowed money at twelve-and-a-half per cent. Cynics said that any competent creditor of his could expect a yield of forty-five per cent per annum on his capital. Even the 5,000 fabulous silver mines of the Cerro Potosí in what is now Bolivia, which came into production ten years before his abdication, could not amortize his incredible debts.

That he canalized an enormous percentage of the early product of the discoveries away from Spain is sufficiently obvious. That it damaged Spain, however, is apparent only in degree. It is altogether doubtful that Spain was in fact economically competent to handle the inflationary weight and the speed of the flow of treasure which through the century poured out of the New World. That his exactions were resented is well documented, but it is also true that an admiration developed for a Spanish King – even if he was an absentee King – who had so successfully imposed himself upon the will of Europe. Spain had entered the 'Big Time'.

Moreover, his exactions were never absolute. The New World trade was officially a Castilian monopoly. Its nerve centre was Seville. In 1517 when Charles first came to Spain, Seville's population was 25,000. In 1600 it was 100,000. Something of the 25,000,000 pesos of the first plunder of the Indies, more of the 6,000,000,000 pesos which flowed eventually from the mines which the Spaniards and the Portuguese developed, clearly stuck in its passage through. Nor were other benefits entirely lacking. Charles was an autocrat in the strictest sense of the term but he permitted the passionately waspish las Casas not only to survive but, in a measure, to suceed. The *Neuvas Leyes,* the protective laws which were las Casas' inspiration, were promulgated with his consent. They constituted, with the protection they afforded to the Indians, the first amelioration of colonialism in what may possibly have been its most atrocious form. More importantly still, Charles took action to curb and rationalize the

Jakob II of the Fuggers of the Lily with his secretary, Matthäus Schwarz, in 1519

Opposite
The Emperor Charles V rides into battle, painted in 1548 by Titian

spirit of the conquistadors. That no successful attempt was made to set up alsatias and private kingdoms in the opening phase of the New World is largely his achievement.

Charles died and Philip II, his son, succeeded to his father's thrones (less Germany) and to his debts – 2,000,000 ducats.

The Spanish Government declared a moratorium.

There is an ironic quality in the economic fact that the Potosí mines had by his father's death reached an annual production of five million pesos and that by the end of Philip's own reign they would reach thirty-five million. In theory it should have been possible for him to establish a superb stability. In fact Philip was overtaken by a slow tide of inflation in which the new superabundance of silver combined with the huge discoveries of the previous century in Saxony to upset values throughout Europe.

Little of the new silver was available in Spain for industrial and economic investment. What surplus there was was absorbed in a nightmare spiral of external payments to purchase manufactured goods which Spain by now should have been able to manufacture for herself, to pay for foreign wars that had only indirect connection with herself, and to satisfy the legion of bankers – no longer now from Augsburg alone but from Milan and Florence and the Low Countries – who had permeated the Spanish economy.

Estimates of the real value of the Indies Treasure are unreliable. Merriman suggests that by the middle of Philip's reign it was rather more than ten per cent of all the revenues from European sources. Governmental expenditure because of endemic war in Europe was heavier than revenue. The Indies Treasure represented escape from bankruptcy. Which explains the paradox of Renaissance Spain that, commanding the richest of the new discoveries, she remained poor.

England all through the first phase of the discoveries was in a process of social revolution. The monastic system had been destroyed. The proceeds of destruction had created a middle class. It formed a new level between an aristocracy enriched with monastic spoils and a new industrial mass formed out of a peasantry dispossessed of land but substantially re-established in an embryo cottage industry.

Britain as a whole had finally recovered from the shattering impact of the Black Death. England had a population of between three and four million, solvent, if hardly prosperous, on a considerable output of wool, an extensive production of cloth, and a sufficient agriculture.

The difference in the character of the countries is reflected broadly in the sea ventures.

The coast of Guinea was discovered on behalf of a Prince. A King and a Queen sent out Columbus to search for the Indies. Magellan's circumnavigation of the world was completed for an Emperor. John Hawkins, principal entrepreneur of England's entry into the carve-up of a new-discovered world, was the son of a small town mayor of the West of England, operating a private enterprise on a joint-stock basis.

Sir Walter Ralegh

The nature and increase of this type of enterprise had two consequences. By its attacks on the Indies Treasure in transit it threatened Philip's precarious solvency. In the intervals when it failed to do so, Philip's Treasure threatened the peace of Europe. Ralegh, between efforts to acquire more of it, said with superb moral indignation, 'It is his Indian Gold that endangereth and disturbeth all the nations of Europe.'

The reiteration of such enterprises eventually helped to shatter Philip's alliance with England. On the other hand, it played an incomparable part in the technical perfection of a Royal Navy adequate to an island's special needs.

The navy of the English kings has an ancient history. It has also alarming discontinuities. Under the Tudors it developed strongly once the weakness of

Henry VII's early years was over. Under Henry VIII it improved numerically, advanced technically, and was inculcated with a fighting spirit. Under Edward VI and Mary it rotted metaphorically and literally. Burghley persuaded Elizabeth, who was a realist, of its importance, but its principal growth stems from the interloping which produced ships, privately built, that were effectively warships and men who traded as merchant seamen and were effective fighting men. It produced, in addition, captains of imagination.

John Hawkins is inadequately assessed in many of the historical studies of the Elizabethan age. Too much has been made of his voyages, too little of the dour, disinterested brilliance of his administration. Drake, kaleidoscopic and flamboyant, overtook him in the public consciousness. Hawkins is the weightier man. The report he wrote for Burghley before he took office is precise, informed and angry. The Queen was being cheated in shipbuilding contracts and in timber purchases, in upkeep, in new building 'which proceeds of the wilful covetousness of one man and to set forth his glory'.

Burghley made him Treasurer of the Navy.

It is wholly typical of the man that his agreements with Burghley are known as the First Bargain and the Second Bargain. He was essentially a businessman. Under him the substructure of the Navy moved forward from strength to power as the threats of Philip of Spain grew with his ambition. Hawkins rationalized upkeep and secured new efficiencies at diminished expenditure. He reduced ships' complements and saved money in wages and lives by cutting down the death rate in disease from overcrowding. He produced the new galleons of the *Revenge* class. He remodelled existing ships to match them as far as possible by removing top-hamper. He applied, to what had been a Home Defence navy, the potentials of the distant water strength of the interlopers.

What part he had in the strategy which delayed the Armada and gained time for England is difficult to estimate, but it bears his hallmark, and it produced, in one of its most remarkable episodes, an odd example of historical ingratitude. Drake, making his pre-emptive strike on Cadiz, had attacked the springing point of the Spanish discoveries. With victory, he withdrew first to Lagos, then, defiantly to Sagres, the conceptual centre of *all* modern discovery – and incontinently burned what was left of Henry's 'palace', heaving the guns from the cliff.

Simultaneously he collected the entire fleet of ships that carried the output of barrel staves for the season of 1587. These too he burned.

Lack of barrel staves became an important item in the delay over the sailing of the Armada. Head winds, when it sailed, forced it into Corunna to make good the leakage from the old casks that had had to be used. Wine went sour in rotten barrels. In the event it was impossible for the Spanish fleet to re-supply on the Lowland coast.

Casualties in action had been astonishingly low: the Spaniards lost the great galleass at Calais, two ships in the confusion of Gravelines and two driven ashore; but off the Scheldt a Protestant God 'blew with his wind and they were scattered'; and off the Orkneys and Northern Ireland as they fled north-about round the British Isles and closed the land again in hope of water, He blew a second time. Of 130 ships that sailed from Corunna sixty-three were lost.

The abysmal strategy that had failed to provide a base at the end of the gauntlet of the Channel, incompetent tactics that had rejected all opportunity to destroy the English fleet before the junction with Parma, and finally the condition of Medina's ships, ended the dream of Spanish sea power despite all subsequent attempts.

The English won in an exercise of the most exquisite pragmatism.

The defeat of the Armada did not cause, though it contributed to, the decadence of the seventeenth century. Parma carried on and won his victories in the Low Countries, but Henry of Navarre won France. Protestantism was restrained but not expunged. Philip's successor ejected the Moriscos but destroyed the middle class in Spain. Philip IV forfeited Portugal in a welter of mismanagement. Culturally brilliant in a late flowering of the Renaissance, Spain declined inexorably to the status of a second class power.

Portugal emerged from her tutelage agitated and sustained herself by valorous improvisation, losing colonies and markets and points of power like leaves in autumn. Only when Brazil belatedly discovered gold and diamonds in the state of Minas Gerais at the end of the century, was she able finally to shake off the effects of the Spanish hold.

Britain – the name begins now to move slowly into general use – set up her joint-stock Empire. The decision of Elizabeth in the year after the Armada to grant to 'The Governor and Company of Merchants Trading Into the East Indies' a fifteen-year monopoly of the trade that had been Portugal's by prior right, is one of the determinants of history.

Portuguese traders off the Malabar coast employing native labour

Chapter XV

The World Refashioned

The consequences of the second phase of the conquest have, in the exploited countries, a matching complexity. It is simplest again to consider, separately, each of the principal areas involved.

Historically they are earliest apparent in Western Africa. The slave trade, opening with the captures at the Rio do Ouro, is the first effect, human or economic, of Henry the Navigator's psychological triumph at Cape Bojador. Its impact on Africa is vital to all consideration of subsequent developments.

The vast fecund area which supplied the slaves until the Congo also was brought into production was bound absolutely to the south and west by the Atlantic. Its tribes were not boat peoples. The northern side of the area was walled by the Sahara and, though the wall was not impregnable, the keys to its gates were in the hands of the Arab and the Azenegue. The single open frontier lay to the east and exit was free to the tribes of the eastern sectors through the riverine area and the tropical rain forest to the savannahs of the uplands. Under population pressures limited elements moved more or less continuously to join the slow general flux of Black Africa to the south where the Bushman and the Hottentot had preceded them. Within the area the population was static except in terms of the milling-around of local war. It was a mosaic of semi-hostile communities, coalescing into small empires as leaders appeared and disappeared. For the most part it existed in a late Iron Age environment, with occasional artistic efflorescences. War was endemic and its twin prizes were land and slaves.

In the north from the seventh century onward there was an increasing Arab influence. The area as a whole therefore was conditioned to a degree of interference at the hands of a superior civilization.

In the opening stages of the discoveries slavery in the areas of Portuguese interest was physically insignificant, and no moral issues were involved. In contemporary thought slaves existed under God and *Las Siete Partidas,* the Spanish version of the social code that stemmed from Justinian. Numbers involved, despite the sad market at Lagos, were irrelevant against the vast background of Africa.

A quarter of a century after the discovery of the West Indies there was a significant up-turn. In 1517 the first *Asiento* was issued. It gave permission for the importation of 4,000 Negroes into the Indies over a period of eight years and it initiated the direct traffic between Africa and the Caribbean. It had become necessary to begin filling the vacuum created by the destruction of the population of the islands, and of Española in particular, by disease and punitive war.

It is doubtful if Africa, as such, was even aware of the first phase of the trade. All that differentiated it from the slavery of immemorial custom was that a small proportion of the coffles – the inhuman slave caravans – took a route to the coast instead of away from it.

The second phase was more plainly apparent.

In the absence of demographic statistics for the Africa of the seventeenth and eighteenth centuries exact figures are impossible. Estimates, however, are instructive. The present population of the areas directly involved in the main period of the transatlantic traffic is approximately 100,000,000. Though it has grown sharply in the last century, it is improbable that it has doubled since the peak of the slaving period. If an average of 50,000,000 for the area is accepted through the relevant years, and the estimate discussed earlier of 14,000,000 slaves shipped and as many destroyed in the process is applied to it, it is possible to form an estimate of effect.

The transatlantic trade persisted for 440 years. The annual extraction rate was therefore approximately 63,000 a year. In the middle of the eighteenth century it is known to have risen to about 100,000 a year and in 1835 it is claimed to have topped 135,000. An average of 63,000 over the whole period is clearly in keeping with this.

Against a population background of fifty million the figures suggest that the average individual had an 800 to 1 chance against involvement.

Whether this is higher than the average chance of involvement in ordinary tribal warfare, normal internecine slavery, or the ancient Arab traffic is not capable of proof. That it increased the possibilities of involvement is of course logical. Whether it increased simultaneously the brutalities and bestialities inherent in the traffic is open to surmise but incapable of proof. It was at all times barbarous. Portuguese responsibility begins at the coast, but it is the overriding responsibility of the market. Not until the Scotsman Mungo Park reached the Niger at Ségou in 1769 was there an effective European penetration inland.

Little suggests that in the year of the Niger's discovery the trade was more, or less, atrocious in principle than it had been in 1481. It was then, and at all times, inhuman. None the less it is important to note that it did not destroy West Africa – either in its social structure, as has too frequently been claimed, or in its economy. The extraction rate reached its high point in the first half of the nineteenth century, the population rose to 100,000,000 in the first half of the twentieth century. Though a high proportion of the rise may be attributed to an enforced *pax Britannica* through the second half of the period and to the introduction of better food grains, an improved protein intake, higher medical standards and organized trade, it is manifest that at no time was the regenerative potential of Western Africa significantly affected. As a community West Africa survived – with its penchant for tribal annihilation largely unimpaired, as the recent war in Biafra made plain.

The consequences in the Caribbean are very simply interwoven with those of Africa. In 1535, according to las Casas, there were only 500 Indians left alive in Española. In 1795, it is claimed, there were 2,000,000 Negroes. The first consequence of the African slave trade was the Africanization of the islands. For reasons ranging from prevailing winds to crop changes and agricultural innovation, rather more than a third of all slaves transported from Guinea were landed there.

The economic factor was sugar.

It will be remembered that Columbus picked up cane cuttings at Gomera on the outward passage of the Second Voyage. New stocks followed from Madeira. In the confused state of Española following the destruction of Navidad its progress was slow. With more settled conditions it went ahead: by 1516 a *trapiche*, a horse-powered mill, was operating in Española and producing almost 1,000 lb of sugar a day. Despite the swift surge of gold-hungry men to the mainland which followed the conquest of Mexico, and the shortage of labour as the Taino population faded, it flourished. In rapid succession *trapiches* were taken over by the *ingenio*, the water-powered mill which could, according to Oviedo, produce 2,000 lb per day, and which required 120 men to feed it. Las Casas reported that almost fifty *ingenios* were operating by the half century, and the profit of a single *ingenio* was reckoned at 10,000 ducats a year.

The demand for slaves exploded, the market was assured.

Sugar spread to Cuba, to Jamaica, to Costa Rica, in due course to Mexico, Peru and Brazil. Sales prospects in a Europe that had barely moved out of the honey-sugar stage were unlimited. It was one of the most powerful of the magnets that drew the Dutch, the English, the French, the Danes not to raid but to settle. As possibilities expanded the power of Spain diminished.

The Dutch landed first, on the rock of St Eustatius twelve years after the Armada. The English took St Kitts in 1623, the French forced a way on to the island two years later. One by one they fell: St Croix, Nevis, Antigua, Tobago, and just before the end of the century, Española itself.

Barbados offers perhaps the clearest picture of what actually happened. Easternmost island of the Caribbean, it had been missed by Columbus. Subsequently the Spaniards eliminated its population. Its early history, inevitably,

Above
Disembarking African slaves for sale in Brazil

Right
Sugar: slaves feeding cane into a mill on a Brazilian estate and, *below*, stoking the boiler with sugar-cane waste

242

is confused but in 1627 English settlers landed and fourteen years later sugar cuttings were smuggled in from Pernambuco, to a mixed and unflourishing agriculture.

Sugar is a labour intensive crop. Before its arrival the needs of the island had been served by a mixture of slaves and indentured English, '. . . a sort of loose vagrant people, vicious and destitute of means to live at home, being either unfit for labour, or such as could find none to employ themselves about, or had so misbehaved themselves by whoring, thieving, or other debauchery that none could set them to work.'

No doubt their defects were considerable – though petitions to Parliament at the time suggest that there was another side to the picture – but they were neither numerically, nor in terms of balance, capable of meeting the requirements of a sugar explosion. In 1641 there were 18,000 whites on the island, and 5,000 Negroes. Twenty years later there were 10,000 whites and 40,000 Negroes. In the 1750s the 166 square miles of Barbados sugar were judged to exceed all the New England Colonies in economic importance, and the sugar magnates were buying their way into Parliament and into English society.

Sugar was Europe's first gift to the Americas. It flourished to become the earliest factor in the break-up of the Spanish Empire of the Caribbean.

America's first gift to Europe was syphilis: despite Herndon Hudson's monumental study of *Treponematosis*, there is still no indisputable reference to the disease in Europe before Columbus led his triumphant procession into Barcelona to lay proof of his discovery of the Americas before *los Reyes Catolicos*. The Indians who carried the parrots in his procession carried the spirochete of a disease that was common to all Central America, and las Casas is entirely positive that the Spaniards acquired it in the islands. Oviedo says that it reached Spain by the time of the second voyage. De Isla describes the epidemic which began in Barcelona in 1493. Soldiers from Barcelona moving to Italy for Charles VIII's campaign against the Kingdom of Naples spread it across Europe.

The interchange of good and evil is a limitless field of study. Europe's second gift to the Americas was the smallpox, a vastly swifter and more determined killer. Yellow fever, on the other hand, was almost certainly the epidemic disease *Xekik* which ravaged Yucatan eight years before Columbus sighted Española, and which heralded the breakdown of the Maya. Spanish ships transported it back to Africa. Malaria, on sound evidence, was brought from Guinea and reached epidemic proportions in the Caribbean as early as 1493. Hookworm moved in with the first Negro slaves and took root.

The pendulum swings back and forth, operating at times at both ends of its swing. Sugar, for example, substituted superbly for the simple economy of the Taino, made such demands on slavery and attracted so much competition that it ended by ousting the Spaniards almost altogether. Exported to Europe, it transformed the European dietary – and drastically altered the incidence of dental caries.

The potato, taken back to Europe long before Sir Walter Ralegh, found a

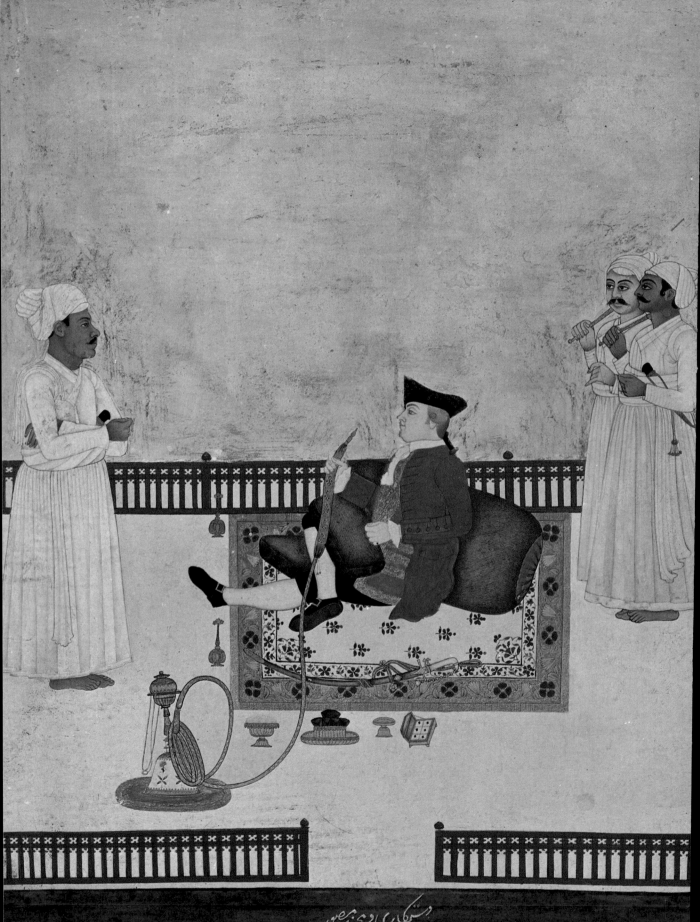

دستکاری دمحمد مصور

militaro-dietetic justification as an easily storable strategic food in Ireland in the endless war against the English. With its success it was elevated beyond economics to an article of Irish faith. When *Phytophthora* destroyed the crops in the famines of the nineteenth century it destroyed with them the economy of Ireland.

The tomato, shipped back to Portugal or Spain at about the same time acquired, as the love-apple, a delicious aura of aphrodisia. It needed as a result two-and-a-half centuries to achieve respectability as a salad vegetable.

The banana, on the other hand, was taken from the Canaries to Española, having reached the Canaries by complex routes from Asia.

Another gift remains. Hernando Columbo records its appearance in his account of his father's arrival at the island of Cuba: '. . . on the way they met many people who carried a firebrand to light certain herbs the smoke of which they inhale, and also to make a fire to roast those roots of which they had given the Christians to eat and which are their principal food'.

Tobacco *and* potatoes, both. The herbs were brought back to Europe while Walter Ralegh was still a boy at Hayes Barton, and it was Jean Nicot, ambassador of France at the court of Lisbon, who sent home the seeds of *Tabacum* to Catherine de Medici and affixed his name to nicotine. 400 years after, tobacco still drifts indeterminately between blessing and curse, and lung cancer may be America's last gift to Europe.

The ultimate phase of the Spanish-American adventure is embodied in the consequences of the mainland conquests.

In an earlier chapter it was stated that the pre-Colombian population – 45,000,000 by recent research – was reduced to 2,000,000 by the second half of the sixteenth century in a disastrous combination of exotic epidemics like smallpox, and endemic plagues like *Xekik*, against a background of simple slaughter. In the face of human disruption of this order an orderly economic progression is clearly impossible.

The tradition that the wealth of the Indies was the Treasure of the Aztecs or the Gold of the Inca is possibly ineradicable. Spanish records, admittedly incomplete, suggest certain alternatives. Von Humboldt's estimate, based on surviving papers, is that 'Plunder' totalled in fact no more than 25,000,000 pesos (with the peso roughly the equivalent of the silver dollar). The estimate is generally accepted; real wealth came later in the conquest.

By one of the odd quirks of history it has been largely forgotten that the principal export of the central American area through the period before and during the rape of Mexico, was the product of the great beds of pearl oysters that fringed the coast of Venezuela from Margarita to Aruba. It is estimated that its value exceeded that of all other shipments from the area for more than a generation. The enormous, and slightly vulgar *arrangements* of pearls with which Elizabeth armoured her virgin breast came certainly from this source – and almost as certainly by simple piracy.

Gold and silver production, on the other hand, began with the resumption of operations on alluvial workings in Mexico precisely as it had begun in Española.

An Englishman, possibly Dr William Fullerton, at leisure in Bengal in 1760

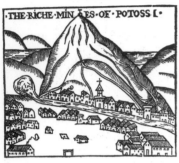

THE
DISCOVERIE AND CONQVEST
of the Prouinces of *PERV*, and
the *Nauigation in the South
Sea*, along that Coast.
And also of the ritche *Mines*
of *POTOSI*.

¶ *Imprinted at London by* Richard Ihones. *Febru.6.1581.*

Potosí, 1581

Right
Indians on Española
smoking and lighting a fire

It shifted to rock mining only when new techniques were developed and new equipment became available. Following this, its value overtook all else.

The story of the Potosí find illustrates it more dazzlingly than anything else. In 1545 a shepherd on the conical peak of Potosí in the Eastern Andes fell and falling, grabbed at a clump of grass to save himself. When he recovered he found the grass roots crusted with silver nodules. With ruthless speed the entire mountain of Potosí was eviscerated. New mines in the Cerro Potosí were prospected and worked, giant finds of mercury speeded and cheapened the processing, the village where the shepherd had lived expanded to a city of 160,000 people 14,000 feet up in the high mountains. By the eighteenth century 1,000,000,000 pesos worth of silver had been extracted.

Gold fell behind in the table of values. In the century and a half after Columbus 16,000 tons of silver reached Europe – 180 tons of gold. At the end of Spanish sovereignty 6,000,000,000 pesos worth of silver had been shipped, legally; no statistics exist for the illicit traffic.

How much, in blunt terms, stuck in the Americas? In Mexico, Peru and Brazil, little more than the altar fronts and the haloes of the innumerable Madonnas. Potosí had at its height a population of 160,000, when Simon Bolivar liberated the city in 1825 it had shrunk to 8,000. Little was left anywhere in the colonies. Some was lost in transit – by acts of God as when the Plate Fleet ran in a hurricane on to the Florida reefs – by acts of the devil, as when Drake raided the Isthmus or the Dutchman Piet Hein captured the entire treasure *flota* in 1628 and forced Spain to sequester 1,000,000 ducats consigned to private individuals in the following year.

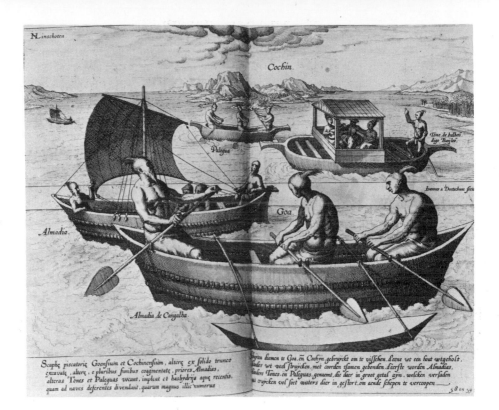

In Goa and Cochin the Portuguese established a trading system using native craft: two types of vessel are illustrated and named

Little enough, as has been said, was left in Spain. The position is aciduously encapsulated by de Figueros at the height of Charles V's operations: 'Our Spain is the Indies of the Genoese'.

Wide differences existed between the conquest of the East and of the West. In the East it was essentially a takeover; the acquisition of an intricately existing trade. The Moghul – correctly the Timurid – Empire had, like Islam, visible parallels with the Caliphate of Cordoba; the Hindu kingdoms, with their involuted religious systems, were perhaps less easy to understand but life patterns were none the less comparable with those of Renaissance Europe at innumerable points. It was simpler, therefore, to establish a *modus vivendi* in the East than in Africa or the New World. Operations were further conditioned by the matter of distances: Calicut and Cochin were four times as far from support and reinforcement as Arguim and Mina on the West Coast of Africa; Macao was 4,000 miles farther still. Trade had of necessity to be established on a system of equitable compromise, reinforced by an invisible threat of power. It was made possible by d'Almeida's destruction – at the very outset of operations – of the combined Arab/Egyptian fleet at Diu, even if that was inspired largely by revenge for the death of d'Almeida's son. Victory at Diu left Albuquerque, the Viceroy, in a position to begin the immense expansion which took the Portuguese to Malacca and the control of the spice trade just thirteen years after the arrival of da Gama. In 1550 Portugal was at the zenith of her power in the East. Ormuz at the entrance to the Persian Gulf was in her hands. Macao on the coast of China was about to fall into them. St Francis Xavier was at Nagasaki in Japan, and the Malaccas had entered an alliance.

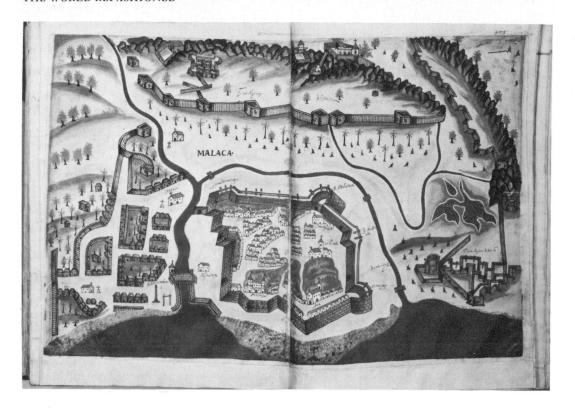

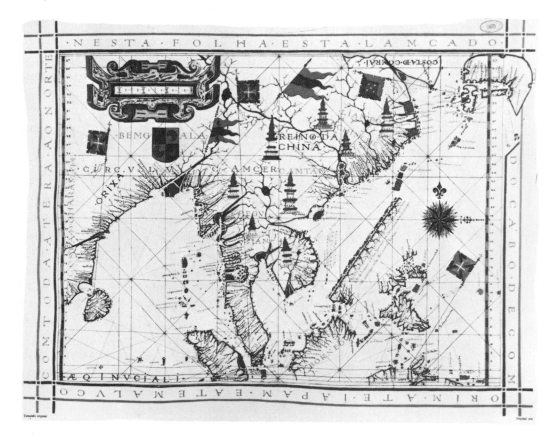

Above
The headquarters of the
Dutch East India Company
in Bengal, 1665

Left
From the port of Malacca
above the Portuguese took
control of the spice trade;
below China and the East
Indies, from the Atlas of
Fernão Vaz Dourado, 1571

None the less, by 1600 the end was already discernible.

England had set up the structure of that incredible private empire, the East India Company. Holland was shaping the Dutch East India Company. Fleets more powerful than Portugal could envisage were entering the Indian Ocean and a century of monopoly was over.

The end product of Dias and Covilhão and da Gama was the establishment of the most arrogant, the most powerful and the richest joint-stock empires that the world has ever seen. They were not Portuguese.

Through the changes India remained, substantially, unchanged. In the East Indies, focal points vital to trade were reshaped but the rest survived. China continued remote and inaccessible except to slow impertinences along her coastal fringe. Japan withdrew into an exquisite lacquered shell and Jesuits and Traders both were confined to the artificial island in the harbour of Nagasaki. The traditional economies of the Eastern peoples, the complexity of their social structures, the endurance of their religions, their age, their dignity, their sense of ineffable superiority conspired to preserve them from destruction. They bowed to *force majeure* and waited for the invader to decay – it took four centuries, but it happened.

The names of the great explorers shout like a tucket of trumpets: Dias de Novais, Cristoforo Colombo, Vasco da Gama, Magalhãis, Hawkins, Drake.

The name of the first great colonist of North America was John Smith.

Princess Pocahontas and her father Chief Powhaton. In the background an Indian village burns.

About it there is an entirely deceptive aura of English pragmatism – deceptive because, in an era of infinite adventure, John Smith scaled the heights of the picaresque. The first heroic figure of joint-stock colonialism, he was born on a Lincolnshire farm. He fought as a boy in the Netherlands against Spain. He was captured in Hungary fighting the Turks – and escaped desperately through Russia. He sailed in 1607 with three ships of the London Company – *Susan Constant, Godspeed,* and *Delivery* – for the Chesapeake Bay, and safely in the Chesapeake was disallowed his promised seat on the Council of the new colony on a charge of being associated with attempted mutiny. In December, trading with the Indians for urgently needed food, he was captured far up the Chickahominy and saved from execution with all the circumstance of romance by Pocahontas, thirteen-year-old daughter of the Chief Powhaton. On his return to the settlement he was accused of hazarding the men who had left with him and a move was made to hang him. He was rescued once more by the timely arrival of the first replenishment fleet. By the following September he was President of the Colony, had brought order into the chaos of Jamestown, completed the fort, regularized fishing and agriculture, and crowned Powhaton.

The vicissitudes of Jamestown which followed Smith's return to England after injury in a gunpowder accident, the wreck of the new administration on the island of Barbados, the decimation of the population, are an integral part of the history of the North American foundation.

Smith called the English colonies, with a characteristic truculence, 'the pigs of my sow', and in a large sense they were.

If Jon Skolp and João Vaz Corte-Real really reached Newfoundland as early

254

as 1476, then both Denmark and Portugal, and subsequently the Cabots under whatever king, failed to capitalize the earliest discoveries. France made tentative gestures only; Spain, with Ponce de Leon, poked with a romantic ineffectiveness about the southern shores. Holland and Sweden came in uncertainly and late.

The joint-stock companies found the money and the manpower where the nations hesitated, but the history of North America for a century and a half is in real terms one of company promoters jostling for position and experimenting in power.

The English boasted the best company promoters. The positive era begins with Wolfe's capture of Quebec in the interest of God, the Crown and the Hudson's Bay Company. New England swallowed New France as it had already swallowed the New Netherlands and New Amsterdam. Acquisitive change was inherent and unavoidable in the nature of seventeenth-century colonization. No more than an oyster could young and vigorous colonies tolerate a foreign body in their midst and the flux of time elevated ambition and potential alike.

England was too large and too angular to be treated as the nucleus of a pearl but the Thirteen Colonies were young, activist and pioneering in an age before pioneering had become a suspect activity. Something in the nature of a Declaration of Independence was inevitable from the first – only its date was indeterminate. On 2 July 1776, when the Congress resolved that 'these United Colonies are, and of right ought to be Free and Independent States', the decision was, except for the temporary abstention of the State of New York, unanimous.

It was a young decision. The influence of youth is not a phenomenon peculiar to the late twentieth century. When the first federal census of America was taken after the separation, the population was about 4,000,000 of whom 2,000,000 were under the age of sixteen, and its promulgation may be considered as the start point of the penultimate consequences of the explorations.

From the day when John Smith's life was saved by Pocahontas there had been a powerful impulsion towards the West. It had been contained within limits partly by humanitarian developments in Europe, partly by the entirely practical determination of English governments to avoid the cost and difficulty of Indian wars. The Royal Proclamation of 1763, which delimited a vast Indian reservation between the Appalachians and the Mississippi where settlement was to be prohibited, was a factor of importance – especially amongst the young – in the progression of opinion towards independence. The 'Plan for the Future Management of Indian Affairs' in 1764 was still remembered as a grievance ten years later. With the establishment of independence a slow relentless drift towards the West began.

It was not, in any sense, the product of a population explosion. If the Atlantic coastline at the Declaration is calculated at about 1,300 miles, it would have required a belt of land less than fifty miles in depth to accommodate the then population of 3,500,000 at the present day United States density of fifty-four per square mile. It is difficult to offer precise reasons for the drift. There was some preliminary investigation and exploration and prospecting, but for the long-drawn-out dispossession of the eastern tribes there is no discernible reason except land-hunger – or more candidly, land-greed.

It set in motion the last of the four genocides of the Great Discoveries.

The pace of the advance is low for the first three-quarters of a century after Independence. Probably, despite the frontier stories, the actual killing was not heavy. Deaths from exotic diseases were not on the same scale as in Mexico or Peru or the Islands, basically because of the wide dispersion of the Indian population. There were fewer than 2,000,000 Indians in North America in John Smith's day. But genocide is not death only, it is the destruction of habitat, of grazing for food animals, of the innumerable small constituents of a way of life.

Tribes moved from the advancing frontier because of these things, and came into collision with other tribes whose habitat they encroached upon. It was not a chain reaction, it was more like a series of collisions increasing in a narrowing space. In the mid-nineteenth century it accelerated with the discovery of gold in California. The speed of movement and the number of whites moving by themselves increased the totals. In California there were 100,000 Indians before gold was found in 1849. Fifteen years later there were 30,000. At the end of the century 19,000. The first elements of the gold rush carried cholera with them, and the Pawnees were wrecked as a nation. Successive waves of Europeans were involved in Indian fighting. Who began it is irrelevant but there was endemic war on the plains from the sixties on. In the seventies smallpox hit the Black Foot, the Assiniboin and the Cree. Tribes were dispossessed of grazing altogether. The attempt to regularize the allotment of land in the late eighties resulted in the loss of 86,000,000 acres of tribal land out of 138,000,000.

By the end of the century it was customary to talk of the Vanishing Indian. Remarkably, he did not vanish. By 1915 the Indian population was stable. By 1920 it had begun to increase. Numerically, the Indian is today secure: nationally, the slow, painful and continuing tragedy of the Navajo demonstrates that there are immense ecological problems still to be solved.

The ultimate effect of the Discoveries on the modern world cannot be measured in terms of mathematics; its limits, like its origins, are indefinite.

That the Discoveries were the splendid flowering of a Renaissance dream is, as their history indicates, a myth. The simple evidence is that they were begun before the Renaissance spread to Portugal and that they were generated not by intellectual inspiration but by strictly practical intention. Henry of Portugal ordered Zarco and Teixeira 'to sail in search of the Land of Guinea' for the declared purpose of securing an entry into the ancient but existing trade in gold, ivory, slaves and malaguetta pepper. João II sent Bartolomeu Dias down the Atlantic to find a way round Africa to a vast and flourishing eastern trade in 'gold, precious stones, pepper, cloves, cinnamon and rhubarb'. Columbus, wholly immersed in Portuguese methods and concepts, secured his long-sought subsidy by proposing to cross the Western Ocean to Cipangu with its known 'pearls, precious stones, gold, silver and spices' (and a written guarantee of ten per cent on their value). Charles V fitting out the renegade Magellan with his five ships instructed him to sail west '. . . for the discovery of the spicery'.

The common factor is spice – the winter dietary of medieval Europe made startling demands on flavourings. Gold, silver and jewels appear with variable emphasis, spice is always listed. That it was in due course overtaken by pearls, gold, silver, sugar and slavery – in that order – is inherent in the nature of the areas involved. Essentially, discovery was a matter of commercial endeavour.

It is possible, indeed, with only a moderate exercise in cynicism to construct a theory that the explorations played a greater part in the Renaissance than the Renaissance played in them. The argument is beguilingly simple. The great efflorescence that began at the end of the fifteenth century was uniquely spontaneous. Its continuing triumph, on the other hand, was by the evidence due primarily to patronage. Patronage flourishes, the rest being equal, in accordance with the availability of money. Money was available in Europe because, substantially before Michelangelo and Leonardo da Vinci and Raphael and Titian had reached the summits of artistic perception, the loot of the Islands, and Mexico and Peru had been disseminated through Europe. Much, perhaps most of it, had passed through the hands of the great banking families: the Medici in Florence (Lorenzo was Michelangelo's first patron), the bankers of Milan under the Sforzas, the bankers of Genoa under Doria, and above all the Church of Rome which took its share with the passion and precision of the English pirates.

How much of the money that funded the great churches, the pictures, the letters and the science of the Renaissance came from the Americas will never,

Fruits and spices of the East Indies: areca-nuts, coconuts and pepper

perhaps, be determined with accuracy. What is entirely certain is that all Europe, as Charles V paid or neglected to pay his armies by the Spanish Road, shared in it. Even France, outside Charles' aegis and in the early stages herself only a moderate participant in sea venturing, helped to cream off the profits. Carew, the English Ambassador to Paris in 1507 as the French Renaissance burgeoned with its borrowings from Italy, wrote '. . . after the arrival of the Indian Fleets the treasure they bring in is suddenly dispersed, and most of it carried into France in lieu of the corn which hath been brought thence'.

One other participation in the profits is less certain. How much of the Indies treasure that went to Augsburg in payment of Charles' debts to the Fuggers was expended on the arts is not determinable. Everywhere else in Europe at that time great painting, superb sculpture, incredible achievements in literature began to be subsidized by money which came from the East, from the Spiceries and most of all from the Americas and the silver flood of Potosí.

The debt of the Renaissance to the Discoveries is palpable. Their debt to the Renaissance is less easy to define. It lies mostly in the new availability of classical geography, the rapid developments in mathematics, and above all in the improvements to astronomical and navigational instruments – though the major Discoveries preceded most of these.

Probably the most immediate contribution was the advance in cartography. It is at once the index of the achievement of the explorations themselves and an indication of the speed of the advance of knowledge. It can best be measured from Martin Behaim to Gerhardus Mercator. Behaim, a Bavarian, had, like Columbus, married the daughter of a Captain General of an island in the Azores; he had made a voyage to Guinea (though not with Cão as he claimed); and he was acquainted with Diogo Gomes whose account of the voyage to the Gambia he wrote from dictation. He was, like Columbus, deeply immersed in the Portuguese maritime community, and presumptively abreast of current information. He was clearly aware, for example, of the Florentine Toscanelli's theories, and presumably therefore of his correspondence with Columbus.

Equipped with this knowledge he returned to Nuremberg in 1492 – the year of Columbus' departure – and constructed a globe. It uses Toscanelli's approximate positions for Cathay and Cipangu, it perpetuates the extraordinary fabrication of the *Ginea Portogalexe*, it shows no knowledge whatever of Dias' voyage, and it is erroneous in almost every material particular. Its distinction is that it is the oldest surviving globe, and its importance lies in the fact that it supplies the measure of available geographical knowledge in the year in which Columbus sailed on the First Voyage – outside, that is, closely knit groups in Lisbon and Seville.

Seventy-five years later, Gerhardus Mercator of Rupelmonde published the superb Chart of the World which he entitled *Nova et Aucta Orbis Terrae . . .*

The projection that he used – though his name has been attached to it – had been used before, but Mercator embodied in it the results of the principal voyages, supplemented them with the lesser ventures, and to an Old World drawn with singular accuracy, he positioned a New World whose outlines were

Gerhardus Mercator of Rupelmonde

Right
Martin Behaim's globe of 1492

The north-west sections of
Mercator's chart of 1567,
showing the mythical
Northern Land

to require eventual amendment only in detail. The great Southern Continent, built up on seamen's assumptions and the rumours of Australia and Antarctica is, with the lesser Northern Land, the single blemish on the masterpiece of cartography.

After Mercator man knew the shape of his world. The terror of the unknown – and its fascination – were both gone.

Precisely a hundred years later Josiah Child, the tough Governor of the East India Company, wrote in his *New Discourse of Trade,* '. . . if we keep the trade of our said plantations entirely to England, England would have no less inhabitants, but rather an increase of people by such evacuation, because that one Englishman, with the Blacks that work with him, accounting what they eat, use and wear, would make employment for four men in England'.

It is the earliest, bluntest English exposition of the principles of mercantilism in respect of colonies, and it made plain the growing realization of their profitability. Within a generation Charles Davenant put the position in more orthodox terms by announcing that England's commerce with the New World had reached a level of £2,000,000 a year, and that her share of the Triangular Trade now accounted for substantially more than a third of the total profits of British exports.

Child's declaration is the primary statement of the credo of a modern world. On the basis of its principles the Triangular Trade developed in its staggering proportions. On it the economic pattern of an emergent Britain was formulated.

The simplicity of the Triangular Trade needs restating. Ships loaded at British West Coast ports – though London retained a substantial share – with trade goods. These were bartered on the West Coast of Africa for slaves. The slaves were carried in the same ships to the West Indies and sold there for money, for sugar, for tropical goods or for tobacco. The cargoes were carried back to England or the Continent and sold for cash.

The defect of the time was that the potential of the Triangular Trade was greater than the productivity of English trade goods.

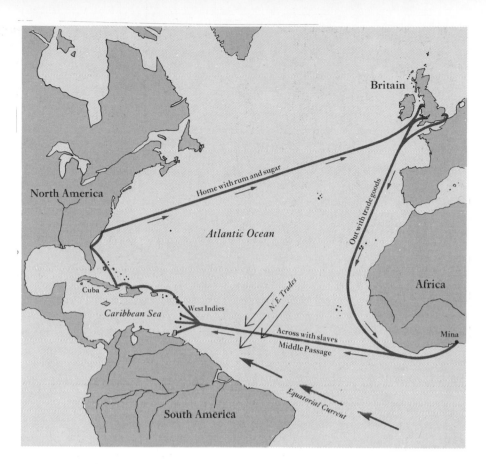

The Triangular Trade

There is no accident in the fact that the primary inventions of the industrial revolution – Kay's 'new invented shuttle', Hargreaves' Spinning Jenny, Cartwright's power loom – were made in the interests of accelerated textile production or that the inventions in power were first applied to the new machines: the new use of the horse, the use of water, the use of steam.

The chain of causation is exquisitely clear. It begins with the passage of Cape Bojador, it moves through the discoveries to the Triangular Trade, it expands with the textile inventions, it proceeds to the steam locomotive, the paddle steamer, electricity, the internal combustion engine, the aircraft and nuclear power.

Linked within the chain are colonial wars and power struggles over population, pollution and the exhaustion of natural resources.

That invention would have happened without the Discoveries is of course certain – man is an experimental animal. That it would have happened in the same manner and above all at the same breathless speed is at least doubtful. The shape of mankind is a consequence of that speed. Little in the world today, even in its most fantastic features, lacks some point of origin in the Discoveries, in the Americas, in the fertilization of the New World.

The last links in the chain are clear. There is no difference in principle between Gil Eanes landing on the beach beyond Cape Bojador to bring back St Mary's rose and Neil Armstrong stepping down to the surface of the moon to bring back a handful of moon dust.

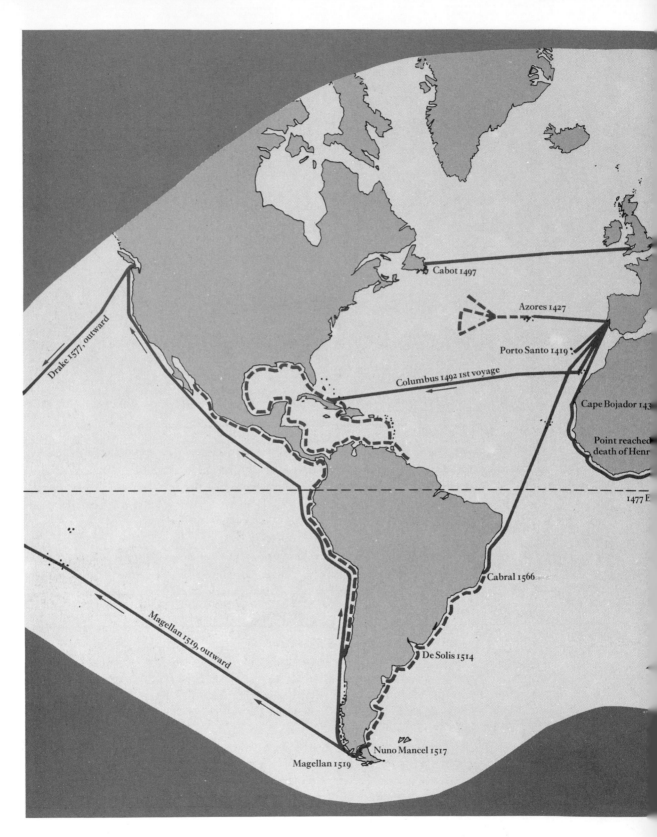

Cabot 1497

Azores 1427

Porto Santo 1419

Columbus 1492 1st voyage

Cape Bojador 143

Point reached
death of Henr

Drake 1577, outward

1477 E

Cabral 1566

Magellan 1519, outward

De Solis 1514

Nuno Mancel 1517

Magellan 1519

The World in the Sixteenth Century. The great voyages were based on lesser ones preceding them.

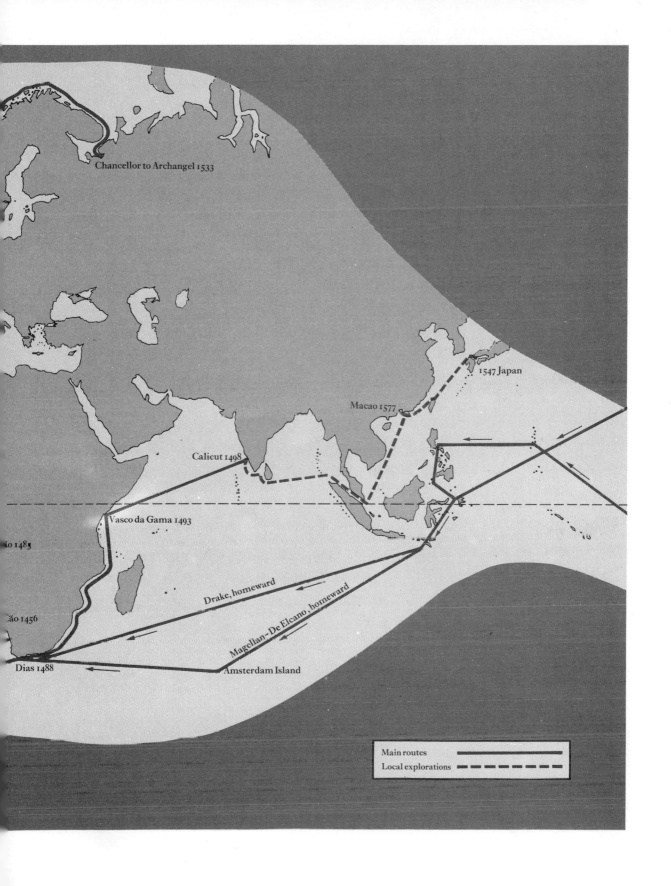

Chancellor to Archangel 1533

1547 Japan

Macao 1577

Calicut 1498

Vasco da Gama 1493

...o 148_

Drake, homeward

...ão 1456

Magellan~De Elcano, homeward

Dias 1488

Amsterdam Island

Main routes
Local explorations

Illustrations and Acknowledgments

Page numbers in **bold type** denote colour illustrations.

ENDPAPERS

Map of the World by J. B. Vrient from *Itinerario, Voyage ofte Schipvaert*, 1596. British Museum. Photo: John R. Freeman.

12 From *Crónica dos Feitos da Guiné*, Zurara. Biblioteca Nacional, Lisbon.

14 From *The Regiment of the Astrolabe*, Sacrobosco, 1509. Courtesy of the Trustees of the British Museum.

15 Genealogy. Biblioteca Nacional, Lisbon.

17 *Portolano* attributed to Petrus Vesconte, *c*1327. Courtesy of the Trustees of the British Museum.

18 Medieval ship-building. Mansell Collection.

20 From *Crónica da Tomada de Ceuta*, Zurara. Biblioteca Nacional, Lisbon.

23 Engraving of Ceuta. Portuguese Trade Office, London.

25 Hispano-Moresque bowl, early 15th century. Victoria and Albert Museum.

26-7 From *Geographia*, Ptolemy, 1482. British Museum. Photo: John R. Freeman.

28 From an illuminated psalter, 13th century. Courtesy of the Trustees of the British Museum.

33 Pots of Naquada II period. British Museum. Photo: John R. Freeman.

34 Ship model from the Great Pyramid. Photo: John G. Ross.

35 (above) Relief from Dair al Bahri, *c*1600 BC. Photo: Science Museum, London. (below) Relief from tomb of Sahu Re, *c*2600 BC. Photo: Science Museum, London.

37 (above) Ship model from Tutankhamun's tomb. Cairo Museum. Photo: John G. Ross. (below) Painting of Egyptian ships, 12th dynasty. Cairo Museum. Photo: John G. Ross.

38 Nile mosaic from the Praeneste, 1st century AD. Photo: John G. Ross.

41 Glandular seals of sard, Middle Minoan period, 1750-1600 BC. Courtesy of the Trustees of the British Museum.

43 False-necked jar, Late Minoan period, 1300 BC. Courtesy of the Trustees of the British Museum.

45 Red-figure vase, 400-380 BC. Courtesy of the Trustees of the British Museum.

46 (above) Bireme from Assyrian tomb, 700 BC. British Museum. Photo: Radio Times Hulton Picture Library. (below) Bas-relief panel from Sennacherib's palace, Nineveh. British Museum. Photo: John R. Freeman.

50 Drawing from Athenian black-figure vase, *c*540 BC. British Museum. Photo: Science Museum, London.

52 Mosaic from Piazza Armerina, Villa Romana del Casale. Photo: Scala, Florence.

53 From *Sinopsis Historiarum*, Juan Skylitzes. Biblioteca Nacional, Madrid. Photo: MAS, Barcelona.

54 From *A History of the Goths, Swedes and Vandals*, Olaus Magnus, facsimile of Rome edition 1555. British Museum. Photo: John R. Freeman.

55 From an Anglo-Saxon manuscript, 10th century. Courtesy of the Trustees of the British Museum.

56 Prow of the Oseberg ship. Universitetets Oldsaksamling, Oslo.

58 (above) Head of picture stone, Lindisfarne Priory, 8-9th century. Photo: Department of the Environment, Crown Copyright reserved. (below) Mammen axe, found at Bjerringhöj, Jutland, 10th century. Danish National Museum, Copenhagen.

59 (above) Gokstad ship. Universitetets Oldsaksamling, Oslo. (below) Nydam ship. Schleswig-Holsteinisches Landesmuseum für Vor- und Frühgeschichte, Schleswig.

60 Oseberg ship. Universitetets Oldsaksamling, Oslo.

61 'Academician' head-post, Oseberg find. Universitetets Oldsaksamling, Oslo.

62 (above) From *Sinopsis Historiarum*, Juan Skylitzes. Biblioteca Nacional, Madrid. Photo: MAS, Barcelona. (below) From *A History of the Goths, Swedes and Vandals*, Olaus Magnus, facsimile of Rome edition 1555. British Museum. Photo: John R. Freeman.

63 (above) Gundestrup bowl, (below) Roman drinking service 1st century AD. Danish National Museum, Copenhagen.

66 (above) Viking ships. Pierpont Morgan Library, New York.

66-7 From *A History of the Goths, Swedes and Vandals*, Olaus Magnus, facsimile of Rome edition 1555. British Museum. Photo: John R. Freeman.

69 Pendant cross found at Birka. Statens Historiska Museum, Stockholm. Photo: ATA, Stockholm.

70-1 Vinland map. Copyright© 1965 by Yale University.

73 Ship on figured stone, *c*800. Statens Historiska Museum, Stockholm. Photo: ATA, Stockholm.

76 (above) From the retable of St Auta, *The Martyrdom of the 11,000 Virgins*, mid 16th century. Museu Nacional de Arte Antiga, Lisbon. (below) Model of Portuguese caravel. Science Museum, London.

77 From the Walter de Millemete manuscript. Christ Church Library. By permission of the Governing Body of Christ Church, Oxford.

78 Spanish astrolabe, *c*1585. National Maritime Museum, London.

79 From a 16th-century manuscript. Istanbul University Library. Photo: Aldus Publications, London.

80 (left) Italian ship's compass, 16th century. National Maritime Museum, London. (right) Chinese compass. Musée de la Marine, Paris.

81-3 Three sections from the Catalan Atlas, Abraham Cresques, 1375. British Museum. Photo: John R. Freeman.

84 From an illuminated manuscript. Courtesy of the Trustees of the British Museum.

85 Detail from *The Art of Good Government*, Lorenzetti. Palazzo Publico, Sienna. Photo: Scala, Florence.

86 *Portolano* by Grazioso Benincasa, 1463. Courtesy of the Trustees of the British Museum.

88 From a 15th-century manuscript. Courtesy of the Trustees of the British Museum.

90 Monument raised to Prince Henry by Leopoldo de Almeida at the Tagus, Lisbon. Photo: F. P. Marjay.

91 (above) Chapel at Sagres. Photo: F. P. Marjay. (below) *Mappa mundi* by Borgia, 1450. British Museum. Photo: John R. Freeman.

93 Saint Vincent panel. Museu Nacional de Arte Antiga, Lisbon.

94 Portrait of João I, 15th century. Museu Nacional de Arte Antiga, Lisbon.

97 João de Castro. Portuguese Trade Office, London.

98 Vale da Ribeira da Cruz, Flores. Portuguese Trade Office, London. Photo: Arpad Elfer.

102 (left) From
Anacephalaeoses . . . Lusitaniae,
P. Antonio Vasconcellos,
Academia das Ciências, Lisbon.
(right) From
Retratos e Elogios dos Varões, Sousa
Madeda. Biblioteca Nacional, Lisbon.

103 From *Civitates Orbis Terrarum,*
Georgius Braun, 1577.
Biblioteca Nacional, Lisbon.

107 Map by Lazaro Luis from
Portugaliae Monumenta Cartographica,
1563.
Academia das Ciências, Lisbon.

109 Chart by Diogo Homen, 1558.
Courtesy of the
Trustees of the British Museum.

111 From *Brevis Narratiosorum,*
J. Lemoyne de Morgues, 1564.
Service Hydrographique de la Marine.
Photo: Giraudon.

112 Detail from
Landscape with the Fall of Icarus,
Pieter Breugel the Elder,
mid 16th century.
Musées Royaux des Beaux-Arts,
Brussels.
Photo: Giraudon.

114 *Portuguese Carracks off a Rocky Coast,*
attributed to Cornelis Anthoniszoon,
c1530.
National Maritime Museum, London.

115 From *Les Singularitez de la
France antarctique,* Jacques Thevet, 1558.
British Museum.
Photo: John R. Freeman.

117 Benin ivory salt, 17th century.
British Museum.
Photo: John R. Freeman.

118 From a manuscript of 1590.
British Museum.
Photo: Aldus Publications, London.

121 From *Les Livres du Graunt Caam,*
Marco Polo, c1400.
Ms. Bodley 264, fol. 218.
Bodleian Library, Oxford.

122 (above) From a woodcut, 1557.
Radio Times Hulton Picture Library.
(below) Italian nocturnal, 16th century.
National Maritime Museum, London.

124 Letter from Prince Henry.
Arquivo Nacional da Torre do Tombo,
Lisbon.

127 Laurentian *portolano,* facsimile.
British Museum.
Photo: John R. Freeman.

129 From *Les Livres du Graunt Caam,*
Marco Polo, c1400.
Ms. Bodley 264, fol. 231v.
Bodleian Library, Oxford.

130 The Cape of Good Hope from
Cape Point.
Cape Peninsula Publicity Association.

132 Afonso V.
British Museum.
Photo: Aldus Publications.

133 *Portolano* by Grazioso Benincasa, 1468.
Courtesy of the
Trustees of the British Museum.

134 Engraving of Lisbon,
16th century.
Portuguese Trade Office, London.

136 From *A History of Ancient Geography,*
E. H. Bunbury, London, 1879.
Reproduced from the original volume
in the George Peabody Department,
Enoch Pratt Free Library, Baltimore.
Used by permission.

137 (left) Sandglass, 16th century.
National Maritime Museum, London.
(right) Portuguese astrolabe.
Sociedade de Geografia, Lisbon.
Portuguese Trade Office, London.

138 Map by Filipe Pigafetta, from
Regnum Congo, De Bry, 1598.
Biblioteca Nacional, Lisbon.

140 *Padrão* erected at Cape Santa Cruz by
Diogo Cão, 1485.
Sociedade de Geografia, Lisbon.
Portuguese Trade Office, London.

141 *Guinea Portogalexe*
chart by Cristofero Soligo, c1485.
Courtesy of the
Trustees of the British Museum.

142 *Mappa mundi*
by Henricus Martellus, c1489.
Courtesy of the
Trustees of the British Museum.

144 (above) 'Cantino' map, 1502.
Biblioteca Estense, Modena.
Portuguese Trade Office, London.
(below) Engraving of fortress of Mina,
built 1482.
Portuguese Trade Office, London.

147 Benin ivory salt, 17th century.
British Museum.
Photo: John R. Freeman.

148 Portrait of Columbus
by unknown artist.
Civico Museo Storico, Como.

150 Engraving of Genoa,
from the *Nuremberg Chronicles,* 1493.
Mansell Collection.

152-3 Eastern sections of the Catalan Atlas,
Abraham Cresques, 1375.
British Museum.
Photo: John R. Freeman.

156 Portrait of João II.
Kunsthistorisches Museum, Vienna.

158-9 Model of the *Santa Maria.*
Science Museum, London.

160 (left) Martin Alonso Pinzón.
Museo Naval, Madrid.
Photo: MAS, Barcelona.
(right) Portrait of Christopher Columbus
attributed to Ridolfo Ghirlandaio, c1525,
a copy from a lost original.
Museo Civico Navale, Genoa.

161 From *Navigatio ac Itinerarium
Johannis Hugonis Linscotani . . .,* 1599.
Academia das Ciências, Lisbon.
Portuguese Trade Office, London.

162 (above) Map signed 'Raro', from
*Petri Martyris de Angleria de
Orbe Novo Decades,*
Alcalà de Henares, 1516.
Biblioteca Universitaria, Bologna.
(below) Facsimile of map by
Giovanni Matteo Contarini, 1506.
Courtesy of the
Trustees of the British Museum.

163 (left) Engraving. Mansell Collection.
(right) From *De Insulis Inventis,*
Columbus' letter to Sanchez, 1493.
Mansell Collection.

164 From *De Insulis Inventis,*
Columbus' letter to Sanchez, 1493.
New York Public Library.

165 Map painted on ox-hide by
Juan de la Cosa, 1500.
New York Public Library.

166 Miniature from a 1646 revision
by Pedro Barretto de Resende of
Livro do Estado da India Oriental,
António Boccaro, 1614.
Courtesy of the
Trustees of the British Museum.

168 (above) A carrack before the wind.
After Pieter Breugel the Elder, c1535.
National Maritime Museum, London.
(below) Trom *Théâtre de l' Univers,*
Ortelius, 1574.
Reproduced from the original volume
in the George Peabody Department,
Enoch Pratt Free Library, Baltimore.
Used by permission.

169 From a 1646 revision by
Pedro Barretto de Resende of
Livro do Estado da India Oriental,
António Bocarro, 1614.
Courtesy of the
Trustees of the British Museum.

170 Portrait of Queen Isabella.
Palacio Real, Madrid.
Photo: MAS, Barcelona.

171 From *Livro das Armadas.*
Ministério da Marinha, Lisbon.
Photo: F. P. Marjay.

174 The Island of Quiloa.
Portuguese Trade Office, London.

176 From *Civitates Orbis Terrarum,*
Georgius Braun, 1577.
Biblioteca Nacional, Lisbon.

177 (left) French engraving.
Arquivo Histórico Ultramarino, Lisbon.
Portuguese Trade Office, London.
(right) From *Livro das Armadas.*
Academia das Ciências, Lisbon.
Portuguese Trade Office, London.
(below) Tomb at the
Church of the Jeronimos, Lisbon.
Photo: F. P. Marjay.

178 Engraving of Pedro Alvares Cabral.
Portuguese Trade Office, London.

179 From an engraving by De Bry.
British Museum.
Photo: John R. Freeman.

181 Map of Brazil.

Portuguese Trade Office, London.
183 Portrait of Magellan.
Uffizi, Florence.
Photo: Scala, Florence.
184 Map of South America,
Diego Homen, 1558.
Warren C. Shearman Collection,
History Division, Los Angeles County
Museum of Natural History.
Photo: American Heritage Publishing
Co., Inc.
186 (above) *Mappa Salviati*, 1525-30.
Biblioteca Medicea-Laurenziana,
Florence.
(below) Fleet in the Bay of Santa Lucia,
Rio de Janeiro.
Portuguese Trade Office, London.
187 From *Americae . . .*, De Bry.
Biblioteca Nacional, Lisbon.
188 Map of South America.
Photo: Fine Art Engravers, London.
189 Engraving of Magellan's fleet.
Portuguese Trade Office, London.
191 (above) From *Johan Schöner . . .*,
Coote, 1888.
New York Public Library.
(below) From *Americae . . .*, De Bry.
Biblioteca Nacional, Lisbon.
193 Engraving of Magellan.
Portuguese Trade Office, London.
194 Portrait of Henry VIII
by Hans Holbein the Younger.
Thyssen Collection, Lugano.
Photo: National Gallery, London.
197 Plymouth in the 16th century.
British Museum.
Photo: John R. Freeman.
198 From *Les Singularitez de la
France antarctique*, Jacques Thevet, 1558.
British Museum.
Photo: John R. Freeman.
199 Engraving by S. Rawl, 1824.
National Maritime Museum, London.
201 Portrait of Sir John Hawkins, 1591.
City Museum and Art Gallery,
Plymouth.
Photo: Tom Molland.
202 Portrait of Sir Francis Drake
by Marc Gheeraerts, 1580.
National Maritime Museum, London.
203 Portrait of Philip II by Lucas de Heere.
Museo del Prado, Madrid.
Photo: Manso.
205 Portrait of Elizabeth I, c1575.
National Portrait Gallery, London.
206 From the Anthony Roll.
Pepys Library, Magdalene College,
Cambridge.
211 Map by Diego Gutiérrez, 1562.
British Museum.
Photo: John R. Freeman.
215 From *Historia . . .*,
Antonio de Herrera y Tordesillas, 1601.
New York Public Library.
216 Engraving of North American Indians.
British Museum.

217 (above) From *De Insulis Inventis*,
Columbus' letter to Sanchez, 1493.
Mansell Collection.
(below) From *Antiguedades Mexicanas*,
1892, copied from *Lienzo de Tlaxcala*,
Mexican illustrated document of
1550-64.
British Museum.
Photo: John R. Freeman.
219 One of a series of six paintings
on mother-of-pearl attributed to
Miguel González, end 17th century.
Museo de America, Madrid.
220 Detail from the earliest known painting
from South America,
by Adrián Sánchez Galque, 1599.
Museo de America, Madrid.
222 (above) From *Americae . . .*, De Bry.
British Museum.
Photo: John R. Freeman.
(left) From facsimile of
Nueva Coronica y Buen Gobierno,
Peruvian codex compiled by
Felipe Huaman Poma de Ayala,
completed 1613.
Courtesy of the publishers,
Institute of Ethnology, Paris.
(right) From *Archivo de las Indias*,
Seville.
Photo: MAS, Barcelona.
225 (left) Peruvian hammered gold vase.
Dumbarton Oaks, Washington.
Photo: Nickolas Muray.
(right) After drawing by Aztec artist
Paso y Troncoso.
Biblioteca Medicea-Laurenziana,
Florence.
(below) Engraving showing gathering of
Atahualpa's treasure.
Photo: Larousse, Paris.
228 Engraving.
British Museum.
Photo: John R. Freeman.
229 From *Les Singularitez de la
France antarctique*, Jacques Thevet, 1558.
British Museum.
Photo: John R. Freeman.
231 (above) Indigo plantation.
Radio Times Hulton Picture Library.
(below) Lithograph by Deroy
after Rugendas.
Mansell Collection.
232 From *Lendas da India*, Gaspar Correia.
Arquivo Nacional da Torre do Tombo,
Lisbon.
233 Engraving.
British Museum.
Photo: John R. Freeman.
234 Charles V by Titian, 1548.
Museo del Prado, Madrid.
235 Jakob Fugger, c1519.
Herzog Anton Ulrich-Museum,
Brunswick.
237 Portrait of Sir Walter Ralegh.
National Portrait Gallery.

239 Engraving.
British Museum.
Photo: John R. Freeman.
242 Lithograph by Deroy after Rugendas.
Mansell Collection.
243 (above) Engraving, 1845.
(below) Engraving, 1876.
Mansell Collection.
244 Painting by John White.
British Museum.
Photo: John R. Freeman.
245 Printed cotton bedspread
from Golconda, 17th century.
Victoria and Albert Museum.
Photo: A. C. Cooper.
246-7 Japanese screen of Kano Namban
Byobu school, 16th century.
Musée Guimet, Paris.
Photo: Giraudon.
248 Miniature portrait by Dip Chand, c1760.
Victoria and Albert Museum.
Photo: A. C. Cooper.
250 (left) From *The Discoverie and
Conquest of the Provinces of Peru . . .*, 1581.
Radio Times Hulton Picture Library.
(right) From *Les Singularitez de la
France antarctique*, Jacques Thevet, 1558.
British Museum.
Photo: John R. Freeman.
251 From *Itinerario . . .*, Linschoten, 1596.
British Museum.
Photo: John R. Freeman.
252 (above) Plan of Malacca from a
1646 revision by
Pedro Barretto de Resende of
Livro do Estado da India Oriental,
Antonio Boccaro, 1614.
Courtesy of the
Trustees of the British Museum.
(below) From the Atlas of
Fernão Vaz Dourado, 1571.
Arquivo Nacional da Torre do Tombo,
Lisbon.
Portuguese Trade Office, London.
253 Painting by H. van Schuylenburgh, 1665.
Rijksmuseum, Amsterdam.
254 Engraving.
British Museum.
Photo: John R. Freeman.
257 From *Itinerario . . .*, Linschoten, 1596.
British Museum.
Photo: John R. Freeman.
258 From *Académie des Sciences et des Arts*,
Isaac Bullart, 1682.
Reproduced from the original volume
in the George Peabody Department,
Enoch Pratt Free Library, Baltimore.
Used by permission.
259 Nuremberg globe, 1492.
Germanisches Nationalmuseum,
Nuremberg.
260 Sections from
Nova et Aucta Orbis Terrae . . .,
Mercator, 1567.
British Museum.
Photo: John R. Freeman.

Figures in **bold type** refer to colour plates;
those in *italics* to black-and-white illustrations.

Abraham of Beja, Rabbi, 169
Adahu, a Berber, 105, 106,
  108, 110, 226
Afonso, Diogo, 114
Afonso, João, 16, 24
Afonso I, 16
Afonso IV, 74
Afonso v, 20, 88, 89, 113, 118,
  123, 124, 128, 131, 132, *132*, 134,
  135, 154
Agricola, 53
Ahmad al Kader, 73
Ailly, Pierre d', Cardinal, 85, 154
Akra Sidheros, 39
Albergaria, Vasco de, 23
Albuquerque, Afonso d', 232,
  233, 251
Alcácer *see* Ksar es Seghir
Alcantara, 137
Alcobaça, Monastery of, 119, 126
Alday, James, 198
Aldeigjuborg, 61
Alfarrobeira, 118
Alfragan, 155
Algarve, the, 16, 20, 90, 116
Algeciras, 62
Algeciras Bay, 21, 22
Algoa Bay, 146
Aljubarrota, 15
Almagro, Diego de, 221, 223, 224
Almeida, Francisco de, 178, 251
Almeida, Lopez d', 89
Al Muhet, 175
Als, 57
Álvares, Nuno, 89
Amalfi, 78
Amsterdam Island, 192
Anaximander, 51
Andersen, Magnus, 57
Angel, 210
Angra dos Ruivos, 104
Angra Pequena, 145
Anse aux Meadows, L', 72-3
Antilia, 142
Ants, the, 99
apoika system, 49, 51
Apolonius of Perge, 78
Appius Claudius, 51
Arabs, 230, 232, 240
Araouane, 92
Arawak, 217
Arctic, the, 51; fur trade of, 61
Arfet, Ana de, 96
Arguim, 113, 116, 230
Aristotle, 13, 224
Arles, 64
Armada, Spanish (1588), 238-9

Arnarson, Ingar, 67
Arte de Marear (of Faleiro), 180
Arzila, 101, 136
Asiento, 240
Assiniboin Indians, 256
astrolabe, 78, *78*, 85, *122*, 137,
  137, 172
Aswan, 13, 34, 51
Atahualpa, 221, 223
Ataide, Vasco de, 24
Aveiro, João Afonso de, 137, 143
Avis, House of, 15, 87
Axem, 132
Azambuja, Diogo de, 137, 143
Azamor, 178
Azenegues, 105, 115, 226, 240
Azores, 74, 99, 101, 126
Aztecs, 217-218, 221, 227, 248
Azurara, Gomes Eanes de, *see*
  Zurara

Bab el Mandeb, Straits of, 32, 50
Babeque, Island of, 163
Badarian period, 33
Baghdad, Caliphate of, 73
Bahia dos Vaqueiros, 145
Balboa, Vasco Núñez de, 178,
  179, 211
Baldaia, Afonso Gonçalves,
  75, 89, 104
Baluchistan, 36
bananas, 249
Banda Islands, 178, 185, 189
Barbacini, the, 131
Barbados, 242
Barbara, 196
Barbosa, Duarte, 190
Barboza, Beatriz, 180, 182
barca, 19, 75, 77, 95
Barcelos, Count of, 19, 23, 87, 92,
  101, 113, 118, 119
barinel, 19, 104
Barker, Andrew, 210
barley, 31, 39
Barros, João da, 106, 142, 155
Bastidas, Rodrigo de, 179
Behaim, Martin, 21, 89, 123,
  127, 258, *259*
Benedict, 212
Benin, 128, 200
Berbers, 115
Bernaldez, Lorenzo, 207
Berrio, 171, *171*, 174
Béthencourt, Jean de, 75, 96, 98
Béthencourt, Maciot de, 98, 119
Birka, 59
Bjorn Ironside, 62, 64

Black Foot Indians, 256
Black ship, 58
Blanche of Navarre, 19
boats, early, 30-5, 39, 57
Bobadilla, Francisco de, 229
bombardes, 171
Book of Virtuous Well-Doing, The,
  85
Borburata, 207
Braganza, Catherine of, 135
Braganza, Duke of, 143
Braganzas, 113, 119, 126
Brattahlid, 69, 72
Brazil, 179, 196, 239
'British Empire', coining of term,
  212
Burghley, William Cecil, Lord,
  198, 206, 208, 213, 238
bussen, 78
'Byblos' boats, 34
Bymba, 207
Byzantium, 53, 61

Cabo da Santa Marta, 139, 140
Cabot, John, 194, 195
Cabot, Sebastian, 195, 196, 198,
  199, 200, 203
Cabral, Gonçalo Velho, 98, 99, 100
Cabral, Pedro Álvares, 172, *178*
  179
Cacafuego, 213
Cadamosto, Alvise da, 21, 75, 92,
  120-1, 123, 131
Cadiz, 47, 62
Cajamarca, 223
Calicut, 77, 169, 176, *176*
Callinicus, 53
Callixtus III, Pope, 120, 123
Cambay, Gulf of, 36
camel routes, 123
Caminha, Pedro Vaz da, 179-80
Cananor, 169, 178
Canary Islands, 74, 97, 100, 101,
  119, 125, 126, 135, 196, 203
Cantor, 123
Canute, 58
Cão, Diogo, 12, 135-42, 143, 145,
  155, 258
Caonabo, 214, 216
Cape Agulhas, 77
Cape Bojador, 74, 75, 92, 99, 100,
  103, 125, 126, 145
Cape Branco, 106, 110, 113,
  115, 121
Cape Cod, 195
Cape Cross, 143
Cape Europa, 21

Cape Farewell, 68
Cape Las Virgines, 187
Cape Ledo, 131
Cape Lobo, 138, 139
Cape Lopo Gonçalves, 137
Cape Masurado, 132
Cape Non, 75, 92, 99
Cape of Good Hope, **130**, 145, 146
Cape of Masts, 116
Cape Padrone, 146, 172
Cape St Catherine, 134, 138
Cape St Vincent, 21, 149
Cape Santa Maria, 138-9, 140, 141
Cape Verde, 114, 123, 135, 172
Cape Verde Islands, 89, 116, 123,
  126, 131, 229
caravel, 75, 77, 105, 106, *144*
caravela latin, 158
caravela redonda, 76, 158
Caribbean, 108, 217, 229, 240,
  241, 244
Caribs, 227
Cartagena, 208
Cartagena, Juan de, 185, 187
Carthage, 47, 52, 53
cartography, 258
Carvalho, 190, 192
Cassiterides Islands, 47
Castello d'Altar Pedroso, 138
Castile, 233
Castro, João de, 92, 97, 98, 99, 100
Catalan Atlas of 1375, 75, **81-3**,
  152
Catalan Map of 1429, 98
Cathay, 195, 258
Cebu, 190
Cecil, William, *see* Burghley, Lord
Cempoala, 218, 221
Ceuta, 15-9, 21-4, *23*, 47, 86, 92,
  101-3, 114
Chancellor, Richard, 200
Charlemagne, 54, 62
Charles v, 178, 180, 182, 192-3,
  196, 198, 235-6, *235*, 251, 256,
  258
Charles VIII, 157
Charles the Bald, 62
charts, maritime, 80
Chesapeake Bay, 195, 254
Child, Josiah, 260
Cholula, massacre at, 218
Christofer of the Tower, 78
Christopher III, 118
Chronicle of Portugal, 19
Cipangu, 155, 156, 163, 164, 189,
  195, 256, 258
Cisneros, Jimenes de, *182*

Clement VI, Pope, 74-5
Clinton, Lord Admiral, 206
Cockeram, Martin, 196
coffles, 240
Cogominho, Nuno Fernandes, 16
Coimbra, 118
Colombo, Bartolomeu, 150, 157, 215, 228
Colombo, Diego (brother of Christopher), 216
Colombo, Diego (son of Christopher), 156, 157
Colombo, Domenico, 149
Colombo, Hernando, 149, 150, 151, 154, 156, 160, 248
Columbus, Christopher, 108, 142-3, **148**, 149-51, 154-8, *160*, 160-1, 163-4, 170, 195, 214, *215*, 216, *217*, 227-9, 242, 256
Comnenus, Manuel, 108
compass, 78, 80, *80*, 137
Concepción, 178, 180, 182, 185, 186, 187, 188, 190
Conga, 208
Congo, River, 138, *138*, 139
Conosciemento de todos los Reynos, 96
Constantinople, 119
Corte-Real, João Vaz, 254
Cortés, Hernán, 179, 217, *217*, 218, **219**, 221, 235
Costa, Soeiro da, 132
Covilha, 90
Covilhão, Pedro de, 110, 143, 155, 167, 169, 172, 173
Cree Indians, 256
Cresques, Abraham, 75, **81-3**, *152-3*
Cresques, Jahuda, 95
Crete, 39, 41, 42, 43
Crónica da Tomada de Ceuta, 20, *20*
Crónica do descobrimento de conquista de Guiné, 21, 90, 118
Crossness, 69, 73
cross-staff, *122*, 137
Crotone, 53

Danegeld, 62
Danes, early expeditions of, 58, 62, 64
Danzig, 59
Darius, 50
Davenant, Charles, 260
Davis Strait, 195
Décadas da Ásia, 142
Declaration of Independence,

American, 255
Deed, John, 212
Delivery, 254
De Naturis Rerum, 78
Denmark, 54, 255
Denmark Strait, 67
Deseado, 188
De Sphaera Mundi, 14, *14*
Dias, Bartolomeu, 77, 109, 127, 137, 140, 143, 145-6, 157, 158, 167, 170-2, 180, 256
Dias, Dinis, 114, 116
Dias Point, 145
Dicuil, 65
Dido, 47
Diniz, King, 16, 18
Diu, battle of, 178, 251
Dnieper, River, 61
Dominica, 207
Dorestad, 62
Dorians, 44, 49
Doughty, Thomas, 212
Dragon ships, 54, **55**, 57, 58, *73*, 75
dragon's blood, 97, 120
Drake, Sir Francis, **202**, 208, 210, 212, 213, 238
Drepana, 52
Drobin, 59
Duarte, King, 16, 18, 19, 21, 22, 85, 88, 101, 103, 104
Ducket, Lionel, 203
dugout canoes, 31, 33, 39, 57, 61
Dulmo, Fernão, 143, 156
Dutch East India Company, *252*, 253
Dvina, River, 61

Eanes, Gil, 75, 89, 100, 103, 104, 124, 145
East India Company, 253, 260
Egypt, 35-6, 42; early ships of, 33-4, **37**
Eheumerus the Messanian, 51
einkorn, 39
Elbe, River, 62
Elcano, Juan Sebastian de, 178, 182, 185, 187, 190, 192, 193
Elizabeth I, 194, 204, *205*, 206, 207, 208, 212, 238, 239
Elizabeth, 212
Elorriaga, 185
Emmer wheat, 31, 39
Enriquez, Don Martin, 209, 210
Eratosthenes, 13, 51, 155
Eric's fjord, 68, 72
Ericsson, Leif, 54, 68, 69, 72,

see also Leif's huts
Ericsson, Thorwald, 69
Eric the Red, 67, 68, 69
Eridu, 32, 33
Escolar, Pero de, 132
Española, *162*, *163*, 164, 203, 208, 214, 218, 228, *228*, 229, 240, 241-2, *250*
Espinosa, Gomez de, 192
Etesian wind, 35, 39, 42
Ethiopia, 108
Eudoxus of Cyzicus, 51
Eugenius, Pope, 87, 106
Euphrates, River, 33, 34, 36, 224

Faleiro, Francisco, 180
Faleiro, Ruy, 180, 182
Faro, 90
Faroe Islands, 65, 66
Fayal, 96
Fendek, el, 101
Ferdinand V, King of Aragon, 135, 149, 157, 195, *215*
Fernandes, Álvaro, 116
Fernandes, João, 114, 115, 121
Fernandes, Valentim, 123
Fernando, Prince, 89, 101-2, *102*, 104, 135
Ferrar, Jaime, 75
Ferreira, Gonçalo, 131
Fertile Crescent, 30, 39
Fez, 22; King of, 135
Finnbogi, 69
Firedrake, H.M.S., 21-2
flat earth controversy, 13-14
Flateyjarbók, 65
Flensborg fjord, 57
Floki, 66, 67
Flores, *98*, 99
Florida, 207
Florin, Jean, 221
flota, 209
Fontanarossa, Suzanna, 149
Formigas Rocks, 99
Fortunate Islands, 75
Frederick Barbarossa, 108
Freydis, 69
Friesland, 62
Frobisher, Martin, 200, 210
Fuggers, 235, 258
fusta, 75

galé, 19, 75
Gama, Paulo da, 174
Gama, Vasco da, 77, *166*, 167, 169, 170, 172, 173, 174, 175, 176, 177, *177*

Gambia, River, 123, 128
Gardar, 66
Gazahouet, 24
Genghis Khan, 73, **129**
genocide, 214, 224, 228, 230, 256
Gerard of Cremona, 14
Gibraltar, 17, 22, 92
Gil, Diogo, 116
Gilbert, Humphrey, 210
Ginea Portogalexe, 140, *141*, 258
Girardi, Lorenco, 154
Godfred of Denmark, 62
Godspeed, 254
Gokstad ship, 57, *59*
gold, 24, 29, 110, 123, 132, 135, 230, 248, 250
Gold Coast, 132, 200
Golden Hind, 212, 213
Gomera Island, 118, 242
Gomes, Diogo, 21, 85, 86, 89, 92, 98, 123, 124, 126, 127, 128, 131
Gomes, Fernão, 132, 136, 137, 138, 143
Gonçalves, Antão, 89, 105-6, 108, 110, 114, 115, 118, 119, 120, 226, 227
Gonçalves, Lopo, 134
Gonsalves, Ruy, 22-3
Gonson, Benjamin, 203, 206, 211
Gotland, 59
Grace of God, 210
Granada, 24, 29, 33, 115
Grand Canary, 75, 98, 99
Grand Catalan Company, 233
Greece, 51
Greek Fire, 53, *53*
Greenland, 58, 67, 68, 69
Green Sea of Darkness, 99-100
Grenville, Sir Richard, 210, 212
Gresham, Sir Thomas, 198
Grijalva, Juan de, 218
Grim Kamban, 65, 66
Guacanagarí, 164, 216
Guam, Island of, 189, 190
Guanahani, 214
Guanches, 74, 98, 119
Guinea, 95, 97-8, 99-100, 101, 113ff, 118, 119, 120, 124-5, 126, 132, 137, 196, 198, 203, 214
gunpowder, 78
Gunnbjorn's Skerry, 67, 68
guns, 78

Hacilar, 30
Hadhramaut coast, 32, 50
hafskip, 67

Haiti *see* Española
Hamilcar, 52, 53
Hangchow, 155
Hannibal, 52-3
Harrapa, 36
Hasdrubal, 52
Hassuna culture, 31
Hasting, 62
Hatshepsut, Queen, 34, *35*, 42
Hawkins, John, Sir, 194, 196, 200, **201**, 203-4, 206-12, 213, 236-7, 238
Hawkins, Katherine, 203
Hawkins, William, 196, 198, 200
Hawkins, William, the younger, 212
Hebrides, 53, 65
Hecateus, map of, *136*
Hein, Piet, 250
Helgi, 69
Henrique (Magellan's slave), 189, 190
Henry IV of Navarre, 239
Henry IV (of England), 78
Henry V, 29
Henry VII, 157, 195, 238
Henry VIII, *194*, 195, 196, 198
Henry, Prince, 'The Navigator', *12*, 13, 14-15, 16, 17, 75, *90*, 93; sent to Porto, 19; assault of Ceuta, 21-4; at Ceuta, 29, 92; education of, 85-6; voyages of, 87; character of, 87, 88, 89; appointed Governor of the Algarve, 90, 100; four phases of career, 90, 92; maritime administration, 95ff., 128, 131; finances and debts of, 97-8, 119, 126, 230; appointed Governor of Order of Christ, 98, 100; his attack on Tangier, 101-3; motivation of, 110, 124-5; cooperation with Braganzas, 118-9; death of, 123-4.
Hercules, 41-2
Herjolfsen, Bjarni, 68, 72, 95
Herodotus, 13, 47, 49, 86
Herons, Isle of, *see* Arguim
Heroonopolis, 50
Hippalus, 51
Hipparchus, 78
Holy Haven, the, 95
Holywood, John, *see* Sacrobosco
Homen, Hector, 89, 104
hookworm, 244
Ho Presto Joam das indias, 108, *see also* Prester John
Hormuz, 169, *169*
Hottentots, 146
Howard, Lord Admiral, 198
Huascar, 221, 223
Huayna Capac, 221
Hudson's Bay, 200
Hudson's Bay Company, 255
Hyksos, 42

Ibn Mâdjid, 175, 176
Iceland, discovery of, 66, 67
Imago Mundi, 154
imramha, 66
Incas, 221, 223, 227
Incense Coast, 32
India, 119, 126-8, 135, 137, 139, 146, 170, 177, 179-80, 198, 214, 253
India, Further, 108, 127, 128, 137
India, Greater, 108
India, Lesser, 108
India, Nearer, 108, 128
Indian Ocean, 139, 146, 173, 175-6, 178
Indians, North American, 255-6
Indicopleustes, Cosmas, 108
Indies, 106, 109, 232, 235, 236, 237
Indus, River, 50
Indus valley, 36
ingenio, 242
Innocent VIII, Pope, 139, 140
Iona, 61
Ionians, 49
Ireland, 50, 51, 61, 62
Irish navigations, 65-6
Isabela, 204, 216, *217*, 228
Isabella, Queen, 135, 149, 157-8, 170, *170*, *215*, 227
Ivan the Terrible, 200
ivory trade, 47, 132, 135

Jacome, Master, 95
Jakob II of the Fuggers, *234*, 235
Jamestown, 254
Jan Mayen Land, 151
Jarmo, 30, 31, 32, 39
Jesus of Lubeck, 206, *206*, 208, 209, 210
Jeufosse, Island of, 62
Joana of Castile, 135
João I, King, 14-15, *15*, 16, 17, 19, 21-2, *84*, 85, 87-8, *88*, 92, **94**, 100-1, 135
João II, King (great grandson of João I), 90, **93**, 135-6, 138, 139, 140, 142-3, 146, 155, 156, *156*, 157, 167, 169, 170, 256
João, Prince (son of João I), 89, 101, *102*
John of Gaunt, 15, *15*, **84**
joint-stock companies, 255
Joseph, Master, 155
Joseph of Lamego, 169
Journal of Marco Polo, 85
Judith, 208, 210
Jutland amber, 58

Karpathos, 39
Kasos, 39
Khoi Khoi, 146
Khufu, 34
knarr, 67, 75
Knossos, 39, 40, 42, 43

Ksar es Seghir, 87, 101, 119, 124
Kunene River, 139, 142
Kvalsund ship, 57

Labrador, 68
La Cerda, Louis de, 75
La Cosa, Juan de (master of the *Santa Maria*), 164
La Cosa, Juan de (cartographer and pilot), **165**
Lactantius Firmianus, 13
Ladoga, Lake, 61
La Gallega, 158
La Gorda, 229
Lagos, 21, 90, 99, 100, 106, 110, 115, 116
Lambay, 61
Lançarote, 113, 116, 226
Landnamabók, 66
Lanzarote, 75, 118, *118*
Lapu Lapu, Chief, 190
La Salle, Gadifer de, 75
Las Casas, Bartolomé de, 229, 235, 241, 242, 244
Laudonnière, René de, 207
Leakeys, the, 30
Leicester, Robert Dudley, Earl of, 206, 212
Leif's huts, 69, 72, 73
Leiria, 18
Lemkin, Raphael, 214
Leonor, Queen Regent, 15, 87, 105, 113, 178
Lincoln, Lord Admiral, 212
Lindisfarne, 54, *58*, 61
Linear B, 43
Lisbon, 16, 19, 62, 74, 90, 178
Lodge, Thomas, 203
Loire, River, 62
Lok, John, 200, 210
London Company, 254
Long ships, 58
Lopes, Diogo, 104
Lopes, Fernão, 19, 20
Lopez of Seville, 75
Lothair, Emperor, 62
Lothal, 36
Louis XI, King, 135
Lourenço, Teresa, 15
Lovell, John, 208
Luanda, 137
Lucira, 139
Lucira Grande, 140
Luli, King of Tyre, 44, *46*
Luna, 64
Luque, Hernando de, 221
Lutterell, Sir John, 198

Macao, 203, 251
Machin of Bristol, 96
Mactan, Island of, 190
Madeira Islands, 89, 95, 96, 98, 99, 126
Magellan, Fernão de, 178-80, 182, 183, 185-90, *186*, 192-3, *193*, 235, 256

Magellan, Straits of, 187-8, *188*, 212
Maghrurin, the, 74
Maglemosian culture, 57
Major, R. H., 86
Malacca, 251
Malaga, 22
malaguetta pepper, 142
malaria, 217, 244
Malindi, 175, 176
Malocello, 74
Mandeville, Sir John, 14
Mandeville's Travels, 14
Manoel the Fortunate, King, 170, 178
Manoel, Nuno, 180, 185
mappae mundi, 74, 80, *91*, 98
Marchena, Antonio de, 157
Margarita Island, 207
Marigold, 212
Markland, 69, 72
Martellus, Henricus, 142, *142*
Matthew, 195
Matthew of Pisa, 19
Mayas, 227, 244
measles, 217
Medina Sidonia, Duke of, 157
Melilla, 24, 47
Mendoza, Luis de, 187
Menezes, Pedro de, 24, 29, 101
Mercator, Gerhardus, 258, *258*, 260
Mesta, the, 233
Milos, 40, 42
Mina, 132, *144*, 151, 154, 172, 200, 230
Minion, 208, 210
Minoans, 39, 40, 42, 43, 58
Minos, 36, 40, 42
Mitombi, River, 203
Moçambique, 173
Moçtezuma, Emperor, 217, *217*, 218, 221
Mogadishu, 47, 49
Moghul Empire, 251
Mohammed II, 119
Mohenjo Daro, 36
Moluccas, 182, 185, 192
Mombasa, 175
Moniz, Garcia, 23
Mons, Graupius, battle of, 53
Monte Cristi, 214
Morocco, 101, 124
Moscovy Company, 200
Mossel Bay, 172
Moustique Bay, 164
Mycenae, 42, 43, 44, 49

Naar, Island of, 113
Nadd-Odd, 66, 72, 95
Namib desert, 142
Naquada II period, 33, *33*
Narvaez, Pánfilo de, 221
Natal, 173
nau, 19, 75, *76*, 77, *144*, 171, 172

Nauplia, 42
Navajo Indians, 256
Navidad, 164, *164*, 214, *215*
navy, Royal, 237-8
Necho, King of Egypt, 47, 49
Neckham, Roger, 78
Negroes, 115, 229, 240, 241
Negus, the, 110, 169
New Discourse of Trade, 260
Newfoundland, 68, 69, 195, 196
Nicholas V, Pope, 120
Nicot, Jean, 248
Niger, River, 241
Nile, River, 33, 35, 36, 47
Nimes, 64
Niña, 158, 160, 161, 227
Ninan Cuyoche, 221
Noirmoutier, 62
Noli, Antonio da, 123, 131
Nombre de Dios, 210
Nomi Mansa, 123, 126
Normanni, 73
Norsemen, 66, *66*, 72, 73
Northumberland, John Dudley, Duke of, 198
North-West Passage, 200
Norway, 54
Norwegians, early expeditions of, 58, 61-2, 64
Nova et Aucta Orbis Terrae, 258, 260, *260*
Nuestra Senora de la Concepción, 212-3
Nydam ship, 57, *59*

obsidian, 32, 40
Ogane of Ethiopia, the, 128, 143
Ojeda, Alonso de, 179, 221
Olduvai, 30
On Ocean, 51
Oran, 24
Ordás, Diego de, 218
Order of Christ, 87, 98, 104, 119, 126
Orkneys, 53, 65
Ormen Lange, 58
Ortiz, Diogo, Bishop, 136, 143, 155, 171
Oseberg ship, **56**, 57, *60*
Ostrich, Henry, 198
Oviedo, Gonzalo Fernández de, 214, 242, 244
Ovityimbo, 142
Oxenham, John, 210, 212, 213

Pacheco, Gonçalo, 116
Pacheo, Duarte, 146
padrões, 138, 140, *140*, 143, *144*, 172
Paesi nuovamente ritrovati, 120
Paiva, Afonso de, 143, 167, 169
Palos, 135, 158
Panchea, 51
Papar, 67
Park, Mungo, 241

Parmenides, 51
Paul, 196, 198
Pawnee Indians, 256
pearl oysters, 248
Pedro I, 15
Pedro, Prince, 16, 18, 19, 21, 22, 85, 88, 98-9, 101, 105, 113, 119
Pelican, 212
Peloponnese, 42, 44
Pembroke, Earl of, 206
Peraza y Bobadilla, Doña Beatriz de, 160
Pereira, Nuno Álvares, 20
Perestrello, Bartolomeu, 95, 96, 151
Perestrello, Dona Felipa, 151, 154, 156
Perez, Juan, 157
Perigrinus, Peter, 145
periplus, 72, 80
Periplus of Scylax of Caryanda, 50
Pessanha (Pezagno), Manoel, 16
Philip II, King of Spain, 200, 203, *203*, 204, 207, 236, 237, 238
Philip III, King of Spain, 239
Philip IV, King of Spain, 239
Philippa, Queen, *15*, 15-16, 21, 88, *88*
Philippine Islands, 189, 190
Philips, John, 196, 198
Phoenicians, 44, 47, 49, 51
Pico de Teide, 74
Pigafetta, Antonio, 189
Pillars of Hercules, 17, 64
pilot books, 50, 80
Pinta, 158, 160, 161
Pinteado, Antonio, 200
Pinzón, Martin Alonso, *160*, 161, 163
Pinzón, Vicente Yañez, 158
Pires, Diogo, 114
Pires, Gomes, 116
Pires, Inês, of Galicia, 88
Pisa, 64
Pizarro, Francisco, 196, 221, 222, 223, 224, *225*
'Plan for the Future Management of Indian Affairs' (1764), 255
Plate, River, 185, 196
Pó, Fernando, 132, 136
Pocahontas, 254, *254*
Polo, Marco, 154, 155
Polotsk, 61
Ponte, Pedro de, 203, 294, 206
Porto, 19
portolani, 17, 80, 85, 95, 96, 98, 116, 126, *127*, 128, *133*, 136
Porto Santo, 95, 96, 99, 151, 154
Portugal, 15ff., 105, 119, 120, 179; expansion of, 75ff., 230; population of, 77; trade of, 203, 230, 232
potato, introduction into Europe of, 244, 248
pot de fer, 77, 78

Potosí mines, 235, 236, *250*, 251
Powhaton, Chief, 254, *254*
Praecelsae Devotionis, 180
Prester John, 108, *109*, 110, 128, **129**, 142, 167, 169
Promontorium Prassim, 139, 140
promontorium sacrum, 13
Ptolemy, **26-7**, 85, 86, 128, 135, 146
Pudsey, John, 196
Puerto de Plata, 204
Punt, 34, 35, *35*
Pylos, 43, 44
Pythagoras, 13, 51
Pytheas of Massalia, 50, 51, 53

quadrant, 85, 137
Quelimane River, 173
Quebec, 255
Quesada, Captain, 185, *187*
Quiloa Island, 174, 175
Quinsay, 154
Quseir, 32, 33

Rabat, 119
Ragnar Lodbrok, 62
Ralegh, Sir Walter, 210, 237, *237*, 244, 248
Raposeira, 90
Recco, Nicholas de, 74
Regiment do Astrolabio e do Quadrante, 136
Regiment of the North, 136
Reginbold of Cologne, 78
Renaissance, 257, 258
René of Anjou, 149
Rio de Janeiro, 185
Rio de la Hacha, 208
Rio do Ouro, 104, 105, 110, 116
Rio Grande, 116
Rio Verde, 131
Robert the Englishman, 145
Rodrigo, Master, 136, 155
Roger I, 73
Rome, 51, 52, 53
Roskilde fjord, 67
Roteiro, 167, 172, 175, *176*
Roxo Island, 132
Royal Proclamation of 1763, 255
Rudolf, Lake, 30
Rule for Raising the Pole, 136
Rule of the Marteloio, 80, 136
Rule of the Sun, 136
Rus, the, 54, 61, *62*
Russia, 61
Rutter, 85

Sacred Cape, the, 13
Sacrobosco, 14, *14*, 85
Sagres, 13, 31, 89, 90, 131; 'court' at, 90
Sahara desert, 113
Sahu Re, 34, *35*
St Augustine, 14
St Basil, 14

St Brendan legends, 66
St Chrysostom, 14
St Francis Xavier, **246-7**, 251
St Gregory, 14
St Gregory pillar, 146
St Jerome, 14
St Jorge, 137
St Mary at Batalha, 124
St Mary of Belem, 90
Sala ben Sala, 22, 24, 102
Salamis, battle of, 50
Sambula, Island of, 206
San Antonio, 178, 180, 185, 186, 187, 188
Sancto Amarco, 204
sand-glass, 85, *85*, 137, *137*
San Domingo, 204
sand table, 19
San Julian, 185, 212
San Juan de Ulua, 209, 210
San Martin, Andres de, 190
San Nicolo of Messina, 80
Santa Cruz, 146
Santa Lucia, 185
Santa Maria, 158, *159*, 161, 164, 214, 226
Santa Maria, Bosque de, 132
Santa Maria, Island of, 99
Santa Maria de la Concepción, 163
Santa Marta, Bahia da, 138, 139, 140
Santángel, Luis de, 157, 158
Santarém, João de, 132
Santiago, 178, 180, 186, 187
São Christovão, 80
São Gabriel, 171, *171*, 175
São Raphael, 171, *171*, 173, 175
Scheldt, River, 62
Schwarz, Matthäus, *234*
Scilly Islands, 47
Scipio, Cnaeus Cornelius, 52
Scylax the Carian, 50
secrecy, policy of, 119, 121, 127, 128, 143
Seine, River, 62
Selvagens Island, 132
Sequeira, Ruy de, 134
Serrão, João, 190
Seven Brothers, 18, 21, 22
Seven Cities, Island of the, 142, 156
Severac, Jordan de, 110
Seville, 62, 235
Shatt el Arab, 32
Shetlands, 65
Sicily, 73
Sierra Leone, 131, 132, 204, 208
Siete Partidas, Las, 240
Silva, Guzman de, 207, 208, 210
silver, 236, 248, 250
Silves, 16, 20, 90
Sintra, Gonçalo de, 114, 116
Sintra, Pedro de, 131-2
Skolp, Jon, 254

Skraelingar, 69
Slavar, 61
Slave trade, 18, 24, 29, 96, 105, 110, 113, 116, 119, 123, 126, 132, 203-8, 224-7, 229, 230, *231*, 240-2, *242*
smallpox, 217, 221, 244, 248, 256
Smith, John, 253-4
Sofala, 169, 178
Soligo, Cristofero, 140
Solis, Dias de, 180
Solomon, 206, 207
Spice Islands, 178, 180, 185
spice trade, 213, 232, 257
Strabo, 13, 44, 47, 49, 51, 86, 135, *136*
Strandhugg, 54, 58, 62
Strandlooper peoples, 146
Straumfjord, 69
sugar, 96, 120, 242, *243*, 244
Suktagen Dor, 36
Susan Constant, 254
Swallow, 206, 210
Swan, 212
Sweden, 54, 61
Swedish expeditions, early, 58-61
syphilis, 244

Tagus, River, 19, 21, 62, 90
Tainos, 217, 227, 228, 229, *229*, 230, 242, 244
Tangier, 16 17, 86, 101, 102, 103, *103*, 104, 119, 134, 135
Teixeira, Tristão Vaz, 89, 95, 96, 116, 214, 256
Telod, 36
Tenochtitlán, 218
Tepe Gawra, 30
tephra, 42, 43
Terra Australis Incognita, 212
Tetouan, 101
Thales of Miletus, 51
Thera, volcano of, 42
Thirteen Christian Brothers, 75
Thorfinn Karlsefni, 69
Thorhall, the Hunter, 69, 72
Thucydides, 40, 49
Thule, 50, 51, 150
Thutmose III, 42
Tiber, River, 51
Tider, 110
Tidor, 192
Tiger, 206
Tigris, River, 33, 34, 36, 39
Timor, 192
Timurid Empire, 251
tin trade, 66
tobacco, 248
Tomar, 104
tomatoes, 248
Tordesillas, Treaty of, 170
Toscanelli, Paolo, 154, 155, 258
Tracker, H.M.S., 67
trapiche, 242
Treatise of the Sphere, 14, *14*

Triana, Rodrigo de, 161
Triangular Trade, 260, 261, *261*
Trinidad, 178, 180, 188, 192
Trinidad, 229
Tristão, Nuno, 75, 89, 105, 106, 110, 114, 116, 226, 227
Trois Fontaines, Alberic de, 108
Trojan War, the, 44, *45*
Truso, 59
Turgeis, 54, 62
Turki, 69
Tyre, 44

Ulfsson, Gunnbjorn, 67, 95
urca Bechalla, 149-50
Ussher, Archbishop, 30
Utnapishtim, 66

Valence, 64
Vallarte, 118
Valverde, Vicente de, 223
varinel, 75
Vatnajökull, 66
Vegas, Ruy Dias de, 19
Veiga, Blasius de, 194, 203, 204
Velasquez, Diego, 218, 221
Veneti, 66
Ventris, Michael, 43
Vespucci, Amerigo, 180
Vesconte, Petrus, *17*
Victoria, 178, 180, 186, 187, 188, 190, *191*, 192, 193
Videro, 66
Vieyra, Mertim, 102
Viking ships, 58
Vinland, 54, 58, 69, *70-1*, 72
Viseu, Duke of, 143
Vivaldis, the, 74
Vizinho, José, 136
Volga, River, 61
Volkhov, River, 61

Wadi Hammamet, 33
Walcheren, Island of, 62
Walsingham, Sir Francis, 212
Willoughby, Sir Hugh, 200
Winter, Sir William, 194, 203, 206, 207, 210, 211, 212
Wollert *see* Vallarte
Wyndham, Thomas, 198, 200

Xeira, Frei João, 21
Xekik (yellow fever), 244, 248
Xerxes, 50

Zacuto, Abraham, 172
Zacuto of Salamanca, 136
Zarco, João Gonçalves, 89, 95, 96, 116, 214, 256
Zaya, 131
Ziusudra, 32, 66
Zurara, 19-24, 29, 75, 85, 87, 90, 95, 99, 100, 105, 108, 113, 114, 116, 124, 126, 127, 151

TERRA COMPENDIOSA DESCRIPTIO